SOUS VIDE AT HOME

SOUS VIDE AT HOME

THE MODERN TECHNIQUE FOR PERFECTLY COOKED MEALS

LISA Q. FETTERMAN

with **MEESHA HALM** and **SCOTT PEABODY**

Photography by **MONICA LO**

TEN SPEED PRESS

Berkeley

CONTENTS

Foreword by Dominique Crenn

COOKING IS AN ANCIENT ART that connects us with our deepest roots. But it is also a modern art that is constantly reinventing itself with new ideas, new materials, and new tools. When sous vide cooking first swept through the food world, some observers regarded it with suspicion, judging it too scientific to be absorbed into the art of cooking. It quickly prompted labels like "molecular gastronomy," which proved intimidating. I prefer the term *modernist cuisine* because it implies the opening up of new avenues to the art of cooking.

Eventually, sous vide found its place in haute cuisine, just as the visual arts made room for photography alongside painting and drawing. But an artistic evolution is not complete until it becomes widely available to the public. And that's why I love Nomiku, one of the first devices to make sous vide cooking at home possible. It's like the little Nikon camera that brought photography out of the studio and into the hands of the people. Nomiku democratizes sous vide, creating an outlet for personal expression.

It's not just the technology, however. It's the people who make Nomiku such a creative force. I remember when I first met Lisa Fetterman. A dynamo fueled by energy and enthusiasm, she was passionate about her Nomiku. I mean, she simply would not rest until I tried her sous vide machine. Once I did, I had to admit it was great. Since then, I've been using the Nomiku at my restaurants, Atelier Crenn and Petit Crenn, and I love it. I have four now.

For me, sous vide is all about texture and about getting consistent results. Nomiku gives its user an intuitive and reliable way to explore sous vide cooking without taking up a lot of space in the kitchen. That's important not only for chefs but also for everyone who loves to cook. The versatility of this tool is continually inspiring. And ultimately, whether everyone is gathered around an open fire or around a Nomiku, cooking is about people, about connection.

I love the way that Nomiku encourages a community to engage in a dialogue that fosters experimentation. For me, that's what is most important: the opening up of an avenue for personal expression. This book is not only a collection of recipes and a guide to a new culinary mode but also an invitation to culinary improvisation—an encouragement to try something new. We can all be artists in the kitchen. We just need the right tools.

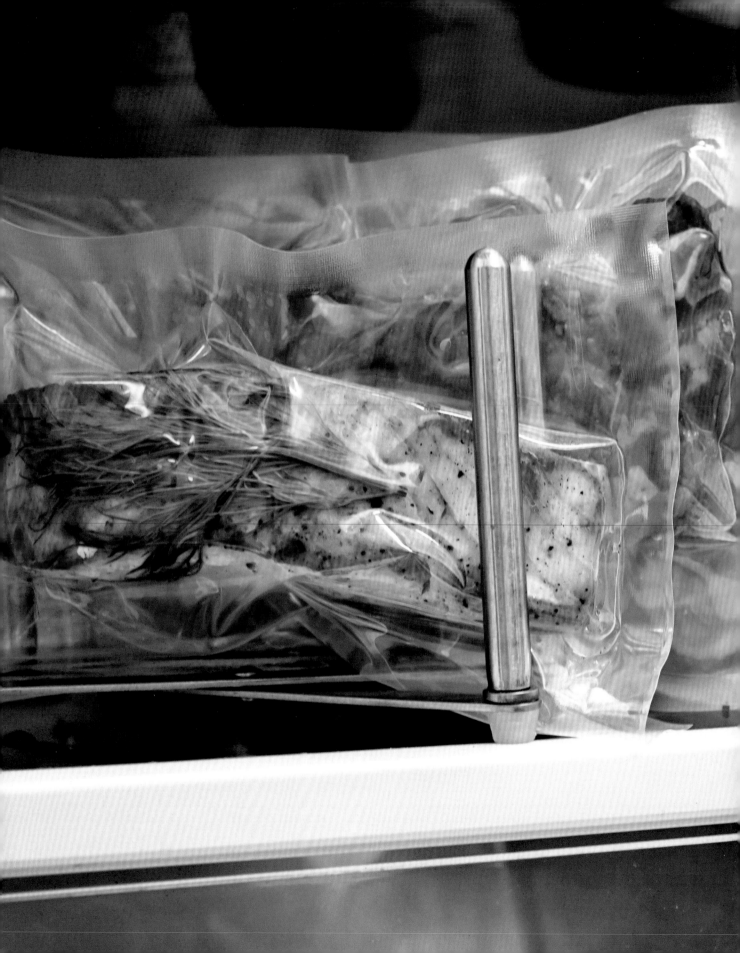

Preface: Nomiku, A Love Story

I WAS SEVEN YEARS OLD when my family moved from China to America. It was hard for me to make friends at school because I didn't know English or even that I had to change my clothes every day. One day, I invited a classmate over for dinner. I desperately wanted her to like me, so I thought long and hard about what to serve that would impress her. I settled on a century egg, a traditional preserved Chinese duck egg with a striking jade-hued yolk surrounded by a translucent amber white. Since it's prized as a delicacy, I figured it was cool. She took one bite, made a little bit of a face, and then sat silently during the rest of the meal. The next day, I was a worried about what the kids at school were going to say to me. As I walked onto the schoolyard, they began circling around me, and I braced myself for the onslaught of teasing. But to my amazement, they started chanting, "Lisa, Lisa, Lisa. Can we come to your house and eat your weird food?" That day internalized for me the power of food to connect us. Even when I didn't know how to behave, food broke through.

From then on, my world changed. I started to idolize the top chefs around the globe and to follow every New York City Michelin-starred restaurant in the media. Sometimes I'd call the restaurants just to see how they answered their phone. I know, a bit stalker-y, right?

When I turned eighteen, I moved to Manhattan and started working in the restaurants of many of my heroes. I spent a year at Mario Batali's Babbo and then worked for Jean-Georges Vongerichten at his eponymous restaurant in Columbus Circle. After I got over being starstruck, I began to notice that purring away in the corner of every top kitchen was a hulking piece of laboratory-grade equipment outfitted with a pump that heated and circulated a giant water bath. Chefs would drop perfectly portioned bags of food into this gurgling beast and pull them out later to prepare their dishes.

I became intrigued by this mysterious contraption that made food that brought me to my knees. What on earth was this sous vide machine? I felt like I had been transported into the future for a moment and had seen what food could be. I wanted to tell everyone about this miraculous device that turned out exquisite, perfectly cooked food night after night during dinner service. I soon became obsessed with the idea of owning one for myself, fantasizing about all of the great recipes that I could make with it. I spent my evenings thinking about how I could fit one into my tiny Lower East Side apartment. (Maybe I could store it in my bathtub?) But I quickly became discouraged when I discovered that a machine cost thousands of dollars. With my grand hopes of culinary invincibility dashed, I resigned myself to the reality that sous vide machines were for professional chefs only, and reluctantly pushed my fantasy of owning one to the back of my mind.

Fast-forward a few years to when I started dating Abe (now my husband), a cute, lanky plasma physicist who I met at a yoga class. We were the only students who showed up, and we hit it off right away. He was as into the food scene as I was, but that's not where the chemistry stopped. A light bulb went off: as I gazed into his adorable saucer-shaped eyes, it dawned on me that a scientist who could create cold fusion at his day job could probably conquer any mechanical challenge.

One evening while Abe and I were cooking dinner at his apartment, I casually lamented, "If only I had a sous vide machine!" Abe, in a geeky suave attempt to impress me, offered to make me one. A few days later, with a handful of hardware finds in tow, Abe and I figured out how to make our own immersion circulator that could attach to any vessel and thereby turn it into a sous vide machine. It wasn't pretty or polished, but it worked, and although I didn't know it then, it was the beginning of something big. We honed our MacGyver invention into a small, easy-to-use, elegant prototype.

The first thing we tried preparing with our prototype was eggs, which we cooked at 64°C. We were amazed at how this precise low temperature was able to yield yolks that were actually thicker than the whites, so that what emerged was a soft, white halo around a custardy yolk. We felt like we were eating liquid sunshine. The egg we shared that night on the sofa was our "aha!" moment, revealing the paramount importance of temperature control. Put aside talent, sweat, and years of culinary-school training. Heat, above all, is the secret ingredient in the kitchen. After that first incredible *eggsperience*, Abe and I wanted to share our discovery with everyone we could. So we set out to develop a DIY immersion circulator kit.

We traveled across the country, teaching people how make their own immersion circulators and learning how to code and solder along the way. In 2011, we decided to take a few of our kits to the New York Maker Faire, a huge gathering that celebrates innovation across a wide range of fields. The night before the opening, we stayed up until five o'clock in the morning, preparing more than two hundred sous vide eggs to hand out. It wasn't until we heard the rumble of the garbage trucks rolling down the block, and my mother showed up at our apartment to haul our kits to the New York Hall of Science in Queens, that we realized we'd stayed up all night. Luckily, as it turned out, hackers of all stripes were just as passionate about good food as we were, and our DIY sous vide kits sold out that week.

Buoyed by our initial success, Abe and I started making makeshift machines for our friends and relatives. Most of them had never heard of sous vide, but they were inspired by the dishes we were preparing in our tiny walk-up. Friends started begging to try out our new machines and reported great success. I watched in awe as one of my cooking-averse friends—a fellow who claimed he could "burn water"—prepared an incredibly juicy, delicious chicken breast with a prototype. It was at that moment that Abe and I turned to each other and knew that this invention was a game changer.

So in 2012, we quit our day jobs and decamped to China to create a polished version of our prototype at the hardware accelerator HAXLR8R (now known as HAX). A week before our wedding, we put our project on Kickstarter, and the rest, as they say, is history. Not long after, we moved to San Francisco to open our headquarters, joined Y Combinator (a start-up accelerator in nearby Mountain View), built a recipe app, and rolled out our Wi-Fi–enabled immersion circulator that you can operate from your smartphone. Which brings us to this cookbook, which I hope will spread the sous vide gospel even farther.

Introduction

MOST PEOPLE ARE DRAWN TO GREAT FOOD, but sadly far fewer enjoy cooking because they lack the experience, knowledge, or ability to make inspired dishes. I want to change that, which is why I founded my company Nomiku. (Nomiku is adapted from the Japanese *nomikui* [飲み食い], which means "eating and drinking.") At Nomiku, we're crazy about food, and our number-one mission is to help home cooks discover the same joys we have found in the kitchen. Cooking brings people together. It's the original social network. At Sunday gatherings over sweet-and-sticky ribs, we catch up with what's going on in one another's life. It is also fun to search your local markets for the best ingredients and then come home to craft dishes together. Constantly inventing new dishes and trying them out on one another is an art as well, one that we passionately pursue at Nomiku. And finally, cooking is entertainment. Preparing a meal at home can be as enjoyable as going out for dinner and a movie, because the act of cooking among friends is its own show.

But home entertaining is most fun when everything is under control. If you've ever tried to cook the perfect rosy medium rare steak, only to cut into it and find just the faintest hint of pink surrounded by gray, you know how disappointing it can feel. If you are cooking steaks for eight guests all at once and are not sure whether your steaks are raw or overcooked, you might wish you had gotten takeout instead. I feel for you. Before home immersion circulators existed, I'd often invite people over to socialize and just end up ordering in. Cooking for a group felt too complicated, and I was always a little worried about not getting things just right.

Now I can prep in advance, and when it's time to sit down to eat with my friends, it takes only a few minutes to put together a meal. Dinner is just waiting for me, bobbing away in the water bath, and I have the peace of mind knowing that it won't overcook because it is being held at a precise temperature. What's even better is that sous vide lets me get out of the kitchen and join my friends, rather than having to watch the stove constantly or worry that I need to get back to cooking. I couldn't imagine throwing a party without it.

Whether you fancy yourself an expert home cook or self-identify as a person who can't boil water, this book will grant you the secret password into sous vide, the greatest culinary invention of the twenty-first century. My goal for this book is to teach you about this remarkable cooking technique which will give you the confidence to tackle culinary challenges, big and small, and help you become the badass cook that you never knew you could be.

Sous vide (French for "under vacuum") refers to a cooking method in which food is sealed in plastic and cooked in a temperature-controlled water bath, but it isn't an esoteric tool relegated to the escapades of *Iron Chef* competitors, gearheads, and food nerds. It's a fail-safe cooking technique that results in amazing textures and flavors that anyone can use to make perfectly cooked dishes, regardless of skill level or training. What you'll soon discover is that when you cook food at exactly the correct temperature, very little can go wrong. Imagine not having to worry about your turkey being dry on Thanksgiving. Imagine preparing salmon that emerges moist, jeweled toned, and delectable to even the pickiest of fish eaters. With sous vide, even fussy desserts like crème brûlée become easy and effortless to master. Simply put your ingredients into a bag, set the temperature, and then sit back (maybe even pour yourself a drink) and let it do its thing. No babysitting, no heartache, and the results will be amazing. Every time. You'll impress your friends and even yourself with how well you'll cook with sous vide.

A BRIEF HISTORY OF SOUS VIDE

Anyone who frequents restaurants has probably eaten food that has been cooked sous vide. It's used everywhere from the world's top-rated restaurants to fast-food companies. The British Royal Navy deploys it to feed its troops on submarines twenty thousand leagues under the sea, and it's how airlines heat up your turkey tetrazzini in the friendly skies.

The magic behind sous vide is consistent heat. Humans have sought methods to moderate and control heat for millennia, whether it be by braising in clay pots, sealing with salt crusts, or burying in pits of smoldering ash. From roasting over a spit to home stoves and ovens with temperature dials, culinary innovations and advancements have been driven by the same burning desire: the quest to tame heat. Although you and I now take these time-honored cooking techniques for granted, Harold McGee, the acclaimed food scientist and author of the groundbreaking book *On Food and Cooking*, reminds us that throughout history, people have witnessed the invention of paradigm-breaking cooking tools that had to fight their way into acceptance in the kitchen.

In the twenty-first century, sous vide machines have ended that quest. Specifically, the thermal immersion circulator, the element responsible for heating, circulating, and maintaining a precise water temperature, provides a tool that can control temperature to a tenth of a degree, resulting in extraordinary flavors and textures not possible with traditional cooking methods. It was originally developed for use in laboratories, where precision heating was required for scientific study. In the 1960s, the technique was adapted by hospitals as a way to sterilize packaged foods for distribution and by large-scale commercial food ventures concerned with improving the efficiency, safety, and storage of their products. The crossover from industrial food service to fine dining didn't take place until 1974, when French biochemist George Pralus was enlisted by three-star Michelin chef Pierre Troisgois to develop a better technique for cooking foie gras at his eponymous restaurant in Roanne, France. Pralus discovered that sealing the fattened liver in a plastic pouch and poaching it at a precise temperature resulted in the least loss of precious fat, so that it retained its vaunted flavor and texture. That discovery is widely considered the birth of the modern sous vide movement.

Around the same time, another French scientist, Dr. Bruno Goussault, was making similar discoveries working with fast-food companies and hospitals to develop sous vide techniques utilizing pasteurization and improving shelf life. In 1986, Goussault went one step further by teaming up with acclaimed French chef Joël Robuchon to create the first all sous vide dining program for SNCF, the French state-owned railway. Goussault went on to bring the technology to other large-scale commercial food-service organizations.

In the United States, vacuum packing, more commonly known as Cryovacking, after the American company Cryovac that manufactured the plastic, has been used since the 1960s to increase food efficiency, safety, and shelf life. But the dining public was initially skeptical of these sterile boil-in-a-bag endeavors that were more closely associated with industrial food-service operations, such as hospitals, airlines, and fast-food conglomerates. It wasn't until Pralus's discovery and Goussault's collaborations with the world's most highly respected chefs throughout Europe and in the United States that sous vide gained acceptance in the professional kitchens. But once it did, it spread rapidly. Since the early 2000s, sous vide has fundamentally reshaped the way that professional restaurants plan, execute, and hold their dishes. Nearly every Michelin-starred restaurant in the world employs some sous vide technique in its kitchen, and a great number of casual restaurants are following suit. Without abandoning their craft, more and more professional chefs are relying on precision heat control and applying the proper combination of temperature and time to turn out optimally prepared meals consistently.

Despite these breakthroughs, temperature-controlled cooking remained the exclusive domain of professional chefs. It wasn't until the past five or six years that sous vide hit its tipping point. The introduction of more affordable and portable immersion circulators such as the Nomiku, which don't require elaborate technical training or a deep-pocket budget, lowered the bar of entry and propelled a sous vide revolution among food bloggers and amateur chefs. This miraculous cooking method is now being used to splendid effect everywhere from Michelin-starred restaurants to Main Street haunts to the kitchens of a new generation of home cooks who were weaned on technology.

HOW TO COOK SOUS VIDE

When it comes to cooking sous vide yourself, you can forget the fancy French name, the history lesson, and the complex underlying science. From a cook's perspective, it couldn't be easier. Here's how it works: An immersion circulator device clamps onto the side of a stockpot and heats and circulates the water to reach and maintain a precise temperature. To operate it, simply fill the pot with water, set the circulator to the desired temperature, and let the water heat up. All the cook needs to do is seal the ingredients in an airtight food-safe plastic bag, drop the sealed ingredients into the bath when it reaches the target temperature, and then wait for the length of time specified in the recipe for the food to cook to perfection. Mind-blowing, right? If you can turn on a faucet and follow simple directions, you can reap the benefits of sous vide.

Take Cover

Slow, long cooking is a hallmark of the sous vide technique. For recipes that require cooking (or holding) the food for several hours in the bath, it's critical that the food remain fully submerged for the duration of the cooking time (see page 13 further explanation). For that reason, if your sous vide unit does not come with a lid, I recommend covering the water bath with plastic wrap or aluminum foil to minimize evaporation, thus preventing the water level from falling too low. It's a good idea to check the water bath every few hours. If the water level has fallen below the machine's minimum, add more water. Although the additional water will briefly lower the overall temperature, that brief fluctuation will have a negligible impact. If you notice at any point that the bag isn't fully submerged, reseal the bag to remove any air, adding weights to the bag if necessary.

The Flavorful Finish

Although sous vide cooking produces amazing results (namely, incomparable juiciness and otherworldly textures), there are a few things that it just can't do. Because the boiling point is never reached, pasta and grains are a no-go, as is baking. Sorry, there's no such thing as sous vide bread. Low-temperature cooking also means a crust or a sear won't form. In other words, your meat won't come out of the bag photo ready. Why, you ask?

The boiled-down explanation (puns always intended) is that the chemistry behind browning meat, the Maillard reaction, happens at temperatures above boiling. Not to be confused with caramelization, which is the browning of sugar, the Maillard reaction involves proteins and carbohydrates. Pronounced "my-YARD" (as in, my browning reaction brings all the boys to Maillard), it's named for Louis-Camille Maillard, the French chemist who first described the reaction. The science involved is complicated, but its interest to you as a cook is simple: it's responsible for creating the delicious, complex flavors we love in everything from meat charred on the grill to toasted bread. So, to get that much lusted-after crust, which adds both a boost of flavor and textural contrast, you'll need to sear it after cooking. That means you're going to have pull out at least one pot or pan. You'll see many different techniques in the following recipes—grilling, frying, pan roasting—with the same goal in mind: golden brown deliciousness.

You can build flavor in other ways, as well. The most straightforward method is to cook the food in question (let's say a steak) unadorned in the bag, remove it, and then season it before searing. The second way is to build flavor proactively by adding aromatics, in the form of a dry rub or marinade, directly to the bag to season the food while it cooks. In some cases, as with Oil-Poached Trout (page 63), this means your food is ready to eat right out of the bag, with the liquid in the bag becoming a sauce to pour on top. Other times, as in the case of General Tso's Chicken (page 89), the meat is seared in a skillet to get a satisfying crust, and then the cooking marinade is reduced for a tasty glaze. Either way, the results are sensational.

Cooking by the Numbers

One of the unique things about sous vide cooking compared with such conventional techniques as grilling, sautéing, and roasting is that you can't rely on the sensory cues of sight, touch, and smell that cooks normally use to determine when food is done. For that, you'll need to depend on a guide that calculates the proper combination of time and temperature. Because of this, it's important not to lower your bagged food into the water bath until it has reached the proper temperature. Just as you need to preheat your oven for good baking results, it's critical for your water bath to be at the correct temperature when the food goes in. Obviously, the amount of time it takes to heat the water bath depends on the size of the water vessel and the desired temperature. To speed up the process, start with hot tap water. (When you cook ingredients at different temperatures end to end, you will start with the higher temperature and drop in a handful of ice cubes to cool down the water quickly.)

For an avid cook, this absence of the typical cues takes some initial adjustment. But once you give yourself over to the rules and trust in the accuracy of your machine, you will be rewarded with the same (most often vastly improved) results with a fraction of the effort.

Celsius vs. Fahrenheit

You'll see that in this book that I've used Celsius as the standard temperature for the water bath. Aside from the fact that sous vide originated in Europe, the rationale behind this is that it allows me to avoid messy decimals. The nice integer for a slow-poached egg at 63°C, for instance, becomes the ungainly 145.4°F. Though it might be tempting to round that number down to nearest degree, those small differences can have a big impact when cooking sous vide. If Fahrenheit is your default mode of thought, fret not; all the sous vide machines on the market will allow you to easily toggle between Celsius and Fahrenheit. In the instances where I call for conventional cooking methods such as frying or baking, I've called for Fahrenheit, since that's the only option for most American appliances.

Cooking Advantages: What's in It for the Home Cook?

Like slow cookers, immersion circulators offer a hands-off approach. The radical improvement of sous vide is in precise temperature control. This puts you in charge of both texture and doneness. The results—succulent meats, silken fish, toothsome vegetables cooked in their own juices, custardy eggs—will come as a revelation. A side benefit of sealing food in a bag is lack of evaporation, which means that there's also no loss of flavor or aroma. Sous vide ensures that your food cooks to the perfect doneness. To illustrate this, let's compare it to conventional methods. Take a medium rare rib-eye steak as an example. When cooked over the high heat of a grill, the proteins in the exterior of the meat will firm up and brown almost immediately. At this point, the outside is cooked, but the inside is still raw. To bring the center to the desired medium rare, or 55°C, you need to keep cooking it. This means that the outer parts of the meat reach well done before the heat penetrates through, causing a band of overcooked gray meat to creep in as you approach your sought-after internal temperature. But when you cook a steak in a water bath set at 55°C, no part of the steak ever gets hotter than medium rare. In other words, it's impossible to overcook it. After an hour, the steak will be a lovely rosy medium rare from edge to center and will stay that way for hours. Because carryover cooking doesn't apply to sous vide, resting your meat before cutting into it becomes much less vital. I've indicated in the recipes when and if you need to rest the meat. If you don't see any note telling you otherwise, you are free to slice right in.

The accuracy of immersion circulators also lets you cook safely at very low temperatures that allow results that would otherwise be impossible. One such sous vide marvel is the slow breaking down of the connective tissue in tough cuts over a period of many hours, resulting in lusciously tender meats that are still medium rare from edge to edge. The ultimate example of this is sous vide short ribs (page 163).

But the appeal of sous vide isn't just the ability to produce flawless, restaurant-quality meals at home. It also gives the home cook peace of mind. With immersion circulators, you'll never go wrong because you apply exact science to the cooking process. Traditional cooking techniques over high heat depend on the cook to determine the correct temperature and length of time required to cook food properly. Sous vide removes the guesswork. By setting the temperature of the water bath to the desired internal temperature of the food once it is cooked, it's impossible to overcook the food, even if you forget about it. This ability to extend the cooking time for most foods without any negative impact is a godsend for people with busy and often unpredictable schedules. It's also a game changer for entertaining. Read more about that and about other meal planning strategies on page 15.

Getting Started

NOW THAT YOU ARE FAMILIAR with the hows and whys of sous vide cooking, there are just a few more things you'll need to know before jumping in. What follows is a short list of additional equipment required, some tried-and-true techniques for sealing without a vacuum machine, and a few safety guidelines to keep in mind.

ESSENTIAL KITCHEN EQUIPMENT

Although sous vide results in professional-quality dishes, you don't need a lot of fancy gear to pull it off. Very little equipment of any kind is required, and most of it is probably already in your kitchen. All of the recipes in this book were tested using a Nomiku, but they will work with any sous vide device. In addition to an immersion circulator, you will need the following items.

A large container for your water bath. Any standard 8- to 12-quart stockpot will work fine. Or you can pick up a 12-quart square polycarbonate food storage container at a restaurant supply store or online for about twenty-five dollars. Check that it can be safely heated up to 95°C (203°F).

Plastic bags. One of the popular misconceptions about sous vide cooking is that you need to seal the bags with an expensive vacuum machine. The purpose of vacuum sealing is to remove all of the air from the bag, and no specialized equipment is necessary to do that (see sidebar on page 12 for detailed instructions). Commercially available freezer-safe ziplock bags do a good job of eliminating air and are completely safe (see the "Food Safety" section, page 12). Just make sure the bags have a double seal (not a sliding closure) and are labeled "freezer-safe," which means that they are also designed to stand up to use in a microwave, where the temperatures are much higher than in sous vide cooking. Plant-based bags won't work, as they will fall apart when heated, though I encourage you to do Mother Nature a favor and recycle any food-safe bags you do choose to use. I most often use gallon-size bags, followed by quart size.

Small weights. Food sealed in ziplock bags (particularly lightweight vegetables) may float to the top of the water bath. In these instances, placing a small weight of one to two pounds into the bag will keep it submerged. Anything from a big handful of pie weights, a pestle, or even a well-scrubbed smooth rock will work.

Tongs and ladles. These tools come in handy when removing bags, jars, or whole eggs from the hot water bath.

Cast-iron pan and/or a kitchen blowtorch. As noted earlier, sous vide cooking results in luscious, tenderly cooked foods, but to achieve that all-important brown crust on a steak or on other foods, a fast heat source is needed. A quick sear in a cast-iron pan will do the trick.

Hard-core gadget lovers can splurge on a kitchen blowtorch (available for under forty dollars) not only for searing meat but also for producing a crackly crust on crème brûlée.

Time and temperature guide. Sous vide cooking is a science, so you'll need to rely on a guide that calculates the proper combination of time and temperature. The book you're holding in your hands contains all of the information you need to cook a wide variety of ingredients, but I couldn't include everything. If there's something you can't find here, log onto Tender, Nomiku's recipe app, which contains the largest repository of crowd-sourced and professional sous vide recipes online, for additional ideas (once you're comfortable, you can even contribute your own!).

VACUUM NOT REQUIRED:
HOW TO SEAL USING THE WATER DISPLACEMENT OR TABLE-EDGE METHOD

Water Displacement Method. To achieve a proper seal and get most of the air out of a bag without using an expensive vacuum sealer, I recommend the water displacement method (aka Archimedes' principle). Place the food (including any marinade or sauce) in a freezer-safe double-sealed ziplock bag. Submerge the open bag into the water with only the seal exposed. Everything below the zippered closing should be covered with water. The barometric pressure of the water will force most of the air out of the bag. When the liquid rises to just below the zipper, seal the bag. You should feel and hear the "click-click-click" as it closes. It's like sous vide music to the ears, assuring you that no water will get into the ingredients. When placing a lot of small items in a bag, strive to arrange all of the pieces in a single layer, without overlapping. This ensures that the pieces will cook through evenly. Once the bag is sealed, run your hand over the pouch again to distribute the contents uniformly before placing the bag in the water bath.

Table-Edge Method. Sealing bags that contain liquid, such as soups, syrups, or alcohol infusions, can be awkward, but here is a hassle-free solution that I call the table-edge method (very scientific sounding, I know). Pour the ingredients into a freezer-safe, double-sealed ziplock bag and partially close the seal. Hold the bag against a table (or counter), with the liquid hanging down and the top of the bag (with the zippered closing) on top of the table. Use the edge of the table to push down on the liquid and then push out any remaining air from the top of the bag before sealing closed.

FOOD SAFETY

When you first begin cooking sous vide, it can seem like a new frontier, full of unknowns and of the potential for error. Because of this, concern about food safety is a topic addressed frequently throughout this book. The good news is that the potential dangers of sous vide are essentially the same as those of any other form of cooking. The primary concern for any type of food safety is to prevent the growth of pathogens (harmful bacteria), and sous vide is no exception.

What it comes down to is that foods hospitable to bacterial growth (meats, seafood, vegetables—basically all fresh foods) can't be kept too long at the so-called temperature danger zone, where they multiply fastest. Food scientists define this danger zone as between 4.4°C (40°F), below which bacteria grow very slowly, and 60°C (140°F), above which most bacteria are killed. They advise that foods should remain in this range for no longer than two hours. This is a good rule of thumb but it breaks down when you look at it closely.

You'll find a number of recipes in this book that call for food to be cooked to below 60°C (140°F), especially in the "Meats" and the "Fish and Shellfish" chapters. Fret not, however, as eliminating pathogens is a function of both time and temperature: food held at a temperature of 55°C (131°F) for many hours is effectively pasteurized (that is, over 99.9 percent of the bacteria are destroyed), which is why you can use sous vide to prepare eggs (see page 22) that are still "raw" but also safe to eat at 57°C (134.6°F). As the temperature rises, the time it takes to pasteurize decreases, which means that cooking at 60°C (140°F) for an hour is more than enough time to make any of the chicken recipes safe to eat. If this seems like a lot of numbers to memorize, be aware that most immersion circulators have a built-in function that will tell you when you fall below a safe temperature.

In the handful of recipes (all in the "Fish and Shellfish" chapter) calling for temperatures below 55°C (131°F), the cooking times are well under one hour, and you're instructed either to serve or to chill the food immediately, which means pathogens have no time to proliferate. The only exception to this is the yogurt recipe (page 260), in which you are actually encouraging the growth of good bacteria, so there's also no cause for concern. (On the topic of chilling your food, check out the ice water bath instructions on page 14 for the most effective method.)

Because precise temperature regulation is so essential for safe sous vide cooking, it's imperative that bagged food is fully immersed in hot circulating water as it cooks. If a bag floats at the water's surface or lays flat at the bottom, you risk exposing a portion of the bagged food to temperatures low enough for bacterial growth. To avoid this, remove as much air as possible when sealing (see page 12 for instructions), so that the bag stays below the water's surface, adding weights to the bag if necessary. For the same reason, the bag shouldn't lie flat at the bottom of the bath or flush against the side; inserting a colander or small rack into the cooking vessel will help prevent this. In any case, what's important is that water is circulating around the bag for the entire duration of cooking, so I recommend checking frequently to ensure that it remains properly immersed. These precautions are doubly important when cooking sous vide for extended time periods, so I've made special note in the relevant recipes.

Another common (and understandable) concern is whether it's safe to cook in plastic. The answer is an emphatic yes. Modern food-safe plastic bags are made from material that is not harmful when heated. With sous vide cooking, the plastic that touches your food is made only of inert polyethylene. There are none of the small-molecule additives like BPA and phthalates that have been used in other containers and have caused concern about potential estrogen-like effects when they leach into foods. As long as you're using freezer-safe bags (which are tested to be safely heated), you're good to go.

To sum up, sous vide is no more dangerous to your health than any traditional cooking method, and when used properly (as in the case of pasteurization), it's actually safer. So put your mind at ease and cook boldly.

Chilling Properly: The Ice Water Bath Method

As I mention above, minimizing the time window for bacterial growth is the key to safe sous vide cooking. For that reason, if you're going to refrigerate food cooked sous vide (rather than eating it immediately), I recommend first rapidly chilling the bag in an ice water bath. When I talk about using an ice water bath to chill food, I don't mean a few ice cubes floating in a bowl. To cool food down efficiently, you want the coldest water possible, which means adding enough ice to bring the water all the way to 32°F. The addition of salt will lower the freezing point of water, making an even colder bath possible. This same principle also enables you to churn ice cream without a machine (page 214). The following instructions will produce an ice water bath ideal for chilling your sous vide foods, but don't feel obliged to follow it slavishly. Think of the ratio as a rough guide.

To make a proper ice water bath, fill a large bowl with ice cubes and add cold tap water equal to about half the volume of ice. Next, add kosher salt equal to about one-fourth the volume of water and then stir until the mixture is very cold (it will be about 28°F within about 30 seconds. The ratio is 1 part salt, 4 parts water, and 8 parts ice, so for a 4-quart bowl filled with ice, add 8 cups cold tap water and 2 cups kosher salt.

HOW TO USE THIS BOOK

Just because it sounds like something Jacques Pépin would say, sous vide isn't only about French cuisine—though it does make a soigné duck confit (page 99). The recipes in this book run the gamut from ramen with pork belly (page 127) and Sriracha chicken (page 79) to Carolina-style pulled pork (page 133) and New York–style pastrami (page 165), with quite a lot of cross-cultural culinary mash-ups in between. You'll find comfort food like fried chicken or waffles and aspirational recipes that you'll want to block off a weekend for, all adapted to stress-free sous vide cooking. And the beauty of sous vide is that it does more than just cook perfectly medium rare steaks and firm-tender vegetables. An immersion circulator can also be your go-to machine for a variety of surprising uses, such as pasteurizing eggs, making yogurt, and infusing booze for mixologist-savvy cocktails.

I have organized the book into chapters by central ingredient (eggs, fish and shellfish, poultry, meats, vegetables, desserts, and, yes, cocktails), with the recipes loosely arranged from the simplest to the most ambitious to teach you how to master different techniques and ingredients. Be sure to read each chapter opener all the way through and then start with the easiest recipes in the chapter and gradually make your way through to the end. That's the best way to build up your sous vide confidence.

Personal tastes vary—one man's perfectly poached salmon is another's sushi—so when possible, I've tried to give you a range of options for achieving your ideal degree of doneness. However, the first time you try a recipe, it's important that you follow the recommended time and temperature to the letter. Of course, there are endless combinations of time and temperature you can use to achieve falling-off-the-bone short ribs or a custardy soft-boiled egg. But as with any cooking method, risks exist if you stray out of bounds, so read the "Food Safety" section on page 12.

Once you've tried a handful of recipes and you're feeling confident, try experimenting a bit. Follow my instructions for time and temperature and then make your own sauce, or serve the food plain if you've got picky eaters to feed. Almost anything can be cooked sous vide.

Proteins such as beef, fish, and eggs do especially well, but other ingredients in your culinary repertoire can be cooked using the sous vide method, as well. You also don't need to throw out your grandmother's recipes. A few simple hacks that can be used to convert your favorites into sous vide recipes are discussed throughout the book.

In an effort to facilitate your meal planning, I've broken the recipes down into two main components: sous vide cooking time and active prep time. The sous vide cooking time (which is hands off) is divided into the minimum time required and an outermost time (indicated in parentheses). The latter takes advantage of sous vide cooking's extremely forgiving buffer zone; however, I don't recommend going beyond it. Even though the food will never rise above the desired temperature, its texture will become unpleasantly mushy after an extended period of time. The active prep time includes prepping ingredients, additional conventional cooking steps such as searing or sautéing, and resting/cooling (which I make specific note of, since this step is not technically active).

AN IMPORTANT NOTE ABOUT SALT

When I call for salt, feel free to use any type you like and season according to your taste. For garnishing, I specify flaky sea salt such as Maldon or fleur de sel, which gives food a nice salty crunch. Again, use whatever finishing salt you have in your cupboard. For measured amounts, however, I always call for kosher salt. In those cases, I am using Crystal Diamond kosher salt, which is lighter than other kosher salts. Other brands can weigh as much as double for the same measured volume, so it is important that you seek out the brand I am using.

MEAL PLANNING AND ENTERTAINING STRATEGIES

In addition to providing inspiration and solutions for getting dinner on the table tonight, sous vide will change forever how you deal with both make-ahead meals and entertaining. In the case of meat and poultry, the fact that the temperature of your water bath is also the target final temperature of your protein means that your steaks and chicken breasts will never be overcooked. This gives you the ability to hold food hot and ready to serve for several hours without compromising the quality. Delayed at the office? No problem. Forgot to walk the dog? Go free Mr. Scruffy! Dinner guests stuck in traffic? No sweat. Pour yourself another drink and know that your tenderloin will still be perfectly medium rare when everyone shows up.

Reheating is also wondrously forgiving: once cooked and properly chilled in an ice water bath (see page 14), most sous vide foods can be refrigerated in the very bag they were cooked in for at least a couple of days. I provide reheating instructions for each recipe where appropriate, but as a general rule, to reheat, simply drop the bag back into the water bath set to about the same temperature used for cooking the food (or a few degrees lower) and heat for 20 to 30 minutes. Resist the urge to rush and reheat your food on the stove top or in the oven, or you risk losing the exceptional texture that you worked so hard (okay, not so hard) to achieve in the first place.

Meal Planning

With a little preplanning, sous vide can quickly become your go-to tool for pulling off easy and delicious midweek meals with minimal effort. In addition to its convenient hands-off nature, the fact that it effectively pasteurizes the food you cook (see the "Food Safety" section on page 12 for an explanation) greatly improves shelf life, which makes it an ideal method for batch cooking. After all, four chicken breasts don't take any more time to cook than one breast does, so you can cook some for dinner tonight and save the rest for use in a stir-fry, pasta, salad, stew, or in sandwiches or wraps.

I like to make a big batch of marinara sauce (page 263) to have on hand for pizzas and pastas, or of homemade stock (page 267) for use in soups and stews. Similarly, I use the recipe for 63°C eggs (page 25) to prepare effortless poached eggs on Sunday that will last for the week ahead. Vegetables are also a snap to prepare sous vide, retaining their flavor, nutrients, and texture. So the next time you buy too much at the farmers' market, instead of watching it rot before you can use it all up, bag a few portions (with or without seasoning) and drop them into your water bath. Chilled and stored, they'll be ready to use throughout the week to add nutrition and heft to omelets, soups, sandwiches, salads, and more.

Entertaining Strategies

Whether you're preparing an intimate dinner or you're the designated tailgate cook, sous vide has your back. The same logic that makes preparing meals in advance more manageable applies to entertaining larger crowds. An immersion circulator propped on a counter or unused workspace (even a dining room table works, if it's close to an electrical outlet) not only frees up valuable stove and oven space but also liberates the cook because the technique is pretty much hands off. For many of the recipes in this book, I've included do-ahead strategies for spreading out the work and for taking advantage of the passive time in which the food is left to do its thing in the water bath. Follow these cues and you'll be able to pull off any special gathering.

Wanna throw a boozy brunch? Not only can you poach a dozen eggs ahead of time, but if you take a few hours during the week to make some liqueur infusions, you can also mix up some dazzling cocktails on the spot. For your next cookout, sous vide a big batch of chicken wings or rib-eye steaks and then throw them on the grill to reheat just before serving. Even desserts for a large crowd can be effortless if planned ahead. Recipes for crème brûlée, *pots de crème,* and dulce de leche can easily be doubled or tripled and then transferred to sweet-looking mason jars after cooking and refrigerated until you're ready for them.

Best of all, because you're dealing with precise cooking times, sous vide gives you the peace of mind of knowing that your preprepped feast won't be undercooked or overcooked.

* * *

At the end of the day, this book is not a manual for a cutting-edge technology. It's an invitation to bring you back into the kitchen. I hope that you'll love making and eating these recipes as much as I do. But even more than that, I hope that this glimpse into how I cook sous vide at home will inspire you to incorporate it into your *own* recipes and to make your everyday cooking easier and more delicious. With an immersion circulator as part of your kitchen arsenal and this book in your hands, you have everything you need to be successful in the kitchen. Now go forth and sous vide!

EGGS

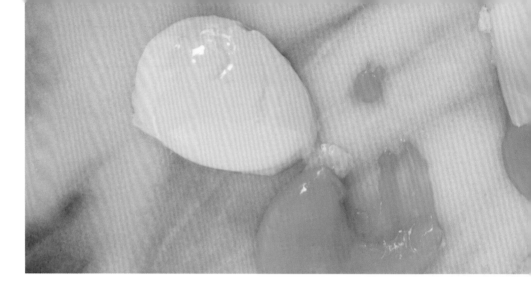

EGGS WERE MY INTRODUCTION TO THE WONDERS OF SOUS VIDE. That silky, unctuous, eye-opening first bite convinced me that I was dealing with something extraordinary. If sous vide is unknown territory for you, I'm pretty sure that your first bite will be enough to persuade you, as well.

It seems fitting to start things off with eggs, not only because it's where my sous vide journey began, but also because the egg is a richly symbolic food. In French cuisine, it has been used as a measure of worth: the pleats of a toque were classically said to represent the number of ways a trained chef could prepare eggs, and the ability to make an omelet has been used as a gauge to establish the skill of a cook being considered for hire. Even in the present day, eggs inspire the culinary imagination, and their extreme versatility offers nearly limitless potential for creativity that belies their ostensible simplicity.

Before I delve any further into my love of sous vide eggs, let's get the issue of terminology out of the way. Some people are all too eager to point out that the phrase *sous vide eggs* is a misnomer because eggs cooked in the shell are not under vacuum, and they have a good point. As I explained in the introduction (and demonstrate throughout the book), however, precise, even heating is actually what makes sous vide revolutionary, so while the distinction is technically correct, it strikes me as a bit pedantic. I certainly won't stop anyone from saying "precise-temperature eggs" or "thermal immersion circulator eggs," but I hope that I'll be forgiven for sticking to saying just "sous vide," with the understanding that you know what I mean.

Owing to their intricate makeup of fat and protein, eggs are remarkably responsive to even minor changes in temperature, which make them an especially good choice for illustrating the power of sous vide cooking. The recipes in this chapter demonstrate how a temperature variation of just a degree or two can cause a dramatic difference in how cooked eggs turn out. I won't delve deeply into the science involved, but the shorthand version is that albumin, the protein that makes up the egg white (which confusingly goes by the similarly named albumen), begins to denature at 60°C, going abruptly from translucent to opaque, which is why it's possible to pasteurize eggs at 57°C, without truly cooking them (as is explained on page 22). Only a few degrees

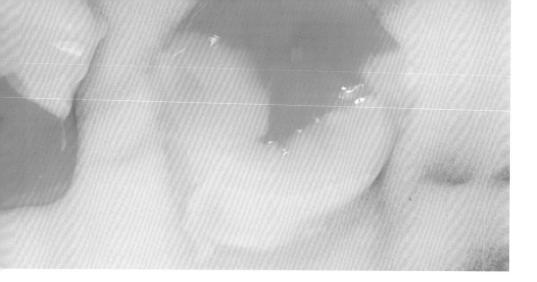

away, at 62°C, the egg will hold its shape, and one degree higher hits a sweet spot, producing my personal favorite temperature for soft cooked (page 25). At 64°C something magical happens: the yolk begins to thicken in such a way that it's semiliquid when warm but still malleable (that is, soft but able to hold a shape) when cold, opening the door to delicious novelties like fried yolks (page 29). Above this temperature, the yolk will be firmly set when cooked for an hour, but if cooked for shorter time periods at higher temperatures, like the 75°C on page 30, the white will be firmer but the yolk will still be soft. When the temperature is raised to 85°C, as I do for the tea eggs on page 36, the result is fully set whites like that of a traditional soft-boiled egg. These slim margins of difference in egg cookery would be impossible using conventional cooking methods.

This mountain of numbers isn't just idle knowledge: you can use this temperature sensitivity to tweak your eggs to create results that are perfect for you. Use the following recipes as guides to the remarkable texture combinations possible with sous vide cooking. They are just some of my tried-and-true approaches to cooking eggs, and all of them are open to customization. If you find egg whites cooked at 63°C a bit too soft for your liking, increase the temperature to 75°C the next time to see if the result suits you better. The possible time and temperature combinations are countless, so experiment boldly. No matter their pedigree, a dozen eggs, even if they're multicolored, free range, grass fed, and home schooled, won't break the bank. If you find that your eggs are *aaalmost* right, but you feel the whites are still a tad too soft or the yolks are a wee bit too runny, ratchet up the temperature a degree (or increase the cooking time) and see if that does the trick. Pretty soon you'll find your Goldilocks egg, one that's *juust* right.

No two cartons of eggs are alike. Commercially sold eggs vary widely in size and in age, and both factors will affect the cooking process. That said, the recipes here have been tested with large eggs and small eggs, extremely fresh eggs and older eggs. Although smaller eggs will cook slightly more quickly, these recipes should produce fine results using any egg that crosses your path. You can control at least one variable, which I recommend in the interest of consistency: rather than bringing your eggs to room temperature first, transfer them from the fridge directly into your preheated water bath. Enough talk, it's time to get cracking.

"RAW" PASTEURIZED EGG

Although eggs are one of the most versatile ingredients at a cook's disposal, the risk of salmonella has sometimes cast raw eggs in a sinister light, as anyone whose mother ever admonished them for eating unbaked cookie dough knows. Luckily, sous vide lets you have your dough and eat it, too. As explained in the "Food Safety" section on page 12, the controlled heat of sous vide makes pasteurization possible even at temperatures below 60°C.

Because minimal protein denaturation occurs even after 2 hours at 57°C, these eggs, when cracked open, will yield yolks that appear unchanged and whites that have turned only slightly opaque (like fogged glass) but still have a raw texture. While this visual difference easily distinguishes them from eggs that are truly raw, the awesome news is that they can still be used exactly like raw eggs. This gives you the freedom to make any recipe that traditionally calls for raw eggs, like the mayonnaise on page 262, without worrying about the risk to pregnant women, young children, the elderly, or anyone with a compromised immune system. So go ahead and fearlessly throw these "raw" eggs into Caesar salad dressings, shake the whites in a whiskey sour for a perfect frothy head, or use them in cookie dough and eat it right in front of your mom just to freak her out.

MAKES 1 or more eggs | **SOUS VIDE COOKING TIME:** 2 hours (or up to 4 hours) | **ACTIVE PREP TIME:** 10 minutes to cool

1 or more large eggs (any quantity is fine)

DO-AHEAD STRATEGY

The chilled finished eggs can be refrigerated for up to 2 weeks.

Preheat your sous vide water bath to 57°C (134.6°F).

When the water reaches the target temperature, using a slotted spoon, carefully lower the eggs (shell and all) directly into the water bath and cook for 2 hours.

When the eggs are ready, using the slotted spoon, transfer them to an ice water bath (see page 14) and chill until completely cold, about 10 minutes. Use immediately or refrigerate until needed.

CRACKING A SOUS VIDE EGG

Although an egg is typically thought of as divided between yolk and white, the white is functionally divided in two parts. The outer "thin" albumin remains watery and mostly unset at 63°C and will fall away from the inner "thick" albumlin once it is out of the shell. At higher temperatures, such as 75°C, the thin albumlin will stick to the shell. In either case, I take this as my guide for how to crack open eggs.

Cracking eggs seems like a no-brainer, but the uniquely fragile consistency of the whites calls for careful handling. To remove the eggs from their shells cleanly without breaking their Platonic ovoid shape, crack the egg against a solid, flat surface like a countertop (definitely not the side of a bowl, which forces shards of shell into the white and risks breaking the yolk). Use one quick, firm strike: think of the action as somewhere between petting a tiny kitten and "hulk smash!" Next, holding the egg over a bowl and using both hands, pull the shell apart in opposite directions. Then, using a slotted spoon, lift the egg from the bowl, giving the spoon a jiggle to make sure that all of the unset white is left behind.

SLOW-POACHED (63°C) EGG

This is my touchstone for sous vide eggs. I call them *poached* for lack of a better word (and because it's what they most closely resemble), even though they're actually slowly cooked in their shell. The archetype for these eggs is the Japanese *onsen tamago*, or "hot springs eggs." In days gone by, people who lived near naturally occurring hot springs in Japan would place their eggs in a basket and lower them into the bubbling water, where the gentle heat would cook them to a soft, custardy consistency. Although not quite as romantic, sous vide can now reproduce the same gloriously silky texture with no need to trek to a geothermal vent, and once you've sampled it, there's no turning back.

I could go on and on about the sensuous texture of these eggs, but the element of convenience is why I'm confident they will become your everyday eggs. At first glance, an hour might seem like a long time to wait for a poached egg, but none of it is active time: you put the eggs in the bath and an hour later they're ready. They can easily be made ahead, so to simplify my hectic morning routine, I like to cook a dozen at the beginning of the week, allowing me to sit down to the perfect poached egg whenever the urge strikes.

MAKES 1 or more poached eggs | **SOUS VIDE COOKING TIME:** 1 hour (or up to 2 hours)

1 or more large eggs

Flaky sea salt (such as Maldon or fleur de sel) and freshly ground black pepper

DO-AHEAD STRATEGY

The finished eggs can be chilled in an ice water bath (see page 14) for 10 minutes and then refrigerated for up to 1 week. Reheat at 60°C (140°F) for 15 minutes.

Preheat your sous vide water bath to 63°C (145.4°F).

When the water reaches the target temperature, using a slotted spoon, carefully lower the eggs (shell and all) directly into the water bath and cook for 1 hour.

At this point, the eggs can be served immediately, kept warm, or cooled down and then stored in the refrigerator. If you're eating the eggs right away, one at a time, crack them into a bowl and transfer them to their intended destination (on toast, over rice, on a salad, or the like). Serve immediately, sprinkled with the salt and pepper.

To use for eggs Florentine, lower the water temperature to 60°C (140°F) and keep the eggs warm for up to 2 hours or until ready to serve. (Lowering the water bath temperature extends the duration of time the eggs can be kept warm.)

PRO TIP

If you plan on making the Eggs Florentine with No-Whisk Hollandaise Sauce on page 26, you'll need 5 of these slow-poached eggs.

EGGS FLORENTINE WITH NO-WHISK HOLLANDAISE SAUCE

Eggs Florentine, Benedict's more refined cousin, features softly cooked eggs nestled on a bed of wilted tender spinach. Of course, the hollandaise sauce is the real star of the show. One of the secrets of an excellent hollandaise is to add liquid to the egg yolks before you mix in the butter, which aerates them and results in a fluffier sauce. Traditional hollandaise requires whisking the yolks carefully in a bain-marie (a stove-top water bath) over low heat to avoid curdling, then gradually adding the butter. Using an egg that has been softly cooked sous vide allows you to pull off a nifty trick: using the white along with the yolk gives the sauce more volume, and since the egg is already cooked, the blender does all of the work, whipping everything together almost instantly so that no fussy whisking is required. If you're a lover of hollandaise (and who isn't?), I guarantee this recipe will win you over.

SERVES 4 | **SOUS VIDE COOKING TIME:** 1 hour (or up to 2 hours done in advance) | **ACTIVE PREP TIME:** 20 minutes

5 Slow-Poached (63°C) Eggs (page 25), held warm at 60°C (140°F)

SPINACH

1 tablespoon unsalted butter

1 tablespoon minced shallot

4 cups loosely packed baby spinach

Big pinch of salt

Pinch of freshly ground black pepper

HOLLANDAISE SAUCE

1 63°C egg (from above)

1 to 2 teaspoons fresh lemon juice

½ cup (4 ounces) unsalted butter, melted and kept warm

Salt

Pinch of cayenne pepper

4 English muffins, properly split using a fork

Cayenne pepper, for finishing

1 tablespoon thinly sliced chives

Have the eggs ready.

To prepare the spinach, heat the butter and shallot in a sauté pan over medium-low heat. When the butter begins to foam, add the spinach, salt, and pepper and stir continuously until the leaves wilt and just begin to give off liquid, about 2 minutes. (Never allow the liquid to boil or the spinach will become stringy.) Transfer the cooked spinach to a sieve set over a bowl and allow the liquid to drain away. Discard the liquid and transfer the spinach to the bowl. Set the bowl aside in a warm place (such as the back of the stove) while you prepare the hollandaise sauce.

To make the hollandaise, remove 1 sous vide egg from the water bath. Crack the egg into a blender, add 1 teaspoon of the lemon juice, and blend on low speed until the mixture is foamy, about 30 seconds. With the blender running, pour in the warm butter in a slow, steady stream. When all of the butter has been added, the mixture should be satiny and thick enough to coat the back of a spoon easily. Add salt to taste, more lemon juice to taste, and the pinch of cayenne.

To assemble, toast the English muffin halves and place each bottom on a plate. Divide the spinach evenly among the muffin bottoms. Following the directions on page 22, one at a time, crack the remaining eggs into a bowl and transfer each egg to a spinach-topped muffin half. Cover each egg with a generous spoonful of warm hollandaise, sprinkle with cayenne pepper and chives, and then the top with the other muffin half. Serve immediately.

DO-AHEAD STRATEGY

This is a perfect brunch dish for company because both the poached eggs (held in their shells) and the finished hollandaise (placed in a quart-size freezer-safe ziplock bag or mason jar) can be kept warm for up to 2 hours at 60°C (140°F). The recipe calls for already-cooked 63°C eggs. You can make them immediately before you start preparing this recipe, in which case you'll need to lower the water bath to 60°C (140°F) to keep them hot. If you're reheating them from cold, first preheat your water bath to 60°C (140°F) and then reheat them in the water bath for 15 minutes before you make the hollandaise.

DEEP-FRIED EGG YOLKS

If your heart is full of adventure but is otherwise very healthy, I recommend these crunchy, gooey treats. The secret behind this culinary marvel lies in cooking the egg at precisely 64°C. This results in yolks that are malleable when cold but still "ooze" when hot. Breading the yolks while they're cold and still firm and then quickly deep-frying them to reheat produces an incredibly indulgent combo: a crunchy shell contrasted with a warm, molten inside. Bite sized but hugely satisfying, they make great appetizers but are also a jaw-dropping garnish for a simple green salad—a sort of glorious hybrid of a poached egg and a crouton.

SERVES 4 as an appetizer | **SOUS VIDE COOKING TIME:** 1 hour | **ACTIVE PREP TIME:** 5 minutes, plus 35 minutes to chill

4 large eggs

½ cup panko (Japanese-style bread crumbs)

Canola or other vegetable oil, for deep-frying

Flaky sea salt (such as Maldon or fleur de sel)

4 small dill leaves, for garnish (optional)

DO-AHEAD STRATEGY

The cooked and cooled eggs can be refrigerated for up to 1 week before you prepare the yolks for deep-frying. Once the egg yolks are fried, they retain their heat well and can be kept at room temperature for 5 to 10 minutes.

Preheat your sous vide water bath to 64°C (147.2°F).

When the water reaches the target temperature, using a slotted spoon, carefully lower the eggs (shell and all) directly into the water bath and cook for 1 hour.

When the eggs are ready, using the slotted spoon, transfer them to an ice water bath (see page 14) and chill until completely cold, about 20 minutes.

Crack 1 egg and drop it into a bowl as directed on page 22. Using your fingers, gently separate the yolk from the white (which will be very delicate and easily fall away) and transfer the yolk to a small plate, then discard the white. Don't worry if a small amount of white remains on the yolk; it will be covered by the bread crumbs. Repeat with the remaining eggs.

Put ¼ cup of the bread crumbs onto a plate or into a shallow bowl large enough to accommodate the yolks in a single layer with about 1 inch between them. Place the yolks onto the bed of crumbs and, using your fingertips or a spoon,

carefully turn the yolks to coat completely. If necessary, gently press the crumbs onto the yolks to make sure they adhere. When all of the yolks are coated, sprinkle the remaining ¼ cup of bread crumbs on top (to "bury" the yolks) and transfer the plate of crumb-covered yolks to the refrigerator for 15 minutes. This cooling step helps to ensure an even crust that won't separate from the yolk.

Line a dinner plate with paper towels and place near the stove. Pour the oil to a depth of about 2 inches into a saucepan and place over medium heat. The oil should come no more than one-third of the way up the side of the pan to ensure it will not boil over the rim once the yolks are added. Heat the oil to 350°F on a high-heat thermometer, or until a few bread crumbs dropped into the hot oil sizzle on contact and then brown within a couple of seconds.

Using the slotted spoon, carefully lower a breaded egg yolk into the hot oil and fry until deep golden brown, 30 to 60 seconds. As it fries, use the slotted spoon to move it around in the oil so that it browns evenly and doesn't rest on the bottom of the pan. Transfer the fried yolk to the towel-lined plate and season immediately with a pinch of the sea salt. Repeat with the remaining egg yolks, frying them one at a time. Avoid the temptation to fry more than a single yolk at a time, because if they stay in the oil too long, you'll end up with hard-cooked yolks, defeating the whole purpose.

To serve, garnish each fried yolk with a dill leaf.

PRO TIP

I prefer the lighter, more irregular pieces of panko over regular bread crumbs because they result in a supercrisp, airy crust and maximum crunchy pleasure time.

FAST-POACHED (75°C) EGG

Though not quite as fast as a traditional poached egg, I still think of these eggs as a quicker version of the Slow-Poached (63°C) Eggs on page 25. With this approach, you can achieve the custardy texture that sets sous vide eggs apart on much shorter notice. However, because the cooking temperature is higher, there is a risk of overcooking. For that reason, unique to this recipe, I give you a range of cooking times: smaller eggs will likely be done after 13 minutes, and larger ones may take an additional 1 to 2 minutes to reach their ideal consistency. Be careful, however, because in that minute or two, the yolk can thicken dramatically. Of course, you can substitute 63°C eggs in any recipe in which you'd use these eggs.

MAKES 1 or more poached eggs | **SOUS VIDE COOKING TIME:** 13 to 15 minutes

1 or more large eggs (any quantity is fine; you'll need 4 eggs for the breakfast sandwiches on page 35)

Flaky sea salt (such as Maldon or fleur de sel) and freshly ground black pepper

DO-AHEAD STRATEGY

Because these eggs cook quickly (and are somewhat finicky), I don't recommend making them ahead. If you're inclined to cook your eggs in advance, I recommend you opt for the Slow-Poached (63°C) Eggs on page 25.

Preheat your sous vide water bath to 75°C (167°F).

When the water reaches the target temperature, using a slotted spoon, carefully lower the eggs (shell and all) directly into the water bath and cook for 13 to 15 minutes, depending on size.

Using the slotted spoon, remove the eggs from the water bath and run them under cool water until they are cool enough to handle, about 30 seconds. They're now ready to be used for the breakfast sandwiches.

If you're eating the eggs right away, one at a time, crack them into a bowl and transfer them to their intended destination (on toast, over rice, on a salad, or the like) as directed on page 22. Sprinkle with the salt and pepper and serve.

QUAIL EGGS WITH POTATO BLINI

A jewel-like quail egg on top of a delicate potato blini contains all of the glory of a sous vide egg in a single miniaturized morsel. Be sure to tell your guests that each canapé should be eaten in one bite. Compared to the plain ol' chicken variety, quail eggs may seem downright rarified, but don't be put off: they're just as simple to cook sous vide—though they take longer than you might expect, given their small size. These blini are show stopping just as they are, but feel free to gussy them up with a dab of caviar or trout roe on top.

MAKES about 12 small blini | **SOUS VIDE COOKING TIME:** 45 minutes (or up to 1½ hours) | **ACTIVE PREP TIME:** 25 minutes

BLINI

1 cup Perfect Mashed Potatoes (about ½ recipe; page 193), cold

Pinch of kosher salt

Pinch of freshly grated or ground nutmeg

Pinch of freshly ground white pepper

1 to 2 tablespoons all-purpose flour

1 large egg

1 tablespoon whole milk, if needed for consistency

Cooking spray or unsalted butter, for greasing the pan

12 quail eggs

About 2 tablespoons crème fraîche, for serving

12 small dill leaves

Flaky sea salt (such as Maldon or fleur de sel)

DO-AHEAD STRATEGY

The batter can be held at room temperature for up to 2 hours or in an airtight container in the refrigerator for up to 2 days. The blini can be made, cooled, packed in an airtight container, and refrigerated for up to 3 days or frozen for up to 1 month. To reheat from the fridge, warm them for 5 minutes in a 350°F oven, or for 10 minutes if from the freezer. In either case, they'll be hot and puff somewhat when ready. The cooked quail eggs can be chilled in their shells in an ice bath for 10 minutes then stored in the fridge for up to 1 week. Reheat in a 60°C (140°F) water bath for 10 minutes before serving.

CONTINUED >

Preheat your sous vide water bath to 64°C (147.2°F).

To make the blini, in a bowl, whisk together the potatoes, salt, nutmeg, pepper, 1 tablespoon of the flour, and the egg until a smooth batter forms. To test if the consistency is correct, using the whisk, lift some of the batter above the bowl. If the batter falls slowly but still holds its shape, the consistency is good. If the batter clings to the whisk, mix in the milk. If the batter is too thin, whisk in the remaining 1 tablespoon flour. Set the batter aside while you begin cooking the quail eggs in the water bath. (The batter can be held at room temperature for up to 2 hours or in the fridge for 1 to 2 days.)

When the water reaches the target temperature, using a slotted spoon, carefully lower the eggs (shell and all) directly into the water bath and cook for 45 minutes.

About 10 minutes before the eggs are ready, begin cooking the blini. Have a sheet pan ready. Preheat a large nonstick sauté pan or skillet over medium heat for 1 to 2 minutes. When the pan is hot, lightly coat the bottom with cooking spray; it should sizzle on contact. Spoon 1½ to 2 tablespoons batter into the pan to form each 1½-inch round blin, spacing the blini at least 2 inches apart. You should be able to cook about 6 blini at a time, depending on the size of the pan. Cook the blini until the edges begin to set and the bottoms are golden brown, about 2 minutes. Using a small offset spatula, flip the blini and lightly press down on the top of each one with the spatula to spread the batter slightly.

The blini should be roughly ¼ inch thick and lacy. Cook on the second side until they begin to puff slightly at the center, about 1½ minutes. Transfer the blini to the sheet pan in a single layer and set aside. Repeat with the remaining batter. You should have about 12 blini. If you're not serving the blini right away, keep them warm in a 250°F oven for up to 15 minutes.

When the quail eggs are ready, using the slotted spoon, carefully remove them from the water bath. One at a time, gently crack the eggs against a solid, flat surface and slide them from their shell onto a large plate. Alternatively, using a sharp knife or kitchen shears, cut off ¼ inch from the pointed end of each shell and then gently shake the quail egg out whole.

To serve, place the blini in a single layer on a serving tray. Put ½ teaspoon of the crème fraîche on center of each blini and then gently top with a quail egg, dill leaf, and pinch of salt.

PRO TIP

If you want picture-perfect round blini and are feeling especially cheffy, spoon the batter into a piping bag fitted with a ½-inch round tip (or into a ziplock plastic bag and cut off one corner tip) and pipe the batter directly into the pan.

BREAKFAST EGG SANDWICH WITH SERRANO HAM, MANCHEGO, AND SALSA VERDE

I turn to Spain for this grown-up version of green eggs and ham (you may want them *con café*, you may want them every day). The sharpness of the salsa verde with salty, savory *jamón serrano* and manchego cheese makes for a Spanish flavor bonanza. Add a flaky croissant and seductive sous vide egg, and you'll wonder why ham, egg, and cheese sandwiches are served any other way. Despite being a sophisticated combination of flavors, it's a rather simple breakfast dish to pull off, particularly since it calls for my quicker 75°C version of a soft-cooked egg.

SERVES 4 | **SOUS VIDE COOKING TIME:** 13 to 15 minutes (done in advance) | **ACTIVE PREP TIME:** 15 minutes

SALSA VERDE

¼ cup finely chopped fresh flat-leaf parsley

1 tablespoon finely minced shallot

Finely grated zest of ½ lemon (about 1 teaspoon)

¼ cup extra-virgin olive oil

Kosher salt and freshly ground black pepper

4 Fast-Poached (75°C) Eggs (page 30)

4 croissants

4 ounces thinly sliced serrano or other dry-cured ham (such as prosciutto or country ham)

3 to 4 ounces manchego cheese, thinly shaved with a cheese plane or vegetable peeler

DO-AHEAD STRATEGY

If you want to make this a snap to prepare for a morning meal, you can make the salsa verde and shave the cheese up to 3 days in advance and keep them refrigerated.

Up to 2 hours before you plan to serve your sandwiches, make the salsa verde. In a small bowl, whisk together the parsley, shallot, lemon zest, and oil. Season with salt and pepper and set aside.

Preheat the oven or toaster oven to 350°F.

When you're ready to assemble the sandwiches, cook the eggs as directed. When they are ready, one at a time, crack them into a small bowl as directed on page 22 and set aside.

Slice the croissants in half lengthwise, keeping the two halves together, and then toast them until just heated through, about 5 minutes.

To assemble the sandwiches, place the bottom half of each croissant, cut side up, on a plate and divide the ham evenly among them. Using a slotted spoon, one at a time, lift the eggs from the bowl, giving the spoon a jiggle to make sure that all of the unset white is left behind, and place them on top of the ham. Spoon a heaping tablespoon of the salsa verde over each egg and then top with the cheese, dividing it evenly. Close the sandwiches with the croissant tops, cut side down. Serve immediately.

PRO TIP

The salsa verde has a better taste and texture if the ingredients are chopped by hand. But if you're pressed for time, a blender or small food processor can be used.

CHINESE TEA EGGS

This is my rendition of traditional Chinese tea eggs, also known as marbled eggs because of the beautiful variegated pattern the tea makes as it seeps through the cracks in the shell. Typically, tea eggs are hard boiled on the stove top, but by using sous vide, the eggs have tender whites with still-runny yolks. A word to the wise: this is one instance where a fresher egg isn't necessarily better. The longer an egg is stored, the more air will penetrate the shell, making for easier peeling, so a farm-fresh egg is not your best choice here. As for the flavoring, it's critical to use naturally brewed soy sauce that lists soybeans as the main ingredient, as opposed to processed versions made with hydrolyzed soy protein and corn syrup, which have a harsh, artificial taste. Additionally, I prefer to use *Lapsang souchong*, a smoked black tea. The resulting combination of smoky, sweet, and salty makes these eggceptionally snackable.

SERVES 6 as an appetizer | **SOUS VIDE COOKING TIME:** 12 minutes | **ACTIVE PREP TIME:** 5 minutes, plus 10 minutes to chill and 24 to 48 hours to marinate

¾ cup soy sauce

¾ cup water

1 tablespoon mirin (Japanese sweet cooking wine)

¼ cup firmly packed dark brown sugar

3 tablespoons loose-leaf Lapsang souchong or your favorite black tea

6 large eggs

DO-AHEAD STRATEGY

The cooked and cooled eggs can be refrigerated for up to 1 week. After 2 days, drain the eggs and discard the marinade to prevent them from overcuring.

Preheat your sous vide water bath to 85°C (185°F).

While the water is heating, make the tea marinade. In a small saucepan, combine the soy sauce, water, mirin, brown sugar, and tea leaves and bring to a simmer over medium heat, stirring to dissolve the sugar. When the liquid is at a simmer, remove the pan from the heat and let the mixture steep for 4 minutes. Pour the marinade into a fine-mesh sieve set over a bowl or liquid measuring cup and discard the contents of the sieve.

When the water reaches the target temperature, using a slotted spoon, carefully lower the eggs into the water bath and cook for 12 minutes.

When the eggs are ready, using the slotted spoon, transfer them to an ice water bath (see page 14) and chill until completely cold, about 10 minutes.

Remove the eggs from the ice water bath. One at a time, carefully crack the entire surface of each eggshell against a countertop, or with the back of a spoon. It's important when cracking the shell to apply the correct amount of force: firm enough to crack the membrane around the egg and create fissures but not hard enough to break it apart. When you have finished cracking their shells, the eggs should have a flaky, scaly exterior but still be intact.

Gently place the eggs in a 1 quart size ziplock bag or a small, narrow container and pour the marinade on top. Make sure that the eggs are completely immersed. Seal the bag or cover the container and then refrigerate the eggs in the tea mixture for at least 24 hours or for up to 48 hours.

To serve, remove the eggs from the refrigerator, take them out of the bag (discarding any liquid), and carefully peel them. Don't worry if the whites tear a little bit in the process; they'll still be delicious. At this point, the eggs are ready to eat, but they'll taste even better if you let them come to room temperature for 30 minutes before serving.

PRO TIP

You can use this recipe to make soft-boiled eggs. Skip the marinating step after chilling the eggs and they're ready to peel. Similarly, to produce hard-boiled eggs, follow the directions for soft-boiled eggs but increase the cooking time to 25 minutes.

FISH AND SHELLFISH

AS ANYONE WHO HAS DEVOURED A TOWERING *PLATEAU DE FRUITS DE MER* KNOWS, seafood is a veritable (sunken) treasure trove of delicacies. Cooking seafood yourself can be intimidating, however, as the raw materials are highly perishable and typically expensive. What's more, environmental concerns about endangered species and the depletion of ocean ecosystems make getting it right feel especially onerous. But it's not just the exclusivity and the price that has made seafood cookery the calling card of many temples of gastronomy. It's also the skill level normally required to achieve superior results. If the thought of cooking shrimp flawlessly has you humming the *Mission: Impossible* theme tune to yourself, I'm here to reassure you that sous vide is the ideal technique for the job.

The fact that fish and shellfish are such delicate products is the very reason that sous vide is so well suited to the task of cooking them. I'm a firm believer that sous vide means never having to endure overcooked food again, and nowhere is that better illustrated than here. More than any other protein, seafood, whether a fin fish like salmon, a crustacean like shrimp, or a mollusk like scallop, goes from tender and succulent to dry and rubbery in seconds. The key to avoiding this is restraint— to applying heat judiciously and to knowing when to stop. In the past, this required considerable knowledge and finesse, but sous vide takes out the guesswork.

By utilizing very low, controlled cooking temperatures, you will not only improve on classics (like the perfectly crispy fish and chips on page 59 and the never-tough garlic shrimp on page 55) but will also achieve pristine, barely cooked textures that would otherwise be impossible (see the scallop sashimi on page 43). If you are accustomed to fish that's cooked well done, the meltingly soft texture found in some of the

following recipes (particularly the salmon on page 57) may come as a surprise. As always, sous vide cooking is supremely adaptable to your tastes, so feel free to raise the temperatures if you prefer your catch on the firm side. Try increasing the cooking temperature of the water bath in increments of 5°C while experimenting.

The flipside of this careful cooking is speed: with the exception of the octopus on page 49, the fish and shellfish in the following dishes all cook in well under an hour (markedly faster than meat or poultry). Because of this, regardless of whether you're cooking a casual weekday meal (like the salmon with salad on page 57) or a show-stopping centerpiece (like the lobster on page 65), the final dish comes together quickly and perfectly cooked. Another difference you'll notice in this chapter is that, unlike my instructions for serving meat or poultry, I generally don't recommend chilling and reheating these dishes. Sous vide can give you wonderful results, but seafood is still a limited-engagement affair.

I always say that fancy is my baseline, but more than anywhere else in this book, this is where you don't want to stint on sourcing. As wonderful as it is, one thing sous vide cooking definitely can't do is cover up the defects of inferior seafood. Because quality and freshness are especially important, I recommend frequenting a shop where you can actually talk to the fishmonger. "Develop a relationship with your fishmonger" may sound hokey, but it's good advice. I suggest checking out the Monterey Bay Aquarium Seafood Watch (www.seafoodwatch.org), as well. It's an excellent resource to help you choose sustainable options (often with the added benefit of higher quality). So, with the confidence to select and cook seafood fearlessly, it's now time to dive in to deliciousness!

SCALLOP SASHIMI WITH GRAPEFRUIT-YUZU VINAIGRETTE

Even when compared with other seafood, scallops are extremely delicate: their supremely tender meat gives them an almost melt-in-your-mouth texture, which means they're at their best when nearly uncooked. If they are exposed to high heat for too long, they quickly become dry and rubbery—no thanks! My solution is to cook them in an extremely low temperature sous vide bath. By using this "barely cooked" approach, the scallops firm up somewhat but lose none of their luscious texture.

The quality of the finished dish will depend heavily on the freshness of the scallops, as you will be serving them barely cooked. For this reason, I always recommend dry-packed scallops over wet-packed ones, which have been soaked in a chemical solution to plump them up and extend their shelf life at the cost of both flavor and texture. If the scallops are sitting in a milky liquid at the shop, they are likely wet packed. If in doubt, double-check with the seafood purveyor. Diver scallops, which are harvested by hand, are tops in terms of quality, so get them if you can!

Don't be scared off by the esoteric ingredients called for in this recipe. Many of them should be relatively easy to find at a well-stocked Japanese grocery store or online (see Resources, page 273). If you can't find them, you can swap them out for more readily available ingredients with good results, as the sweet scallop and tangy grapefruit are the star players here.

SERVES 4 as an appetizer | **SOUS VIDE COOKING TIME:** 30 minutes (or up to 40 minutes) | **ACTIVE PREP TIME:** 25 minutes, plus 20 minutes to chill

8 ounces dry-packed large sea scallops (4 to 8 scallops)

2 tablespoons red or pink grapefruit juice

1 tablespoon white shoyu (light-colored Japanese soy sauce) or other soy sauce

1 teaspoon bottled yuzu juice or fresh Meyer lemon or lime juice

1 teaspoon red yuzu kosho (Japanese sour, salty chile condiment) or finely minced medium-hot red chile such as Fresno

1 teaspoon mirin (Japanese sweet cooking wine)

1 tablespoon extra-virgin olive oil

8 shiso leaves or large mint leaves

1 head Belgian endive, base trimmed, halved lengthwise, and halves cut lengthwise into ¼-inch-wide wedges or spears

1 avocado, halved, pitted, peeled, and cut lengthwise into ½-inch-thick slices

1 red or pink grapefruit, cut into supremes (see page 44)

Flaky sea salt (such as Maldon or fleur de sel)

DO-AHEAD STRATEGY

The cooked and chilled scallops can be refrigerated in the bag for 1 to 2 days.

CONTINUED >

Set your sous vide water bath to 50°C (122°F).

Place the scallops in a single layer in a gallon-size freezer-safe ziplock bag and seal using the water displacement method (see page 12).

When the water reaches the target temperature, lower the bagged scallops into the water bath and cook for 30 minutes.

When the scallops are ready, remove the bag from the water bath and place in an ice water bath (see page 14) until well chilled, about 20 minutes.

While the scallops are chilling, make the vinaigrette. In a small bowl, whisk together the grapefruit juice, shoyu, *yuzu* juice, *yuzu kosho*, mirin, and oil until well blended; you can also shake together in a small capped jar. Taste the vinaigrette; it should be tangy, salty, and a bit sweet and spicy. Adjust the seasoning if needed.

Transfer the chilled scallops to a cutting board. Discard any accumulated cooking liquid. Using a sharp knife, carefully slice the scallops horizontally into ¼-inch-thick coins. You should get 3 or 4 slices from each scallop, depending on their size.

To serve, place 2 shiso leaves in the center of each chilled plate and arrange the scallop coins and endive wedges on top. Scatter the avocado slices and grapefruit supremes around the scallops and drizzle the vinaigrette liberally over everything. Sprinkle with the salt.

PRO TIP

To serve the scallops hot, omit the ice water bath. After you pull the bag from the water bath, remove the scallops from the bag and pat dry thoroughly. Heat a large sauté pan over high heat and lightly coat the bottom with unsalted butter or olive oil. Add the scallops in a single layer and sear until a golden brown crust forms on the underside, 1 to 2 minutes. Flip the scallops over and cook just until they have firmed up, 30 to 60 seconds. Transfer to a cutting board and proceed as directed for the chilled scallops.

HOW TO MAKE SUPREMES, DIANA ROSS NOT REQUIRED

Cutting a citrus such as a grapefruit into supremes involves removing the pith and membrane that surrounds each segment, so that when you bite down, all you taste is juicy fruit. To do this, using a sharp knife, cut a thin slice off the top and bottom of the fruit, then stand the fruit upright on a cutting board. Following the contour of the fruit, slice downward to remove the peel and pith in wide strips, rotating the fruit after each cut. When you have finished, all of the segments should be exposed and no pith should be visible. Holding the peeled fruit over a bowl, slide the knife blade along both sides of each segment to free it from the membrane, letting it fall into the bowl. Once all of the segments have been removed, squeeze the membrane over the bowl to release any additional juice, which can be used for the vinaigrette or any another recipe.

HALIBUT TOSTADAS

This is my take on Baja-style fish tacos. Typically the fish is fried and wrapped in a soft corn tortilla. Here, I've flipped things around and use fried tortillas for crispiness and cook the fish sous vide. This approach yields moist, tender fish that flakes apart effortlessly and eliminates the mess and hassle of frying the fish. I buy prepared tostadas, which are essentially fried corn tortillas, for the same reason I buy tortilla chips: convenience. They're a pain in the ass to make yourself, and the store-bought kind is perfectly tasty.

These tostadas are fast and easy enough to make for a snack or for a casual meal with friends—just add margaritas. The recipe can be easily doubled or tripled for entertaining.

SERVES 4 as an appetizer, or 2 as a main course | **SOUS VIDE COOKING TIME:** 20 minutes (or up to 30 minutes) |
ACTIVE PREP TIME: 25 minutes

8 ounces skinless halibut or other firm-fleshed, flaky fish fillet (such as snapper or sea bass), about 1 inch thick

Salt and freshly ground black pepper

4 teaspoons extra-virgin olive oil

1 (½-inch-wide) strip lime zest

1 oregano or marjoram sprig, or pinch of dried oregano

AVOCADO CREMA

½ avocado, peeled and pitted

3 tablespoons sour cream

Juice of ½ lime (about 1 tablespoon)

Salt

4 (6-inch) tostadas

1 cup finely shredded cabbage (preferably napa) or romaine lettuce

¼ cup loosely packed fresh cilantro leaves

1 Fresno or other medium-hot red chile, thinly sliced and seeded, if desired

Flaky sea salt (such as Maldon or fleur de sel)

4 lime wedges, for serving

Hot sauce, for serving (optional)

DO-AHEAD STRATEGY

The avocado crema can be made up to 2 hours before serving and kept refrigerated.

CONTINUED >

Preheat your sous vide water bath to 54°C (129°F).

Season the halibut with salt and pepper and then coat with 1 teaspoon of the oil. Place the fish, lime zest, and oregano in a quart-size freezer-safe ziplock bag and seal using the water displacement method (see page 12).

When the water reaches the target temperature, lower the bagged halibut into the water bath (making sure the bag is fully submerged) and cook for 20 minutes.

While the halibut is cooking, make the avocado crema. Put the avocado, sour cream, lime juice, and a pinch of salt into a blender and puree until completely smooth. Taste and adjust the seasoning with more salt if needed. Set aside. This makes a generous amount of crema, but blending a smaller amount is difficult. Don't worry—you'll have no problem dispatching any excess using chips (or broken tostadas) for dipping.

Line a plate with paper towels. When the halibut is ready, remove the bag from the water bath and transfer the halibut to the prepared plate. Discard any accumulated cooking liquid.

Preheat a nonstick sauté pan over medium-high heat. Add the halibut and sear until golden brown on the underside, about 1 minute. Flip the halibut and brown on the second side, about 1 minute more. Transfer the halibut to a bowl and, using your fingers or a fork, flake it into small bite-size pieces, discarding any errant bones.

Place the tostada shells on four plates if serving as an appetizer or divide between two plates if serving as a main course. Spread a generous dollop of the avocado crema on each tostada shell. Scatter the shredded cabbage on top, followed by the fish, cilantro, and chile, dividing each ingredient evenly. Sprinkle with the salt and drizzle evenly with the remaining 3 teaspoons of olive oil. Garnish each tostada with a lime wedge and pass the hot sauce at the table.

GREEK OCTOPUS SALAD

Octopus is notoriously prone to turning out rubbery, so much so that it has even inspired the old wives' tale that a wine cork in the pot will tenderize it. But the key to tender octopus is simple: slow, gentle cooking. Octopus takes far longer to cook than the other types of seafood in this chapter, but the results are reliably tender, with no magic tricks required. The deep, briny taste of octopus stands up wonderfully to bright, bold Mediterranean flavors—which is why I turned to Greece as inspiration for this salad.

In the United States, octopuses are most commonly sold frozen (or thawed), but it turns out that's a good thing, since frozen is better than fresh unless, perhaps, you're friends with an octopus fisherman. That's because not only does freezing do a great job of preserving freshness (fresh octopus spoils quickly), but it also helps to pretenderize the octopus.

SERVES 6 as an appetizer, 4 as a light main course | **SOUS VIDE COOKING TIME:** 4 hours (or up to 6 hours) |
ACTIVE PREP TIME: 30 minutes, plus 30 minutes to cool

OCTOPUS

1 fresh or frozen (thawed) whole octopus, about 3 pounds

3 (½-inch-wide) strips lemon zest (from about ½ lemon)

2 bay leaves

2 marjoram or oregano sprigs, or ¼ teaspoon dried oregano

1 teaspoon fresh lemon juice

1 teaspoon kosher salt

OLIVE VINAIGRETTE

3 cloves Garlic Confit (page 265), crushed, or 1 clove fresh garlic, minced

½ red onion, thinly sliced (about ¼ cup)

1 teaspoon chopped fresh marjoram or oregano, or ¼ teaspoon dried oregano

1 teaspoon finely grated lemon zest (from about ½ lemon)

1 tablespoon fresh lemon juice

1 tablespoon red wine vinegar

½ cup coarsely chopped Kalamata olives

¼ cup extra-virgin olive oil

3 tablespoons chopped fresh flat-leaf parsley

SALAD

1 tablespoon extra-virgin olive oil

½ cup cherry tomatoes, halved crosswise

2 cups baby arugula

Kosher salt and freshly ground black pepper

DO-AHEAD STRATEGY

The cooked and chilled octopus can be refrigerated in the bag for up to 3 days. Just before serving, drain well and sear as directed. The vinaigrette can be made up to 3 days in advance and refrigerated; remove from the fridge 30 minutes before serving.

CONTINUED >

Preheat your sous vide water bath to 84°C (183°F).

Put the octopus, lemon zest, bay leaves, marjoram, lemon juice, and salt into a gallon-size freezer-safe ziplock bag and seal using the water displacement method (see page 12).

When the water reaches the target temperature, lower the bagged octopus into the water bath (making sure the bag is fully submerged) and cook for 4 hours.

When the octopus is ready, remove the bag from the water bath, transfer it to a ice water bath (see page 14), and chill until completely cold, about 30 minutes. The octopus will have shrunk to less than half its original size and given off a substantial amount of liquid.

While the octopus is chilling, make the vinaigrette. In a large bowl, combine the garlic, red onion, marjoram, lemon zest and juice, vinegar, olives, oil, and parsley and mix well with a wooden spoon.

When the octopus is fully chilled, remove it from the bag and drain off all of the liquid. (The liquid can be discarded or strained and saved for another use.)

To prepare the octopus, cut the arms from the head and then cut each arm crosswise into about 2-inch pieces. The head is not as tasty as the arms, so I prefer to discard it.

To make the salad, coat the portioned octopus pieces with the oil and season lightly with salt and pepper. Preheat a cast-iron skillet or stove-top grill pan over medium-high heat. Add the octopus pieces and sear on the underside until lightly charred, 1 to 2 minutes. Using tongs, flip the pieces over and sear on the second side until lightly charred, 1 to 2 minutes longer.

Transfer the octopus to the bowl holding the vinaigrette and toss to coat the pieces evenly. Add the tomatoes and arugula and toss well, then season to taste with salt and pepper. The olives in the vinaigrette and the octopus will have plenty of salt, so you may not need to add any.

Transfer the salad to a serving platter or bowl and enjoy. Opa!

PRO TIP

The octopus gives off a lot of liquid as it cooks. The purplish liquid, which has a pleasantly briny taste, can be used in a seafood soup or risotto.

VIETNAMESE SHRIMP SUMMER ROLLS

If you've never made summer rolls before, you'll find that they're actually pretty easy; the goal is to form a tight roll that will hold together when dipped into the spicy hoisin sauce. The worst-case scenario is that the roll will split open, which is a little messy but not the end of the world. If the rice wrapper tears when you are rolling, it's okay to wrap the roll in a second rice wrapper circle. I like to work on a marble slab, but any smooth, clean countertop, large plate, or plastic cutting board will work.

SERVES 4 to 6 as an appetizer | **SOUS VIDE COOKING TIME:** 15 minutes (or up to 25 minutes) | **ACTIVE PREP TIME:** 25 minutes, plus 10 minutes to cool

18 peeled and deveined large shrimp (about 1 pound)

1 tablespoon fish sauce

1 teaspoon Sriracha sauce

Finely grated zest of ½ lime

DIPPING SAUCE

¼ cup hoisin sauce

Juice of 1 lime (about 2 tablespoons)

1 tablespoon chile-garlic paste or Sriracha sauce

2 tablespoons unsalted roasted peanuts, chopped

6 (12-inch) round Vietnamese rice wrappers, plus extras as needed to repair tears

3 large leaves green or red leaf lettuce, halved through the central rib

2 ounces dried rice vermicelli, cooked according to package instructions, drained, and rinsed under cold running water

2 Persian cucumbers or ½ English cucumber, seeded and cut into 3-inch-long thin sticks

1 cup loosely packed cilantro sprigs (tender stems with leaves attached)

1 cup loosely packed fresh mint or Thai basil leaves, or a mixture

DO-AHEAD STRATEGY

The cooked and chilled shrimp can be stored in the bag in the refrigerator for up to 3 days. The assembled rolls can be covered with a damp towel (paper or cloth) and refrigerated for up to 4 hours. Just make sure they don't touch one another, as they will stick together. The dipping sauce can be made up to 2 weeks in advance and stored in an airtight container in the refrigerator.

CONTINUED >

Preheat your sous vide water bath to 60°C (140°F).

Place the shrimp, fish sauce, Sriracha sauce, and lime zest in a gallon-size freezer-safe ziplock bag and massage the contents until the shrimp are evenly coated with the marinade. Seal using the water displacement method (see page 12). Push the shrimp around until they are spread out in a single layer.

When the water reaches the target temperature, lower the bagged shrimp into the water bath (making sure the bag is fully submerged) and cook for 15 minutes.

When the shrimp are ready, remove the bag from the water bath, transfer it to an ice water bath (see page 14), and chill until completely cold, about 10 minutes.

Remove the cooled shrimp from the bag and transfer them to a bowl. Discard the liquid in the bag.

To make the dipping sauce, combine the hoisin sauce, lime juice, paste, and peanuts in a small bowl and stir to mix well. Set aside.

When you're ready to assemble the spring rolls, have all of the ingredients on hand on separate plates or in separate bowls: rice wrappers, lettuce, vermicelli, cucumber, cilantro, mint, and shrimp. Have ready a clean, smooth work surface large enough to accommodate a rice wrapper. Fill a large bowl with lukewarm water (for soaking the rice wrapper) and set it alongside the work surface. Lightly oil a large plate or platter. Soak the rice wrappers and assemble the rolls one at a time, as the soaked wrappers will become sticky and difficult to work with if not rolled immediately.

Using your hands, lower a rice wrapper into the bowl of water; if the bowl isn't big enough to completely immerse the wrapper, rotate the wrapper in the water until it's flexible enough to submerge (akin to bending spaghetti to fit it in cooking water). Let the wrapper sit in the water until it no longer holds its shape and collapses to the bottom of the bowl, which should take 30 to 60 seconds.

Carefully lift the softened rice wrapper out of the water, grasping it by the edges and letting the excess water drip back into the bowl. Place the wrapper on the work surface and smooth out any folds or wrinkles. It should be perfectly flat. If a lot of water is still clinging to it, lightly blot off the excess with a kitchen towel. (A little moisture is fine, but

you don't want the wrapper sitting in a puddle of water or the roll won't come together.)

Working quickly, place a lettuce leaf half just inside the edge of the wrapper closest to you, leaving a small border of rice wrapper exposed. The leaf should cover about the bottom one-third of the circle.

Next, lay out about ¼ cup of the cooked vermicelli across the center of the lettuce leaf, extending the noodles to both edges of the leaf. Top with a small handful of the cucumber sticks, enough to match the length of the noodles. Place 2 or 3 cilantro sprigs and 3 or 4 mint leaves on top of the noodles and cucumber (enough so that there's some herb in every bite). Finally, lay 3 shrimp, end to end, on top of the herbs so they extend to the edges of the leaf.

Now you're ready to roll: using your fingertips, lift the edge of the rice wrapper closest to you and fold it over and around the filling ingredients (the lettuce helps with this process; the idea is to encase the loose ingredients). Carefully roll into a rough cylinder just until the filling is wrapped in a single layer of the rice wrapper. At this point, you will have rolled up about half the circle. Fold the left and right sides of the wrapper over the cylinder, closing off the open ends, and then finish rolling the circle into a cylinder, gently applying pressure as you do to make the roll as tight as possible without ripping the wrapper. Once the roll is made, transfer it to the oiled plate. This sounds like a lot of instructions, but the whole process takes only a couple of minutes, I promise! Repeat this process until all of the filling ingredients have been used, making a total of 6 rolls.

Cut the rolls in half crosswise and place the sauce on the side for dipping. If you're concerned about dastardly double dippers, you'll want to divide the sauce into individual small bowls.

PRO TIP

In this recipe, I cook the shrimp at a slightly higher temperature than for Foolproof Garlic Shrimp (page 55), in part because here they're not sautéed after being cooked sous vide. What's more, the higher temperature lends a slightly firmer texture, which I prefer when serving shrimp cold. For that reason, use this recipe when preparing shrimp for cocktails or a raw-bar buffet.

FOOLPROOF GARLIC SHRIMP

If you like shrimp scampi, you'll love this tangy, spicier version that boasts a citrusy garlic butter sauce inspired by Latin American dishes like *camarones al ajillo*. The gentle low temperature of sous vide offers a foolproof way to gently cook the shrimp all the way through without becoming tough, leaving you with wonderfully succulent meat that has just a bit of resistance. The jicama, an atypical addition, adds a wonderful crunchiness and sweetness. Because the shrimp cook quickly, this is a perfect everyday dish that you can get on the table in no time. The shrimp are delicious on their own as an appetizer, but I also enjoy serving them over rice or pasta or with warm tortillas for a heartier main course.

SERVES 6 as an appetizer, or 4 as a main course | **SOUS VIDE COOKING TIME:** 15 to 20 minutes | **ACTIVE PREP TIME:** 25 minutes

1 pound large shrimp, peeled with tails intact and deveined

3 tablespoons extra-virgin olive oil

5 cloves garlic, thinly sliced

1 serrano or jalapeño chile, thinly sliced

Pinch of paprika

½ jicama, peeled and cut into ½-inch dice (about 1 cup)

1 tablespoon unsalted butter

Juice of 1 lime (about 2 tablespoons)

Salt and freshly ground black pepper

3 tablespoons coarsely chopped fresh cilantro

DO-AHEAD STRATEGY

The cooked shrimp can be chilled in the bag in an ice water bath (see page 14) for 10 minutes and then refrigerated in the bag for up to 3 days. To serve, sauté the still-cold shrimp in the garlicky sauce as instructed, adding an extra minute to ensure they warm through completely.

Preheat your sous vide water bath to 55°C (131°F).

Place the shrimp in a gallon-size freezer-safe ziplock bag, arranging them in a single layer with as little overlap as possible to ensure even cooking. Seal the bag using the water displacement method (see page 12).

When the water reaches the target temperature, lower the bagged shrimp into the water bath (making sure the bag is fully submerged) and cook for 15 minutes. When done, the shrimp will have curled slightly and turned evenly pink. If they are still gray in spots, return the bag to the water bath and cook for 5 minutes longer.

Remove the bag from the water bath and, using tongs or a slotted spoon, transfer the shrimp to a plate. Pour the accumulated cooking liquid into a small bowl and set aside to use in the final step.

Heat the oil and garlic in a large sauté pan over medium-low heat and cook, stirring occasionally, until the garlic turns light golden brown, 3 to 5 minutes. Add the chile, paprika, jicama, and shrimp (the shrimp do not need to fit in a single layer). Sauté, tossing or stirring occasionally with a wooden spoon, until both sides of the shrimp turn just slightly darker pink, about 2 minutes total. Be sure not to overcook them at this step! Add the butter, the reserved cooking liquid, and the lime juice to the pan and then remove the pan from the heat and stir until the butter has melted. Season to taste with salt and pepper.

To serve, transfer the shrimp and sauce to a serving bowl and sprinkle with the cilantro.

SALMON WITH MISO-FENNEL SALAD

If you've never eaten sous vide salmon, prepare to be wowed. This is not the dry, stringy salmon you've had at wedding buffets; the buttery texture will convert even the finicky. I find this the ideal way to enjoy salmon, but if you prefer a firmer, more traditional texture and opaque color, cook the salmon for the same amount of time at 60°C. In this recipe, the finished salmon gets topped with a sprinkle of *shichimi togarashi*, aka "seven-flavor chile pepper," a Japanese spice blend that typically includes sesame seeds, citrus zest, and seaweed in addition to coarsely ground dried chile. If you cannot find it, a mixture of toasted sesame seeds and cayenne pepper can replace it here, as the idea is to add a kick of flavor, color, and crunchiness to the custardy salmon.

SERVES 4 as a main course | **SOUS VIDE COOKING TIME:** 20 minutes (or up to 30 minutes) | **ACTIVE PREP TIME:** 20 minutes, plus 20 minutes to brine

2 cups water

¼ cup kosher salt

1 tablespoon sugar

2 pounds salmon fillet (pin bones removed), skin on or off, cut into 4 equal pieces

1 teaspoon canola or other mild vegetable oil

MISO VINAIGRETTE

1½ tablespoons white miso

1 tablespoon fresh lemon juice

1½ teaspoons Dijon mustard

1½ teaspoons honey

½ teaspoon peeled, grated fresh ginger

2 tablespoons canola or other mild vegetable oil

½ teaspoon toasted sesame oil

2 fennel bulbs, thinly shaved lengthwise on a mandoline (about 3 cups)

2 cups loosely packed pea shoots (pea greens) or other mild greens (such as mâche or spinach)

1 teaspoon *shichimi togarashi*, or toasted sesame seeds with a pinch of cayenne pepper added

DO-AHEAD STRATEGY

This isn't a dish that I recommend cooking in advance, unless you intend to serve it cold. If you do, remove the fish from the water bath and immerse it an ice water bath (see page 14) for 15 minutes, or until completely cold, and then store in the bag in the refrigerator for up to 2 days.

CONTINUED >

Preheat your sous vide water bath to 52°C (125.5°F).

While the water is heating, combine the water, salt, and sugar in a wide bowl and stir until the salt and sugar are completely dissolved. Place the salmon pieces in this brine and refrigerate for 20 minutes.

Remove the salmon from the brine and rinse it under cold running water to wash off the excess. Pat the salmon dry with a paper towel. Rub the salmon pieces evenly with the canola oil. Place the salmon in a single layer in a gallon-size freezer-safe ziplock bag and seal using the water displacement method (see page 12).

When the water reaches the target temperature, lower the bagged salmon into the water bath (making sure the bag is fully submerged) and cook for 20 minutes. When the fish is done, it will have turned an opaque pink and will be very delicate, so handle it with care or it will fall apart.

While the fish is cooking, make the miso vinaigrette. In a small bowl, whisk together the miso, lemon juice, mustard, honey, and ginger until blended. Slowly pour in the canola and sesame oils in a thin, steady stream while whisking continuously to emulsify. Set the vinaigrette aside.

When the salmon is ready, gently remove it from the bag and transfer it to a platter or tray. If the salmon pieces were cooked with the skin on and you would like to serve them without the skin, it is extremely easy to remove it now. Simply pull it off, starting at one edge and lifting it off in one piece.

Just before serving, toss the fennel and pea shoots with the vinaigrette, starting with half of the vinaigrette and adding more to taste. If you like salads lightly dressed, you won't want to use all of it.

To serve, arrange the salad on four individual plates, place the warm salmon on top, and sprinkle with the *shichimi togarashi*.

PRO TIP

Brining the salmon before cooking not only seasons it but also prevents the flesh from releasing albumin, the unappetizing-looking white ooze that often besmirches the exterior of cooked salmon. The brine is optional, but it's pretty quick and effortless to include the step, and once you try it with the salmon, you may just want to use it when cooking other types of fish, too.

BEER-BATTERED FISH AND CHIPS

Applying sous vide to this iconic English dish is a win-win proposition: it gives me a great excuse to spout Britishisms, and I can be confident of smashing results every time. This approach ensures that the fish won't overcook, and what's more, it gives off less steam when fried, helping the batter to adhere and giving you marvelously moist, flaky fish swaddled inside a crisp, airy crust. I've called for cod here, but other flaky white fish, such as haddock or pollock, can be substituted.

Of course, chips are practically a must for this ethereal fried fish, so I serve my British-Style Chips alongside. Please note that this recipe calls for preparing the chips sous vide and then frying them along with the fish. Just add a spot of excellent tartar sauce and by Jove, these will be the best fish and chips you've ever had.

SERVES 4 as a main course | **SOUS VIDE COOKING TIME:** 15 minutes (or up to 20 minutes) | **ACTIVE PREP TIME:** 35 minutes, plus 15 minutes to chill

1½ pounds skinless cod fillet, cut into strips 1½ inches wide

Salt

1 teaspoon canola or other mild vegetable oil

BEER BATTER

1½ cups all-purpose flour

¼ cup potato starch or cornstarch

1 teaspoon kosher salt

1 teaspoon baking powder

1 (12-ounce) bottle pilsner or other pale lager

1 tablespoon malt or cider vinegar

TARTAR SAUCE

¼ cup mayonnaise, homemade (page 260) or store-bought

¼ cup sour cream or crème fraîche

3 tablespoons chopped fresh flat-leaf parsley, dill, or tarragon, or a mixture

2 tablespoons minced cornichon or other sour pickle

1 tablespoon minced shallot

1 tablespoon fresh lemon juice

Salt and freshly ground black pepper

British-Style Chips (page 192), cooked in the bag but not fried

Canola or other mild vegetable oil, for deep-frying

Flaky sea salt (such as Maldon or fleur de sel)

DO-AHEAD STRATEGY

This recipe has a long list of components, but many of them can be made ahead. The cooked potatoes and tartar sauce can be made in advance and refrigerated for up to 1 week. The cooked and chilled cod can be refrigerated in the bag for up to 2 days before frying. The beer batter can be made up to 3 hours in advance and kept in the fridge.

CONTINUED >

Preheat your sous vide water bath to 51°C (124°F).

Season the cod strips with salt and then coat them with the oil to prevent them from sticking to one another and the bag. Place the fish in a single layer in a gallon-size freezer-safe ziplock bag and seal using the water displacement method (see page 12).

When the water reaches the target temperature, lower the bagged fish into the water bath (making sure the bag is fully submerged) and cook for 15 minutes.

When the fish is ready, remove the bag from the water bath, transfer it to an ice water bath (see page 14), and chill until completely cold, about 15 minutes.

While the fish is cooking and cooling, prepare the batter and tartar sauce. To make the batter, in a large bowl, whisk together the flour, potato starch, salt, and baking powder until blended, then whisk in the beer and vinegar until well combined. To make the tartar sauce, in a small bowl, stir together the mayonnaise, sour cream, parsley, cornichon, shallot, and lemon juice, mixing well. Season with salt and pepper. Set the batter and sauce aside until you're ready to fry.

Line a sheet pan with paper towels and place near the stove. Preheat the oven to 250°F. Pour the oil to a depth of at least 1½ inches into a cast-iron deep cast iron skillet and place over medium heat. The oil should come no more than one-third of the way up the side of the skillet to ensure it will not boil over the rim once the potatoes and fish are added. Heat the oil on medium heat until a wooden skewer or bamboo chopstick inserted into the center of the oil bubbles immediately, or the oil registers 350°F on a high-heat thermometer.

First, fry the potatoes as directed, transfer to one end of the towel-lined sheet pan, and keep warm in the oven.

Gently remove the chilled fish from the bag and slip the pieces into the bowl of batter. Using your fingertips, turn the pieces in the batter to coat evenly. This is a bit of a delicate operation, as the pieces will flake apart if handled roughly.

Carefully transfer the battered fish to the oil, spacing the pieces at least 2 inches apart. (Depending on the size of your pan, it will take two or three batches to fry all of the pieces.) Fry the fish pieces, without stirring, until the batter turns deep golden brown at the edges, 3 to 4 minutes. Using tongs, flip the pieces over and fry until evenly golden brown, 1 to 2 minutes longer. Transfer the cod to the free end of the towel-lined sheet pan, season with flaky salt, and return the pan to the oven to keep warm. Repeat with the remaining fish.

To serve, set out the fish and chips on a large platter or on a newspaper-lined table. Accompany with the tartar sauce for dipping.

OIL-POACHED TROUT

Cooking fish with oil and herbs in the bag lends it a luxurious texture and a tantalizing aroma—perfect for a mild fish like trout. This method uses a fraction of the oil typically required to submerge fish for poaching, and the gentle heat of the water bath ensures the results will be especially moist.

This is an ultraversatile recipe. I use rainbow trout, but it would work well for other types of fish such as pike, sea trout, or salmon. Just be sure to use the infused herbal oil in the final dish to enjoy the benefits fully. The choice of herbs is also up to you. I like the combination of tarragon and thyme, but you can try other combinations, such as basil and marjoram.

The herb-scented poaching oil becomes the finishing sauce for the dish, eliminating the need for any additional steps. Serve the fish with potatoes, a side of vegetables, or a simple green salad.

SERVES 4 as a main course | **SOUS VIDE COOKING TIME:** 20 minutes (or up to 30 minutes) | **ACTIVE PREP TIME:** 5 minutes

¼ cup extra-virgin olive oil

Finely grated zest and juice of ½ lemon

¼ cup chopped fresh flat-leaf parsley, dill, or fennel fronds, or a mixture

1 tablespoon chopped fresh tarragon or thyme, or a mixture

8 trout fillets, skin on or off (from 4 trout, about 2 pounds total weight)

Salt and freshly ground white or black pepper

Preheat your sous vide water bath to 55°C (131°F).

In a small bowl, stir together the oil, lemon zest and juice, and herbs, mixing well. Season the trout fillets with salt and pepper. Place the fish in a single layer in a gallon-size freezer-safe ziplock bag and pour in the herb oil, then seal using the water displacement method (see page 12).

When the water reaches the target temperature, lower the bagged trout into the water bath (making sure the bag is fully submerged) and cook for 20 minutes.

Remove the bag from the water bath and carefully transfer the trout to a serving platter or shallow, wide bowl, pouring the herb oil in the bag over the top. Serve immediately.

PRO TIP

The trout is also terrific served cold atop a simple green salad or used as the base for a rustic trout spread. In either case, chill the fish in an ice water bath (see page 14) for 10 minutes and then remove the skin from the fillets (if you have cooked them with the skin intact). To turn it into a spread, flake the fish with a fork, discarding any errant bones, and mix in the oil and season with additional salt and pepper (and maybe a dab of mustard).

BUTTER-POACHED LOBSTER WITH COGNAC SAUCE

This recipe is a riff on the popular butter-poached lobster developed by Thomas Keller of the French Laundry. The key is *beurre monté*, a butter sauce that is hot but remains in a stable emulsion. Butter prepared this way can be used as a medium for cooking lobster without separating, which means it will still be creamy and emulsified after the lobster is cooked and can thus be used for the sauce. You can also simply melt butter in the bag with the lobster and serve the lobster with the butter and a lemon wedge. Either way, your lobster will be lusciously succulent and delicious.

The precise low temperature of sous vide cooking ensures perfectly prepared crustaceans every time. However, to properly cook a lobster sous vide, it must be parboiled and shelled first. This might seem like a bit of a hassle, but if you're willing to invest the extra effort, the payoff is a truly indulgent and refined dining experience: perfectly moist, tender meat that doesn't require a bib or a lobster cracker to consume. This recipe is a great candidate for upscale entertaining, and I promise your guests will be impressed. Accompany the lobster with a simple starch, such as rice or even chunks of baguette, to soak up all of the insanely delicious sauce.

SERVES 4 as a main course | **SOUS VIDE COOKING TIME:** 20 minutes (or up to 30 minutes) | **ACTIVE PREP TIME:** 1 hour

4 (1- to 1½-pound) live lobsters (if using 2- to 3-pound lobsters, add 10 minutes cooking time)

Kosher salt

STOCK

1 tablespoon canola or other mild vegetable oil

1 yellow onion, sliced ⅛ inch thick

1 carrot, sliced ⅛ inch thick

1 fennel bulb or celery stalk, sliced ⅛ inch thick

3 cloves garlic, thinly sliced

2 tablespoons tomato paste

1 teaspoon black peppercorns

BEURRE MONTÉ

¼ cup water

Pinch of kosher salt

½ cup (4 ounces) cold unsalted butter, cut into ½-inch cubes

COGNAC SAUCE

1 shallot, minced

½ cup Cognac, brandy, or bourbon

¼ cup dry white wine

1 cup crème fraîche

1 tablespoon fresh lemon juice

1 tablespoon chopped fresh tarragon

1 tablespoon minced fresh chives

Salt and freshly ground white pepper

DO-AHEAD STRATEGY

The lobster can be parboiled and shelled up to 3 days before butter poaching it, as long as it's kept bagged and refrigerated (a good trick for keeping it extra fresh is to put the bag in a bowl of ice in the fridge). The sauce can be prepared in advance, as well, and refrigerated for 3 days.

CONTINUED >

Select a stockpot large enough to accommodate all of the lobsters at the same time. Fill the pot two-thirds full with water, salt the water generously (use about 2 tablespoons salt per 4 cups water), and bring to a boil over high heat. If you do not have a pot large enough to cook all of the lobsters at once, cook the lobsters in batches, dismember them as instructed, setting aside the claws, and then cook all of the claws together as directed. Have ready an ice water bath (see page 14) for shocking the lobsters and the lobster pieces as they emerge from the boiling water.

Working with 1 lobster at a time, place the point of a heavy chef's knife at the joint where the head meets the body (right behind the eyes) and cut downward in one fluid movement, driving the knife, tip first, all of the way through the head. The lobster may continue to move a bit, but rest assured that it's on the express route to a watery grave.

Using tongs, submerge the whole lobsters in the boiling water and cook for 1 minute. Their shells will turn red. Transfer the parboiled lobsters to the ice water bath and chill until cool enough to handle, at least 2 minutes. Remove from the ice water bath and, using a twisting motion, pull the tail and claws from each body. Set aside the tails (and the legs if using). The tomalley (liver) can also be pulled from the body cavity and saved for adding to the sauce later, if desired.

Once all of the lobsters have been dismembered, return the claws to the boiling water, lower the heat to a simmer, and cook for 4 minutes. (They need to be cooked longer so you can remove the meat from the shells.) Transfer the claws to the ice water bath (adding more ice if necessary) and chill until cool enough to handle, at least 2 minutes, and then remove from the ice bath. Discard the lobster cooking water.

Remove the meat from the shells, reserving the shells for the stock. (This process will be easier on your hands if you wear rubber gloves.) To remove the meat from the tail, using kitchen shears or a sharp knife, cut lengthwise along the center of the bottom shell, taking care not to cut into the flesh. With the cut side facing up, grasp both sides of the shell and pull them in opposite directions to crack the shell open, then gently pull the meat free of the shell.

Now, separate the "knuckles" from the claws. Cut all the way through the outside edge of the shell along the "elbow" (shears are particularly helpful for this task) and then pull the shell apart and remove the knuckle meat, or poke it out with a chopstick. To remove the meat from the large pincer section of each claw, crack the back of the shell (behind the upper, larger claw) with kitchen shears or the back of a heavy knife, exposing the base of the meat. Remove the shell from the lower claw by pulling it open until it begins to separate from the meat at the joint, then wiggle it off. (A hard cartilage-like piece will pull out of the meat along with the shell, so be careful not to tear the meat off along with it.) Once the lower shell is removed, pull the claw meat out whole, wrenching apart the cracked shell as needed to release it.

When all of this is done, you should have 4 whole tails, 8 whole claws, and assorted knuckle meat. At this point, the meat can be refrigerated until you're ready to cook it sous vide.

Preheat your sous vide water bath to 55°C (131.2°F). If you prefer your lobster meat a bit firmer, set it to 60°C (140°F).

While the water is heating, start making the stock. Heat the oil in a large stockpot or saucepan over medium-high heat. Add the onion, carrot, fennel, and garlic and cook, stirring constantly, until the onion turns translucent and just begins to color, 2 to 3 minutes. Stir in the tomato paste, followed by the reserved shell pieces, and cook for 1 minute more. Add the peppercorns and enough water to just cover the pieces and bring the mixture to a boil. Turn down the heat and simmer for 20 minutes.

Strain the liquid through a fine-mesh sieve, discarding the solids. Return the liquid to the pot, bring to a boil over high heat, and boil until reduced to about ½ cup intensely flavored liquid. Remove from the heat and set aside to add to the Cognac sauce later.

Once you get the stock going, make the *beurre monté*. Combine the water and salt in a small saucepan and bring to a boil over medium heat. Add the butter a few pieces at a time, blending in each addition with a whisk or an immersion blender and letting the liquid return to a simmer before adding the next piece. It's important to keep the mixture simmering to ensure the butter is heat stable. This will happen almost effortlessly with an immersion blender, but be sure to whisk vigorously if you are incorporating the butter by hand. The finished sauce will be as thick as cream

and should remain the same solid off-white color as the cold butter, with no yellow droplets of oil. If the sauce doesn't emulsify, continue to simmer it and add additional butter. When the *beurre monté* is ready, remove it from the heat.

Allow the *beurre monté* to cool for 5 minutes, then place the cleaned lobster meat in a gallon-size freezer-safe ziplock bag and pour in the *beurre monté*. Seal using the water displacement method (see page 12).

When the water reaches the target temperature, lower the bagged lobster into the water bath (making sure the bag is fully submerged) and cook for 20 minutes.

While the lobster is cooking, make the Cognac sauce. Combine the shallot, Cognac, wine, and reduced stock in a small saucepan and bring to a boil over medium-high heat. Cook until reduced by half, about 5 minutes. Lower the heat to medium and stir in the crème fraîche. If desired, add the reserved lobster tomalley, finely chopped or pureed, to the sauce at this point. Let the mixture simmer until it is thick enough to coat the back of a spoon, about 5 minutes longer, and then turn the heat to its lowest setting and cover the pot to keep the sauce warm until you're ready to finish it.

When the lobster is ready, remove the bag from the water bath. Using a slotted spoon, transfer the lobster pieces to a serving bowl or platter. Pour the *beurre monté* remaining in the bag into the Cognac sauce. Stir in the lemon juice, tarragon, and chives and season with the salt and pepper. The sauce can be poured directly over the lobster or served on the side. Serve immediately.

POULTRY

IN THE WORLD OF POULTRY, CHICKEN IS UNQUESTIONABLY AT THE TOP of the pecking order. It is by far the most popular edible bird and has even surpassed beef and pork as the most widely eaten type of meat in the United States. The ascendancy of fowl makes sense: the mild flavor and affordability of chicken—and of turkey—make it particularly well suited to a number of different cuisines. I took that observation as carte blanche to do some globe-trotting with the recipes in this chapter, borrowing liberally from multiple Asian cultures, the Middle East, France, Italy, the Caribbean, Mexico, and, of course, the United States. Think of this chapter as a melting pot: whether you choose pure Americana with a game-changing Thanksgiving Turkey (page 111), adapt East-meets-West fusion with sweet and tangy General Tso's Chicken (page 89), or tap into traditional Mexican flavors with a seductively complex Duck Mole Rojo (page 103), our feathered friends are an ideal blank canvas on which to build flavor.

Even though poultry takes well to a variety of cooking methods, the following recipes naturally all rely on sous vide to ensure uniformly excellent results. Cooking in a water bath set to the precise degree of the desired internal temperature means never

having to overcook chicken in an effort to avoid a dreaded pink center. In other words, Schrödinger's chicken (which is simultaneously raw and overcooked until you cut into it and find out which) will be a thing of the past. But this chapter goes beyond chicken, as well, to tackle less common poultry options such as duck and quail, which call for a slightly different cooking approach. For instance, I use long, gentle cooking to transform tough duck legs into lusciously tender Duck Confit (page 99).

Finally, this chapter gives you an arsenal of cooking techniques to amp up flavor and texture. You can create incredibly juicy meat and a gloriously crunchy crust by frying (Perfect Fried Chicken, page 93, or Chicken Katsu, page 81), you can stir-fry your own upgraded Chinese takeout (General Tso's Chicken) to produce results that are never greasy or tough, or you can simply sauté a chicken breast (Sriracha Chicken, page 79) with no fear of a dry finish. The pièce de résistance in this chapter is my foolproof, stress-free technique to elevate your Thanksgiving turkey to stratospheric heights— making a menu centerpiece so memorable that it would bring a tear to Martha Stewart's eye. No matter which of these approaches you use, you'll find that sous vide yields some pretty clucking great results.

CHICKEN LIVER MOUSSE WITH GRILLED BREAD AND FIGS

When it comes to bang-for-your-buck appetizers, chicken liver mousse is one of my favorites. Leave it to the French to transform the lowly chicken liver into something decadent with just a whirl in the blender and a little butter (okay, a lot). In the classic preparation, the livers are pureed while still raw and then baked in a mold until cooked and set. In this version, the livers are cooked sous vide before blending, which ensures that they are cooked safely and evenly. It also eliminates the temperamental baking step, which can result in a grainy texture if overcooked even slightly. Another trick I use to make this nosh noteworthy is pink curing salt (a common ingredient in cured meats, it's also known as Prague powder #1). It can be found in specialty butcher shops or online, but I give you the option to replace it with ordinary salt; the finished color won't be as bright, but you won't sacrifice flavor. I love making this silky smooth mousse even more indulgent by serving it with grilled bread and figs, but it's also marvelous unadorned, set out with crackers or crisp bread.

MAKES about 3 cups; **SERVES** 8 to 10 as an appetizer | **SOUS VIDE COOKING TIME:** 30 minutes (or up to 1 hour) | **ACTIVE PREP TIME:** 30 minutes, plus 1 hour to set

MOUSSE

1 pound chicken livers, trimmed of any connective tissue, visible fat, and greenish areas

1 teaspoon kosher salt

½ teaspoon pink curing salt or additional kosher salt

2 thyme sprigs

1 tablespoon unsalted butter, plus ¾ cup (6 ounces) cold unsalted butter, cut into ½-inch cubes

1 tablespoon extra-virgin olive oil

2 shallots, thinly sliced

3 cloves garlic, thinly sliced

½ teaspoon kosher salt

¼ cup sweet fortified wine (such as Madeira, Marsala, or port)

¼ cup brandy or bourbon

½ teaspoon freshly ground white pepper

1 teaspoon fresh lemon juice

1 small loaf country-style or sourdough bread, cut into 1-inch-thick slices (about 8 to 10 slices)

8 ounces figs, halved or quartered lengthwise

2 tablespoons extra-virgin olive oil

1 teaspoon fresh thyme leaves

Flake sea salt (such as Maldon or fleur de sel) and freshly ground black pepper

1 teaspoon high-quality finishing vinegar (such as aged balsamic or Banyuls, optional)

DO-AHEAD STRATEGY

To store the mousse for more than 1 day, seal it with melted fat to prevent it from oxidizing (which would turn the color an unappealing brown) or taking on unwanted flavors. Once the mousse has set, melt 4 tablespoons rendered duck or chicken fat or clarified butter and pour it evenly over the top. You can now cover the container and refrigerate the mousse for up to 2 weeks. Remove it from the fridge and let it come to room temperature for 30 minutes before serving, then simply scrape and lift away the layer of fat.

CONTINUED >

To make the mousse, preheat your sous vide water bath to 68°C (154.4°F).

Season the chicken livers with the kosher salt and pink salt and place in a gallon-size freezer-safe ziplock bag along with the thyme sprigs. Seal using the water displacement method (see page 12).

When the water reaches the target temperature, lower the bagged livers into the water bath (making sure the bag is fully submerged) and cook for 30 minutes, at which point the livers will be firm and pink.

While the livers are cooking, combine the 1 tablespoon of butter and the oil in a saucepan over medium heat and heat until the butter foams. Add the shallots, garlic, and kosher salt and sauté, stirring occasionally, until softened and beginning to brown, about 5 minutes.

Add the wine and brandy, scrape the bottom of the pan with a wooden spoon or spatula to loosen any browned bits, and then simmer until the mixture is syrupy and reduced by about two-thirds, 1 to 2 minutes. Pour the shallot reduction into a blender but do not blend.

When the chicken livers are ready, remove the bag from the water bath and transfer the livers to the blender, discarding the thyme sprigs. Add the white pepper and lemon juice and blend just until the mixture is combined. Add the ¾ cup of cold butter all at once and continue to blend on high speed until the mixture is completely smooth, stopping to scrape down the sides with a rubber spatula as you go. You should have a loose, silky puree with the consistency of batter. (Depending on the strength of your blender, the mousse may not be perfectly smooth; if desired, pass it through a fine-mesh sieve before refrigerating it.) Taste the mousse and adjust the seasoning with salt if needed.

Pour the mousse into a glass or ceramic container such as a ramekin or soufflé dish and cover tightly with plastic wrap, then refrigerate until firmly set, at least 1 hour.

When you're ready to serve the mousse, preheat a stove-top grill pan over medium-high heat. Brush both sides of each bread slice and the cut surfaces of the figs with the oil. Arrange the bread slices on the hot grill pan and grill, turning once, until browned and crisped on both sides, 1 to 2 minutes per side. Remove from the pan. Add the figs, cut side down, to the hot pan and grill until caramelized, 1 to 2 minutes. Remove from the pan.

To serve, spread the mousse on the grilled bread and sprinkle with the thyme, sea salt, and black pepper. Place the bread slices on a platter or tray. Arrange the figs around the bread and drizzle the figs with the vinegar.

JERK CHICKEN WINGS

Jerk chicken is one of Jamaica's most celebrated culinary exports, and with good reason. Here, I bring that combination of sweetness, acidity, warm spices, and chile heat to chicken wings. By cooking the wings directly in the marinade, you're able to quickly coax the flavors of the spice paste into the meat, eliminating the need to marinate them overnight. In addition, cooking the wings low and slow with controlled heat helps break down their collagen, making them ultratender and juicy, ready to be broiled for a crispy finish with no fear of drying them out. I like to take these wings to potlucks because they can be cooked in advance and then rewarmed in an oven or on a grill.

SERVES 6 to 8 as an appetizer | **SOUS VIDE COOKING VIDE TIME:** 2 hours (or up to 6 hours) | **ACTIVE PREP TIME:** 20 minutes, plus 5 minutes to rest

MARINADE

1 bunch green onions, white and green parts, coarsely chopped (about ¾ cup)

1 to 2 Scotch bonnet or habanero chiles, coarsely chopped

2-inch piece fresh ginger, peeled and thinly sliced (about ¼ cup)

5 cloves garlic, coarsely chopped

1 tablespoon fresh thyme leaves

4 teaspoons ground allspice

1 tablespoon freshly ground black pepper

½ teaspoon ground cinnamon

½ teaspoon freshly grated or ground nutmeg

2 teaspoons kosher salt

2 tablespoons dark brown sugar

2 tablespoons soy sauce

Juice of 2 limes (about ¼ cup fresh lime juice)

3 pounds chicken wings separated into sections, discard wing tips or save for making stock

1 lime, cut into wedges, for serving

DO-AHEAD STRATEGY

The jerk marinade can be made in advance and refrigerated for up to 1 week or frozen for up to 2 months. The cooked chicken can be chilled in the bag in an ice water bath (see page 14) for 20 minutes and then refrigerated for up to a week. Increase the time under the broiler to about 15 minutes to ensure that the wings are well browned and heated through.

CONTINUED >

Preheat your sous vide bath to temperature to 77°C (170.6°F).

While the water is heating, make the marinade. Combine all of the ingredients in a blender or food processor and pulse until a rough paste forms, about 1 minute.

In a large bowl, toss the chicken with the marinade, mixing well to coat evenly. Transfer the chicken, along with any marinade left in the bowl, to a gallon-size freezer-safe ziplock bag. Press the bag flat to ensure that the chicken wings are arranged in a single layer and then seal using the water displacement method (see page 12).

When the water reaches the target temperature, lower the bagged wings into the water bath (making sure the bag is fully submerged) and cook for 2 hours.

Remove the bag from the water bath and set aside the wings to rest for 5 minutes. Position an oven rack in the center of the oven and preheat the broiler.

Using tongs, transfer the chicken wings to a nonstick baking pan or a disposable aluminum foil pan, arranging them in a single layer and spooning about ½ cup of the marinade over them, leaving behind the excess for basting. (You can also finish the chicken on a well-oiled grill rack over a hot fire.)

Place the chicken under the broiler and cook until browned and caramelized, about 12 minutes. Every few minutes, spoon or brush some of the extra marinade on top of each wing, which will help to form a delicious crust. Use tongs to flip the wings over as needed to prevent overbrowning. The chicken is done when it is deeply browned, almost black in spots, and the seasoning rub has cooked into an irregular coating, chewy in some areas and crispy in others.

To serve, arrange the chicken on a platter and garnish with the lime wedges. Have ample napkins on hand.

PRO TIP

Store-bought jerk seasoning paste is a totally acceptable substitute for homemade marinade. Walkerswood is a good-quality brand that can be found at Caribbean markets or online (see Resources, page 273). Just swap out the homemade seasoning for a 10-ounce jar.

SRIRACHA CHICKEN

This is my Asian twist on buffalo chicken—sweet, spicy, garlicky, and buttery. Best of all, the dish makes its own sauce: the kicky sriracha marinade combined with the gelatin-rich meat juices that collect in the bag while the chicken is cooking become the basis for a quick pan sauce. All you need to do is sear the chicken in a hot skillet just before serving. It's fantastic spooned over rice or couscous, with lime wedges on the side.

SERVES 4 as a main course | **SOUS VIDE COOKING TIME:** 1 hour (or up to 5 hours) | **ACTIVE PREP TIME:** 10 minutes

4 skin-on, boneless chicken breasts

1 tablespoon honey

2 tablespoons sriracha sauce

Juice of ½ lime (about 1 tablespoon fresh juice)

4 tablespoons cold unsalted butter, cut into small cubes

Kosher salt and freshly ground black pepper

¼ cup coarsely chopped fresh cilantro

4 lime wedges, for serving

DO-AHEAD STRATEGY

The cooked chicken can be chilled in the bag in an ice water bath (see page 14) for 30 minutes and then refrigerated for up to 1 hour. Reheat in a 60°C (140°F) water bath for 20 minutes.

Preheat your sous vide water bath to 60°C (140°F).

Place the chicken breasts in a gallon-size freezer-safe ziplock bag. In a small bowl, whisk together the honey, sriracha, and the lime juice until well blended. Pour the mixture into the bag and give the bag a good shake to ensure that the chicken is coated evenly, then arrange the chicken so that it sits in a single layer. Add 3 tablespoons of the cubed butter and then seal the bag using the water displacement method (see page 12).

When the water reaches the target temperature, lower the bagged chicken into the water bath (making sure the bag is fully submerged) and cook for 1 hour.

Remove the bag from the water bath and transfer the chicken to a plate, making sure to reserve the cooking liquid (you can pour it into a small bowl). Pat the chicken dry with paper towels and season with the salt and pepper.

Place a large sauté pan over medium heat and add the remaining 1 tablespoon butter. When the butter melts, swirl it until the foam has subsided. Add the chicken breasts, skin side down, and cook until the skin is deeply browned and crisped, about 3 minutes. The sugar in the marinade will make the chicken brown quickly, so keep an eye on it. Once the skin has browned, using tongs, flip the chicken over and cook for 30 seconds longer, then transfer the breasts to a cutting board.

To make the sauce, raise the heat to high and add the reserved cooking liquid. Using a wooden spoon or spatula, scrape up any browned bits stuck to the pan and then remove from the heat.

To serve, slice the chicken breasts against the grain and arrange on a serving plate. Pour the sauce over the top and garnish with the lime wedges.

PRO TIP

If you can't find skin-on, boneless chicken breasts, ask your butcher to bone some for you. In a pinch, you can substitute boneless, skinless breasts, but the crispiness and general deliciousness of the skin really makes this dish.

CHICKEN KATSU

Katsu is Japan's superior (in my humble opinion) answer to schnitzel, but like all fried cutlets, it can get dried out on the path to crispiness. Cooking the chicken breast sous vide and then chilling it before breading reduces the risk of the meat drying out during the frying step. What you end up with is perfectly delicious and juicy white meat enveloped in a supercrisp crust, ready to be dunked in *katsu* sauce. This version of *katsu* sauce isn't strictly traditional, but it's easy to whip up and tastes like the genuine article: tangy, sweet, and umami-rich.

SERVES 4 as a main course | **SOUS VIDE COOKING TIME:** 1 hour (or up to 5 hours) | **ACTIVE PREP TIME:** 25 minutes, plus 20 minutes to chill, and 10 minutes to rest

4 skinless, boneless chicken breasts, halved horizontally to produce 8 thin cutlets

Salt

KATSU SAUCE

¼ cup ketchup

2 tablespoons light brown sugar

1 tablespoon cider vinegar

1 tablespoon soy sauce

1 tablespoon Worcestershire sauce

1 tablespoon hoisin sauce

1 teaspoon Sriracha or other hot sauce

½ cup all-purpose flour

2 large eggs, lightly whisked

1½ cups panko (Japanese-style bread crumbs)

Canola or other mild vegetable oil, for frying

4 cups shredded green cabbage

4 lemon wedges, for serving

DO-AHEAD STRATEGY

The cooked and chilled chicken can be refrigerated in the bag(s) for up to 1 week before continuing with the breading step. No reheating is required, since the frying will reheat the chicken without cooking it additionally. The *katsu* sauce can be made ahead and refrigerated in an airtight container for up to 1 month.

CONTINUED >

Preheat your sous vide water bath to 60°C (140°F).

Season the chicken with salt, then place it in a gallon-size freezer-safe ziplock bag in a single layer, without overlapping (you may need two bags, depending on the size of the breasts), then seal using the water displacement method (see page 12).

When the water reaches the target temperature, lower the bagged chicken into the water bath (making sure the bag is fully submerged) and cook for 1 hour, at which point the meat will be opaque and firm to the touch.

While the chicken is cooking, in a small bowl, whisk together the ketchup, sugar, cider vinegar, soy sauce, worcestershire sauce, hoisin sauce, and sriracha until well blended.

When the chicken is ready, remove the bag from the water bath, transfer it to an ice water bath (see page 14), and chill until completely cold, about 20 minutes.

Remove the chicken from the bag, letting any excess liquid drip off, and place on a plate. Discard all of the cooking liquid.

Set up a breading station by placing the flour, eggs, and bread crumbs in 3 separate wide, shallow bowls. Place a large rack on a sheet pan. One at a time, bread the chicken: dredge in the flour, coating evenly and shaking off the excess; then dip into the eggs, allowing the excess to drip off; and then coat both sides with the breadcrumbs, pressing down firmly to ensure that the cutlets are evenly coated. Make sure there aren't any bald patches. As the cutlets are ready, place them in a single layer on the rack. Allow the breaded chicken to rest for at 10 minutes (or up to 30 minutes) to help the crumbs adhere.

Line a sheet pan with paper towels and place near the stove. Pour the oil to a depth of ¾ inch into a large cast-iron skillet and place over medium-high heat. Heat the oil on medium heat until a wooden skewer or bamboo chopstick inserted into the center of the oil bubbles immediately, or the oil registers 360°F on a high-heat thermometer. You may have to tilt the pan to get enough depth for the oil temperature to register on the thermometer.

Carefully transfer the breaded chicken to the oil, spacing the cutlets at least 1 inch apart. (Depending on the size of your pan, you may need to fry the chicken in two batches.) Fry the chicken until deep golden brown on the underside, 2 to 3 minutes. Using tongs, flip the cutlets over and fry until golden brown on the second side, 2 to 3 minutes longer. Transfer the chicken to the towel-lined sheet pan to drain briefly and then season lightly with additional salt.

To serve, slice the chicken crosswise into 1-inch-wide strips. Make a bed of the cabbage on four individual plates, place the chicken strips on top, and then drizzle with some of the *katsu* sauce. Garnish with the lemon wedges and serve the remaining sauce on the side.

VIETNAMESE CARAMEL CHICKEN

Don't let the word *caramel* mislead you—this isn't a dish you'd want to serve over ice cream. Sugar is often found as an ingredient in savory dishes in Southeast Asia, particularly Vietnam. The sweetness in this dish is offset by an aromatic punch from lemongrass and ginger, as well as a spicy kick from Thai chiles (aka bird chiles), resulting in a knockout combo.

This is a shining example of how cooking meat with a flavorful marinade in the bag effortlessly creates the base for a sauce. When made traditionally, this dish requires careful timing to ensure that the chicken is cooked through by the time the sauce is reduced and caramelized. This version delivers a vibrant dish that is just as flavorful as the original, with uniformly cooked tender chunks of chicken every time. I like to serve this dish over brown rice for the extra bit of flavor and nuttiness.

SERVES 4 as a main course | **SOUS VIDE COOKING TIME:** 1½ hours (or up to 5 hours) | **ACTIVE PREP TIME:** 30 minutes

2 pounds skinless, boneless chicken thighs (about 8)

½ cup firmly packed light brown sugar

¼ cup fish sauce

1 tablespoon canola or other mild vegetable oil

4 cloves garlic, chopped (not too finely or it will burn)

3 shallots, thinly sliced

1 tablespoon peeled, chopped fresh ginger (from a 1-inch piece)

2 tablespoons chopped lemongrass, tender inner bulb portion only

1 to 2 red Thai or other fresh red chiles (such as Fresno or finger), thinly sliced

2 tablespoons rice vinegar

Juice of 1 lime (about 2 tablespoons)

1 cup loosely packed fresh Thai basil leaves or regular basil leaves

DO-AHEAD STRATEGY

The cooked chicken can be chilled in the bag in an ice water bath (see page 14) for 30 minutes and then refrigerated for up to 1 week. Reheat at 55°C (131°F) for 30 minutes before proceeding with the final step.

CONTINUED >

Preheat your sous vide water bath to 65°C (149°F).

Place the chicken, brown sugar, and fish sauce in a gallon-size freezer-safe ziplock bag and press the bag flat against a tabletop to ensure that the chicken thighs are arranged in a single layer, with as little overlap as possible, and then seal using the water displacement method (see page 12). If the pieces have piled up on the bottom, press down on the bag again to distribute them evenly.

When the water reaches the target temperature, lower the bagged chicken into the water bath (making sure the bag is fully submerged) and cook for 1½ hours.

When the thighs are ready, remove the bag from the water bath. Open the bag a crack, pour out the cooking liquid into a bowl, and set the liquid aside for making the sauce. Transfer the thighs to a platter or tray. Don't pat the thighs dry; any marinade adhering to them will help them caramelize.

Heat the oil in a large nonstick sauté pan or skillet over medium-high heat. When the oil starts to shimmer, add the chicken thighs in a single layer and cook until lightly browned, 1 to 2 minutes. Using tongs, flip the thighs over and cook for 1 to 2 minutes more. You're looking for an uneven golden brown, with darker bits of caramelization along the edges. (If your pan cannot accommodate the thighs in a single layer, cook them in two batches.) There's no need to clean the pan; any caramelized bits stuck to the pan bottom are desirable. Transfer the thighs to a platter or tray.

With the pan still over medium-high heat, immediately add the garlic, shallots, ginger, lemongrass, and chile and cook, stirring constantly with a wooden spoon, until the vegetables begin to soften, brown, and become fragrant, 1 to 2 minutes. Add the reserved cooking liquid to the pan, bring to a simmer, and cook until thickened and reduced, 3 to 5 minutes. The mixture is ready when it is bubbling slowly, is thick enough to coat a spoon, and has turned a deep mahogany color.

Return the thighs to the pan and continue to cook over the heat for 1 minute, turning and tossing them in the sauce to glaze well. (The pieces may break apart somewhat, but that's okay.) Stir in the vinegar and lime juice, which will cause the sauce to bubble and hiss, and remove the pan from the heat. Add the basil and stir just until it wilts.

To serve, transfer the chicken and any extra sauce to a platter and dig in.

CHICKEN TIKKA MASALA

The origins of chicken tikka masala ultimately lie in India, where the catchall terms *masala* and *tikka* refer to blends of spices and boneless pieces of meat, respectively. That said, this is not traditional Indian fare. The dish is so heavily influenced by British sensibilities that some have declared it a national dish of the U.K., making it a striking illustration of how cuisines merge.

Any curry powder will work for this recipe, but I like using Madras style for its balance of flavor and heat. In any case, when using ground spice mixes, fresher is better, so I recommend purchasing at stores with a rapid turnover of inventory, such as specialty spice shops and ethnic markets (or see Resources, page 273). This recipe eschews the cream or coconut milk that is typically added to this dish, opting instead for yogurt, which makes for a lighter, more brightly flavored sauce that is still satisfyingly creamy (okay, so the butter helps). To round out this dish, serve it over basmati rice or with warm naan.

SERVES 4 as a main course | **SOUS VIDE COOKING TIME:** 2 hours (or up to 5 hours) | **ACTIVE PREP TIME:** 25 minutes

1 tablespoon sugar

2 tablespoons curry powder

1½ teaspoons kosher salt

1 teaspoon paprika

2 pounds skinless, boneless chicken breasts, cut into 1½-inch cubes

2 tablespoons canola or other mild vegetable oil

3 tablespoons unsalted butter

1 shallot, minced

1 tablespoon peeled, minced fresh ginger (from a 1-inch piece)

3 cloves garlic, minced

1½ cups tomato puree (about one 14-ounce can)

1 teaspoon honey

1 tablespoon ground turmeric

½ teaspoon ground cumin

½ teaspoon ground coriander

½ teaspoon cayenne pepper (optional)

1 cup yogurt, homemade (page 260) or whole-milk plain Greek yogurt

Salt and freshly ground black pepper

¼ cup loosely packed fresh cilantro leaves, for garnish

DO-AHEAD STRATEGY

The cooked chicken can be chilled in the bag in an ice water bath (see page 14) for 30 minutes and then refrigerated for up to 1 week. Reheat in a 60°C (140°F) water bath for 30 minutes.

CONTINUED >

Preheat your sous vide water bath to 60°C (140°F).

In a large bowl, stir together the sugar, 1 tablespoon of the curry powder, kosher salt, and paprika. Add the chicken and, using your hands or a rubber spatula, mix together until all of the pieces are evenly coated with the spice mixture.

Heat 1 tablespoon of the oil in a large nonstick skillet over medium-high heat until it shimmers. Add half of the chicken pieces to the pan, placing them in a single layer (the pieces can touch but not overlap). Cook the chicken until the first side is golden brown, about 1 minute (the sugar and spices will cause it to brown rapidly), then, using tongs, flip the pieces over and cook for about 1 minute more. Transfer the chicken to large bowl or plate, leaving behind any oil. If parts of the chicken are still pink, that's fine; you're not trying to create a perfect sear, simply building flavor with some browning.

Lower the heat to medium, add the butter, shallot, ginger, and garlic, and immediately stir with a wooden spoon to prevent scorching. Cook, stirring frequently, until softened, aromatic, and beginning to brown, 3 to 5 minutes. If the mixture is browning too rapidly (which depends on the strength of your burner), add a splash of water to slow things down.

Once the shallot mixture has softened, add the tomato puree, honey, turmeric, cumin, coriander, cayenne (if using), and the remaining 1 tablespoon curry powder and stir to combine. Bring the mixture to a simmer and remove from the heat. Stir in the yogurt and season with salt and pepper.

Transfer the browned chicken pieces and any juices that have collected to a gallon-size freezer-safe ziplock bag. Using a ladle, spoon the sauce mixture into the bag, then seal using the water displacement or table-edge method (see page 12). I recommend the latter method for recipes with a relatively large amount of liquid.

When the water reaches the target temperature, lower the bagged chicken into the water bath (making sure the bag is fully submerged) and cook for 2 hours.

Remove the bag from the water bath and transfer the chicken and sauce to a warm serving bowl. Taste the sauce again and adjust with salt and pepper if needed.

Garnish the chicken with the cilantro leaves and serve over rice or with naan.

GENERAL TSO'S CHICKEN

Not only is its connection to the eponymous nineteenth-century Qing dynasty military leader questionable, General Tso's chicken also has no clear antecedent in traditional Chinese cuisine. As it turns out, the dish was developed by Chinese immigrants in an effort to appeal to the American palate, and judging by its immense popularity today, they were successful. Rather than deep-frying the chicken all the way through, my recipe relies on cooking it sous vide before using a quick stir-fry finish to produce moist, flawlessly cooked chicken with big flavor. For that reason, my version is satisfyingly sweet, sour, and spicy without the greasiness of the takeout standby. The chile-bean paste provides the heat in this recipe, not the Sichuan peppercorns (which have a numbing effect) or dried red Sichuan chiles (which add color and aroma), so leaving either out won't throw things out of whack. (All of these ingredients can be found at a well-stocked Chinese grocery store, or see Resources, page 273.) To make this dish a little heartier, I recommend serving it over brown rice—Tso good!

SERVES 4 as a main course | **SOUS VIDE COOKING TIME:** 1 hour (or up to 5 hours) | **ACTIVE PREP TIME:** 30 minutes

¼ cup chile-bean paste (sold as toban djan or doubanjiang) or garlic-chile paste

¼ cup soy sauce

¼ cup lightly packed light brown sugar

2 tablespoons rice vinegar

½ teaspoon freshly ground black pepper

½ teaspoon ground Sichuan peppercorn (optional)

2 pounds skinless, boneless chicken breasts (about 4 breasts), cut against the grain into ¼-inch-thick slices

3 tablespoons canola or other mild vegetable oil

1 tablespoon peeled, minced fresh ginger (from a 1-inch piece)

3 cloves garlic, minced

3 green onions, white and green parts, thinly sliced (green parts reserved for garnish)

6 or more dried red Sichuan chiles (optional)

1 red bell pepper, seeded and cut into ⅛-inch-wide strips

1 tablespoon cornstarch mixed with 1 tablespoon water

DO-AHEAD STRATEGY

The cooked chicken can be chilled in the bag in an ice water bath (see page 14) for 20 minutes and then refrigerated for up to 1 week. Reheat in a 60°C (140°F) water bath for 20 minutes before stir-frying.

CONTINUED >

Preheat your sous vide water bath to 60°C (140°F).

In a large bowl, stir together the chile-bean paste, soy sauce, brown sugar, vinegar, black peppercorns, and Sichuan pepper, if using. Add the chicken and mix well to coat evenly with the seasoning mixture. Transfer the chicken and marinade to a gallon-size freezer-safe ziplock bag and seal using the water displacement method (see page 12).

When the water reaches the target temperature, lower the bag into the water bath (making sure the bag is fully submerged) and cook for 1 hour.

When the chicken is ready, remove the bag from the water bath and transfer the contents to a bowl. Using a slotted spoon, transfer the chicken pieces to a plate. Reserve the liquid in the bowl for making the sauce.

To finish the dish, heat the oil in a wok or nonstick skillet over high heat until it shimmers. Add the ginger, garlic, green onion, and chiles (if using) all at once, and stir vigorously with a wooden spoon until the mixture is fragrant and begins to turn golden brown, about 30 seconds (it will happen almost immediately, so don't look away!). Add the bell pepper and cook, stirring constantly, until it begins to wilt, about 1 minute. Push the bell pepper to the side of the wok with a wooden spoon and add the chicken. Allow the

chicken to sit, without stirring, for about 1 minute, until the edges brown (the sugar in the marinade will help the chicken brown quickly). Toss or stir the pieces with a wooden spoon and then let them sit until they've browned a bit more, about 1 minute longer. (Remember, the chicken is already cooked, so the stir-frying is only meant to build flavor.)

Add the reserved marinade to the pan, which should boil immediately upon contact. Give the cornstarch-water mixture a good mix and then stir it into the bubbling liquid (it will thicken into a sauce almost instantly) and toss vigorously for just a few seconds to coat the chicken completely.

Remove the pan from the heat and transfer the chicken and sauce to a serving bowl. Sprinkle the reserved green onions on top, and serve immediately with rice on the side.

PRO TIP

The technique employed here—using sous vide to cook bite-size pieces of meat in a flavorful sauce or marinade, then draining them before searing in a skillet—is one of my favorite ways to make fast, easy dishes. It works well with variety of proteins, such as pork, beef, and shrimp.

PERFECT FRIED CHICKEN AND WAFFLES WITH HONEY HOT SAUCE SYRUP

This recipe is the holy grail for anyone in search of world-class fried chicken. Employing sous vide improves and makes foolproof a recipe that can be tricky to get just right. By cooking the chicken sous vide in a flavored buttermilk mixture, you eliminate the need for an overnight brine or marinade. Then, because the chicken is fully cooked before it's deep-fried, it gives off less moisture in the form of steam, which is the biggest reason why the crust doesn't always adhere properly. The end result is the fried chicken of your dreams—crispy and succulent enough to drive away the memory of any past fried chicken disappointments.

The chicken is delicious on its own, but serving it with buttermilk waffles and my own homemade honey hot sauce syrup turns it into something truly indulgent. If you don't want to go through the trouble of making your own waffle batter, feel free to use a premade mix.

SERVES 4 as a main course | **SOUS VIDE COOKING TIME:** 2 hours (or up to 6 hours) | **ACTIVE PREP TIME:** 30 minutes for the chicken, plus 20 minutes to rest, and 25 minutes for the waffles and syrup

MARINADE AND CHICKEN

1 cup buttermilk, preferably whole

1 tablespoon hot sauce, preferably Frank's RedHot

1 teaspoon Worcestershire sauce

1 teaspoon kosher salt

2 thyme sprigs

4 skin-on, bone-in chicken thighs

4 skin-on chicken drumsticks

DRY BREADING MIXTURE

1½ cups all-purpose flour

½ cup potato starch or cornstarch

1 tablespoon freshly ground black pepper

1 tablespoon kosher salt

2 teaspoons paprika

1 teaspoon cayenne pepper

WET BREADING MIXTURE

1 cup buttermilk, preferably whole

1 tablespoon hot sauce, preferably Frank's RedHot

1 teaspoon Worcestershire sauce

1 teaspoon kosher salt

1 teaspoon fresh thyme leaves

WAFFLES

2 cups all-purpose flour (spooned and leveled)

¼ cup lightly packed light brown sugar

2 teaspoons baking powder

1 teaspoon baking soda

1½ teaspoons kosher salt

2 cups buttermilk, preferably whole

½ cup (4 ounces) unsalted butter, melted

2 large eggs

Cooking spray, for greasing the waffle iron

SYRUP

¼ cup honey

1 tablespoon hot sauce, preferably Frank's RedHot

1 tablespoon unsalted butter

Peanut or other vegetable oil, for deep-frying

2 teaspoon fresh thyme leaves, for garnish

DO-AHEAD STRATEGY

The cooked chicken can be chilled in the bag in an ice water bath (see page 14) for 20 minutes and then refrigerated for up to 1 week. Reheat in a 65°C (149°F) water bath for 30 minutes. After the chicken is fried, it can be held in the 250°F oven for up to 1 hour without drying out or losing its perfect crust. As noted, the waffles can be made while the chicken is kept warm in the oven. The syrup, which is best served warm, should be made just before serving.

CONTINUED ›

Preheat your sous vide water bath to 65°C (149°F).

To make the marinade, in a small bowl, stir together the buttermilk, hot sauce, Worcestershire sauce, salt, and thyme, mixing well. Pour the marinade into a gallon-size freezer-safe ziplock bag, add the chicken pieces, and give the bag a good shake to make sure the chicken is evenly coated with the marinade. Seal the bag using the water displacement method (see page 12).

When the water reaches the target temperature, lower the bagged chicken into the water bath (making sure the bag is fully submerged) and cook for 2 hours.

While the chicken is cooking, in a bowl, stir together all of the ingredients for the dry breading mixture. Set up three wide, shallow bowls (pie plates work well). Put one-third of the dry mixture in a bowl and the remaining two-thirds of the mixture in another bowl. In the third bowl, whisk together all of the ingredients for the wet breading mixture. Set a large wire rack on a sheet pan and set aside.

When the chicken is done cooking, remove the bag from the water bath and set aside to cool for 5 minutes. Open the bag, and using tongs, transfer the chicken to a platter, letting the excess marinade drain off. Discard the marinade.

To bread the chicken, you need to designate one hand for wet ingredients and one hand for dry ingredients. With your designated wet hand, place 1 piece of chicken in the bowl containing one-third of the flour mixture. Turn the chicken with your dry hand until it is completely coated and then shake off the excess flour mixture. Still using your dry hand, drop the chicken into the buttermilk mixture and then turn it with your wet hand to coat it completely. Shake off any excess liquid from the chicken and then, still using your wet hand, drop the chicken into the bowl holding two-thirds of the flour mixture. With your dry hand, dredge the chicken thoroughly in the flour mixture. Lift the breaded chicken piece with your dry hand onto the rack. Repeat with the remaining pieces and then let them sit for 10 to 15 minutes, allowing the breading to absorb moisture so that it will better adhere to the chicken.

Line a new sheet pan with a double layer of paper towels and place near the stove. Preheat the oven to 250°F. Pour the oil to a depth of 1 inch (enough to come about halfway up the side of your chicken pieces) into a large cast-iron skillet. Heat the oil on medium heat until a wooden skewer or bamboo chopstick inserted into the center of the oil bubbles immediately, or the oil registers 360°F on a high-heat thermometer.

Gently lower the breaded chicken into the oil (which should bubble vigorously on contact), spacing the pieces at least 1 inch apart. (Depending on the size of your pan, you may need to fry the chicken in two batches.) Fry the chicken, undisturbed, until the underside is deep golden brown and crisp, 3 to 4 minutes. Using tongs, carefully flip the pieces over and continue cooking until the second side is golden brown and crisp, 2 to 3 minutes longer. It's better to err on the side of cooking a little longer to ensure a crisp crust, since there's little risk of overcooking with this method. Once the pieces are fried, transfer them to the sheet pan and place in the oven to keep warm while you make the waffles.

To make the waffles, in a small bowl, whisk together the flour, brown sugar, baking powder, baking soda, and salt. In a larger bowl, whisk together the buttermilk, butter, and eggs until well blended. Add the flour mixture to the buttermilk mixture and whisk together just until combined. Be careful not to overmix or the waffles will be tough (it's okay if the batter has a few lumps).

Preheat your waffle iron according to the manufacturer's instructions, then lightly coat the top and bottom plates of the iron with the cooking spray. Ladle enough of the batter evenly onto the bottom plate to reach to within ½ inch of the edge on all sides, so the waffle has room to spread. Close the waffle iron and cook until the waffle is golden brown and crisp, 3 to 5 minutes; the timing will depend on your waffle iron. Transfer the waffle to another sheet pan and place in the oven to keep warm. Continue to cook waffles until all of the batter is used up. You should have 4 to 8 waffles, depending on the size of your iron.

To make the syrup, whisk together the honey, hot sauce, and butter in a small saucepan over medium-high heat. When the mixture reaches a boil, immediately remove the pan from the heat.

To serve, divide the warm waffles among four individual plates. Arrange a thigh and a drumstick on top, then sprinkle with the thyme and drizzle with the syrup.

DUCK BREAST WITH APRICOT MOSTARDA

Mostarda, a versatile mustard-laced Italian fruit condiment, makes a wonderful match for meats like duck. Its combination of sweetness and acidity, known as *agrodolce* in Italian, provides a contrast to the richness of the meat. While mostarda is great with duck, it also pairs well with grilled pork, as well as with rich cheeses and charcuterie. If you like, other stone fruits, such as plums or nectarines, can be used in place of the apricots.

It can be challenging to achieve a perfect crisp-skinned duck breast. The key is to fully render the layer of fat located beneath the skin without overcooking the lean breast meat. Cooking the duck sous vide ensures it will be perfectly medium rare, but crisping the skin calls for additional work. To achieve this, I call for scoring the skin, which not only helps it to render its fat, but also keeps the skin from curling once seared. If your knife isn't sharp enough, a clean box cutter or razor blade will also work. Moulard ducks are larger than other breeds, and boast a more substantial layer of fat, which makes for buttery meat and skin that's ideal for crisping. For that reason, Moulard breasts are the best choice here, but Muscovy or Pekin breasts can be substituted (the same goes for the other duck recipes in this chapter)—just bear in mind that the latter may be significantly smaller.

SERVES 4 as a main course | **SOUS VIDE COOKING TIME:** 1 hour (or up to 5 hours) | **ACTIVE PREP TIME:** 40 minutes, plus 15 minutes to rest

2 to 4 skin-on, boneless duck breasts (approximately 2 pounds)

1 teaspoon kosher salt

MOSTARDA

2 tablespoons extra-virgin olive oil

2 tablespoons peeled, minced or grated fresh ginger (from a 2-inch piece)

2 shallots, minced

1 tablespoon yellow mustard seeds, cracked with a mortar and pestle

1 teaspoon coriander seeds, cracked with a mortar and pestle

1 teaspoon black peppercorns, cracked with a mortar and pestle

½ teaspoon red pepper flakes (or more, depending on your heat preference)

1 pound fresh apricots, halved, pitted, and each half quartered lengthwise (about 3 cups), or 1½ cups dried apricots, halved and reconstituted in warm water for 1 hour

½ teaspoon kosher salt

3 tablespoons honey

3 tablespoons cider vinegar

1½ teaspoons fresh lemon juice or 1 tablespoon fresh Meyer lemon juice

1 teaspoon fresh thyme leaves

1 teaspoon canola or other mild vegetable oil

1 tablespoon coarsely chopped fresh mint, for garnish (optional)

DO-AHEAD STRATEGY

If you intend to chill and reheat the duck, I recommend salting the meat after it comes out of the bag (see page 117 for an explanation). The cooked duck can be chilled in the bag in an ice water bath (see page 14) for 20 minutes and then refrigerated for up to 1 week. Reheat in a 55°C (131°F) water bath for 20 minutes before proceeding. The mostarda can be made while the duck is cooking, but if you choose to make it afterward, use the rendered duck fat in place of the olive oil, as it will complement the duck flavor nicely.

CONTINUED >

Preheat your sous vide water bath to 55°C (131°F).

Using a very sharp knife, score the skin on each duck breast in a crosshatch pattern: make parallel incisions ¼ inch apart in one direction, then rotate the breast 90 degrees and repeat the parallel incisions. Be careful not to cut all of the way through the fat into the meat.

Season the duck breasts on both sides with the salt. Place the breasts in a single layer a gallon-size freezer-safe ziplock bag and seal using the water displacement method (see page 12).

When the water reaches the target temperature, lower the bagged duck into the water bath (making sure the bag is fully submerged) and cook for 1 hour.

While the duck breasts are cooking, make the mostarda. Heat the olive oil in a large nonstick sauté pan over medium heat until it shimmers. Add the ginger and shallots, and sauté, stirring constantly, until they are aromatic and beginning to brown, 1 to 2 minutes. Add the mustard seeds, coriander, black pepper, and pepper flakes and sauté until aromatic, about 20 seconds. Add the apricots and salt, and toss or stir the mixture with a wooden spoon until the apricots begin to soften and release liquid, 1 to 2 minutes. Add the honey and vinegar, which will bubble and simmer, and then cook until the apricots soften and begin to lose their shape and almost all of the liquid has evaporated, 2 to 3 minutes more. Remove the pan from the heat and stir in the lemon juice and thyme. Transfer the mixture to a bowl and set aside.

When the duck breasts are ready, remove the bag from the water bath and let the breasts rest for 10 minutes, then remove the breasts from the bag and pat them thoroughly dry with paper towels. Discard any liquid in the bag.

Heat the canola oil in a large nonstick sauté pan over medium heat until it shimmers. Add the duck breasts, skin side down, and, using your hand, tongs, or a metal spatula, press the meat against the pan to make sure all of the skin comes in contact with the hot surface. Sear the breasts, without moving them, for 1 to 2 minutes. The skin should turn light golden brown and begin to render fat. If the skin has turned a deeper shade of brown, turn the heat down to low; if the skin is still beige, turn the heat up to medium-high. Cook for 3 to 4 minutes more, at which point the skin should be crisp and deep golden brown and a significant amount of fat should have collected in the pan.

Transfer the seared breasts, skin side up, to a plate, blot away any fat remaining on the skin with a paper towel, and let them rest for 5 minutes before carving. Save the rendered duck fat for another use, such as duck confit (page 99) or chicken liver mousse (page 73), or discard.

To serve, cut each duck breast against the grain on a slight diagonal into ¼-inch-thick slices and arrange the slices on four individual plates. Spoon the mostarda alongside the duck slices and garnish each serving with a sprinkle of the mint, if using.

DUCK CONFIT WITH FRISÉE SALAD

Making this iconic bistro dish at home needn't be daunting. Yes, the recipe does take 2 days to prepare, but almost all of the time required is hands off. The longest step is the curing process, but the length of time is up to you (the full 24 hours will result in a saltier, more traditional confit).

Traditional confit requires fully submerging duck legs in fat, but here you need to put only a small amount of fat in the bag, making it practical to prepare small quantities. What's more, cooking in a water bath conducts heat more efficiently than the typical stove-top or low-oven method, so the duck cooks more uniformly. Once the duck legs are cured and cooked, all that remains to be done is frying them and tossing the salad. So pour yourself a big glass of Côtes du Rhône and consider this your weekend food project. Your friends will be *très* impressed.

SERVES: 4 as a main course | **SOUS VIDE COOKING TIME**: 8 hours (or up to 12 hours) | **ACTIVE PREP TIME**: 45 minutes, plus 12 to 24 hours to cure

½ cup kosher salt

2 tablespoons light brown sugar

½ teaspoon freshly cracked white pepper

½ teaspoon freshly cracked black pepper

¼ teaspoon Chinese five-spice powder

4 skin-on, bone-in duck legs, preferably Moulard (see page 97, for explanation)

4 thyme sprigs

2 fresh or dried bay leaves, broken in half lengthwise

½ cup rendered duck fat (homemade or store-bought) or canola oil

MUSTARD VINAIGRETTE

1 tablespoon minced shallot

1 clove garlic, minced

1 tablespoon whole-grain mustard

1 tablespoon cider vinegar

1 teaspoon honey

Pinch of kosher salt

Pinch of cayenne pepper

2 tablespoons canola oil

1 tablespoon rendered duck fat (from cooking the duck)

2 teaspoons chopped fresh tarragon

Freshly ground black pepper

2 heads frisée, dark green parts and root end trimmed off (kitchen shears work great for this)

DO-AHEAD STRATEGY

The cooked duck can be chilled in the bag in an ice water bath (see page 14) for 30 minutes and then refrigerated up to 2 weeks. It's not necessary to reheat the confit fully in a water bath, as the final frying is sufficient to heat the duck through. Instead, warm the confit in a 60°C (140°F) water bath for 10 minutes, then transfer the duck to a platter or tray, let the cooking liquid stand to separate the fat from the juices, and use the fat for the frying step. Because the duck will still be cold in the center, there's no need for the resting step.

CONTINUED >

The duck must cure for 12 to 24 hours before it can be cooked, so plan accordingly. To make the cure, in a small bowl, stir together the salt, brown sugar, white and black peppers, and five-spice powder. Using a paring knife, cut a circle around the end of the drumstick on each duck leg, making the incision at the thinnest part of the leg and cutting all the way to the bone; this will make it easier to judge when the legs are cooked. Generously coat the duck legs with the salt mixture, place them in a gallon-size freezer-safe ziplock bag, and seal the bag. Refrigerate for at least 12 hours or up to 24 hours.

The next day, preheat your sous vide water bath to 82°C (179.7°F).

Remove the duck legs from the bag. Discard the liquid in the bag and wash the bag out with water and pat it dry. Rinse the duck legs under cold running water, carefully washing away all of the curing mixture. Pat the duck legs dry with paper towels. Place a thyme sprig and ½ bay leaf next to the flesh side of each leg. Place all of the duck legs and the duck fat into the cleaned ziplock bag and seal with the water displacement method (see page 12).

When the water reaches the target temperature, lower the bagged duck legs into the water bath (making sure the bag is fully submerged) and cook for 8 hours. I recommend checking the water bath every few hours to see that the bag is still fully submerged. I also suggest covering the bath with plastic wrap or aluminum foil to minimize evaporation (see page 8 for explanation).

When the legs are ready, the meat will have pulled back where you scored, exposing the bone. Remove the bag from the water bath and let the duck legs cool for 15 minutes. Open the bag and pour the accumulated cooking liquid into a liquid measuring cup or bowl and set aside. Transfer the duck legs to a platter or tray and discard the thyme and bay. Thoroughly pat the legs dry with paper towels and then pull off the extra cartilage and skin at the end of the drumstick, exposing the bone.

The cooking liquid contains both fat and cooking juices; after sitting for 1 to 2 minutes, the fat will rise to the top. Pour off the fat into a large cast-iron skillet, being careful not to include any of the juices. Alternatively, use a small ladle to skim the fat off the top and transfer it to the skillet. Either way, you want the fat in the skillet to reach a depth of at least ½ inch. Reserve 1 tablespoon of the fat for making the vinaigrette.

Heat the fat in the skillet over medium heat until it shimmers and a drop of water flicked into the oil hisses and steams away immediately, or until it registers 350°F on a high-heat thermometer (you may have to tilt the pan to get enough depth for the oil temperature to register on the thermometer). Using tongs, carefully lower the duck legs, skin side down, into the fat; the oil will sizzle and spit, so it's a good idea to use a splatter guard. Fry the duck, undisturbed, until the skin crisps and turns a deep golden brown, about 8 minutes. Using tongs, transfer the duck to a plate and blot away any excess fat with paper towels. Set aside.

To make the vinaigrette, in a small bowl, whisk together the shallot, garlic, mustard, vinegar, honey, salt, and cayenne pepper. Gradually drizzle in the oil a few drops at a time while whisking constantly, followed by the duck fat. Whisk in the tarragon and black pepper to taste.

To serve, toss the frisée with 1 tablespoon of the mustard vinaigrette and then arrange the salad on four individual plates. Top each salad with a warm duck leg. Drizzle the remaining vinaigrette over everything.

PRO TIP

This recipe calls for rendered duck fat for cooking the duck legs and also for frying them. It can be purchased in specialty stores and online (see Resources, page 273), but if you can't find it, canola oil can be substituted. As the duck cooks, it will render fat and imbue flavor into the oil. Regardless of whether you started with duck fat, once you have finished the recipe, you will end up with leftover fat. Don't throw it away. Store it in the fridge for the next time you make confit, use it to seal your chicken liver mousse (page 73), or use it in other recipes. Keep in mind that it will be fairly salty, however, so go lighter on the seasoning when using it in other recipes.

DUCK MOLE ROJO

Traditional mole recipes are always elaborate, involved affairs, and although this one is still somewhat ambitious, I've streamlined it dramatically, and the results are still spectacular. My sous vide approach not only guarantees that the duck will never be tough or dry, it also eliminates the need to keep a close eye on the sauce to prevent it from scorching.

If you don't want to go to the trouble of making the sauce yourself, you can use a store-bought mole base, though the flavors won't be as vivid. Simply mix 4 ounces of the prepared mole sauce with 2 cups chicken stock. Happily, this is a great dish to prepare ahead of time because the flavor is greatly improved the second day. All this mole needs to make a world-class meal is some warm corn tortillas and yellow Spanish rice. So go ahead, take a quack at it.

SERVES 4 as a main course | **SOUS VIDE COOKING TIME:** 8 hours (or up to 12 hours) | **ACTIVE PREP TIME:** 40 minutes

4 skin-on, bone-in duck legs, preferably Moulard, trimmed of excess fat

1 teaspoon kosher salt

1 tablespoon canola or other mild vegetable oil

MOLE SAUCE

2 ancho chiles, stemmed, seeded, and cut into ½-inch-wide strips

2 pasilla chiles, stemmed, seeded, and cut into ½-inch-wide strips

2 guajillo chiles, stemmed, seeded, and cut into ½-inch-wide strips

¼ cup raisins

2 cups chicken stock, homemade (page 267) or store-bought

1 yellow onion, thinly sliced

Pinch of kosher salt, plus 1 teaspoon

3 cloves garlic, thinly sliced

¼ cup tomato paste

¼ cup roasted almonds, ground in a mortar and pestle or spice grinder, or 2 tablespoons almond butter

2 tablespoons natural or Dutch-processed cocoa powder

1 tablespoon dark brown sugar

½ teaspoon freshly ground black pepper

½ teaspoon ground cinnamon (ideally Mexican)

½ teaspoon ground allspice

¼ teaspoon ground cloves

1 tablespoon toasted sesame seeds, for garnish

DO-AHEAD STRATEGY

The sauce can be prepared in advance and refrigerated for up to 1 week or frozen for up to 1 month. The cooked duck and sauce can be chilled in the bag in an ice water bath (see page 14) for 30 minutes and then refrigerated for up to 2 weeks. Reheat in a 65°C (149°F) water bath for 30 minutes.

CONTINUED >

Preheat your sous vide water bath to 80°C (176°F).

Season the duck legs with the salt. Heat the oil in a large cast-iron skillet or sauté pan over medium heat until it shimmers. Add the duck, skin side down, and cook until the skin is golden brown and has rendered much of its fat, 5 to 6 minutes. Using tongs, flip the duck legs over and cook until the flesh side has begun to brown, about 2 minutes more. Transfer the duck to a gallon-size freezer-safe ziplock bag, leaving behind all of the rendered fat in the pan.

To make the sauce, add all of the chiles and the raisins to the fat remaining in the skillet over medium heat and fry, stirring constantly, until the raisins have puffed and the chiles have darkened slightly and smell toasted, 1 to 2 minutes. Using a slotted spoon, transfer the toasted chiles and raisins to a blender and then pour the stock into the blender to submerge them (this will make it easier to blend later).

Pour off all but 3 tablespoons of the rendered fat from the skillet and discard. Return the pan to medium heat, add the onion and the pinch of salt, and stir with a wooden spoon before adding the garlic. Cook the mixture, stirring occasionally, until it has begun to brown and soften, 6 to 7 minutes. Stir in the tomato paste and cook, stirring constantly, until the paste turns a shade darker, about 2 minutes, and then remove from the heat.

Add the onion mixture, almonds, cocoa powder, brown sugar, black pepper, cinnamon, allspice, cloves, and the remaining 1 teaspoon salt and blend on high speed until

the mixture is completely smooth. Taste and add more salt if needed.

Pour the mole sauce into the bag containing the duck legs and seal using the water displacement method (see page 12).

When the water reaches the target temperature, lower the bagged duck and mole mixture into the water bath (making sure the bag is fully submerged) and cook for 8 hours. I recommend checking the water bath every few hours to see that the bag is still fully submerged. I also suggest covering the bath with plastic wrap or aluminum foil to minimize evaporation (see page 8 for explanation).

When the duck is ready, remove the bag from the water and transfer the entire contents of the bag (the duck and the mole sauce) to a serving bowl. Garnish with the sesame seeds and serve with rice and tortillas for soaking up the glorious sauce.

PRO TIP

The three dried chiles called for here, all of which are traditionally used in mole, are only mildly hot, but in concert they produce a great depth of flavor. All three varieties can typically be found in Latin markets (or online, see Resources, page 273), but if you can find only one, you can use it in place of all three. The goal is to end up with roughly one cup of stemmed, seeded, and cut chiles.

QUAIL WITH ZA'ATAR

Quail is prized for its delicate flavor and texture, but its small size and lean meat make it prone to drying out when cooked on the stove top or in the oven. But when cooked sous vide, the meat remains succulent. In this recipe, I infuse the mild-tasting bird with *za'atar*, a bold-flavored Middle Eastern spice mixture, and follow that up with a quick stop on the grill to produce deliciously charred, world-class quail. Sumac, as well as premade za'atar, is available at Middle Eastern markets and online (see Resources, page 273). If you opt for premade za'atar, use 3 tablespoons; you'll still need to add the brown sugar and salt.

This recipe exemplifies how sous vide can produce results that even very experienced cooks can't beat. I can't take credit, but I've eaten quail dishes in acclaimed restaurants that don't hold a candle to this one. These little birds are superb, particularly when served perched atop a couscous salad with orange and fennel.

SERVES 4 as a main course | **SOUS VIDE COOKING TIME:** 1½ hours (or up to 5 hours) | **ACTIVE PREP TIME:** 15 minutes

4 quail

ZA'ATAR SEASONING

1 tablespoon chopped fresh oregano or thyme, or 1 teaspoon dried oregano or thyme

1 tablespoon powdered sumac

1 tablespoon sesame seeds

2 teaspoons ground cumin

1 teaspoon ground coriander

1 teaspoon freshly ground black pepper

1 tablespoon light brown sugar

1½ teaspoons kosher salt

COUSCOUS SALAD

1 cup couscous, cooked according to package instructions

1 fennel bulb, thinly shaved lengthwise on a mandoline (1½ to 2 cups)

1 orange, cut into supremes (see page 44), with juice

¼ cup roasted almonds, coarsely chopped (optional)

2 tablespoons dried currants (optional)

2 tablespoons chopped fresh flat-leaf parsley or fennel fronds, or a mixture

1 teaspoon fresh lemon juice

3 tablespoons extra-virgin olive oil

1 tablespoon extra-virgin olive oil

Flaky sea salt (such as Maldon or fleur de sel)

DO-AHEAD STRATEGY

The homemade *za'atar* seasoning can be stored in a tightly capped container in a cool, dark place for up to 6 months. If you intend to chill and reheat the quail, I recommend salting the meat after it comes out of the bag (see page 127 for an explanation). The cooked quail can be chilled in the bag in an ice water bath (see page 14) for 20 minutes and then refrigerated for up to 1 week. Reheat in a 56°C (132.8°F) water bath for 30 minutes before crisping the skin.

CONTINUED >

Preheat your sous vide water bath to 56°C (132.8°F).

To spatchcock a quail, place it, breast side down, on a work surface. Using kitchen shears, cut through the ribs and flesh on either side of the backbone and then lift out the backbone. Turn the quail cut side down and firmly flatten the bird with the heel of your hand. Repeat with the remaining quail.

To make the seasoning, in a small bowl, stir together the oregano, sumac, sesame seeds, cumin, coriander, and pepper until well blended. Add the brown sugar and salt and mix well. Rub the spice mixture evenly over the quail. You'll want to season both the top side and the underside, but use the majority of the mix to cover the skin side, pressing it in so that it adheres.

Place the quail in a gallon-size freezer-safe ziplock bag in a single layer and seal using the water displacement method (see page 12).

When the water reaches the target temperature, lower the bagged quail into the water bath (making sure the bag is fully submerged) and cook for 1½ hours.

About 20 minutes before the quail are ready, assemble the salad. In a bowl, combine the couscous, fennel, orange supremes and juice, almonds and currants (if using), and parsley and toss to mix. Drizzle with the lemon juice and 3 tablespoons of oil and toss again to coat evenly.

When the quail are ready, remove the bag from the water bath and transfer them to a plate. Discard the liquid in the bag. Pat the skin side of each quail dry with a paper towel before rubbing it all over with the 1 tablespoon of oil.

Preheat a stove-top grill pan over medium-high heat. Place the quail, skin side down, on the pan and cook until the skin has crisped and deeply browned, almost blackened, 2 to 3 minutes. Using tongs, flip the quail over and cook for 1 minute more. (Depending on the size of your pan, you may need to brown the quail in two batches.)

To serve, divide the salad among four individual plates and sprinkle with the sea salt to taste. Place 1 quail on each plate and garnish with a sprinkle of the fennel fronds.

PRO TIP

The term spatchcock *refers to removing the backbone of any kind of poultry (in this instance quail) and then breaking the breastbone and flattening the bird. By pressing the bird flat, it will not only cook faster but nearly all of the skin will make contact with the hot pan, ensuring even browning and crisping. If you'd like, you can ask your butcher to spatchcock the quail for you.*

TURKEY MEATBALLS STUFFED WITH MOZZARELLA AND BASIL

Made with turkey and stuffed with mozzarella, these meatballs break from tradition, but you won't argue with the results. Exceedingly juicy and tender, with a hidden pocket of oozy molten cheese, these are not entry-level meatballs. Cooking the meat slowly keeps it moist and allows you to heat up the cheesy center gradually. This is a case where it doesn't pay to be fancy: for the best results, I use block low-moisture mozzarella, which melts better than its fresh Italian-style kin.

I like to serve these meatballs as an appetizer, but for a more substantial Italian American dish, go full on Tony Soprano and serve them over spaghetti. *Abbondanza!*

SERVES 6 to 8 as an appetizer, or 4 as a main course | **SOUS VIDE COOKING TIME:** 1 hour (or up to 3 hours) | **ACTIVE PREP TIME:** 25 minutes

2 pounds ground turkey, preferably dark meat (90 to 95 percent lean)

1 cup (about 8 ounces) whole-milk ricotta cheese

¾ cup dried bread crumbs

½ cup plus 2 tablespoons grated Parmesan cheese

1 large egg

1 tablespoon chopped fresh flat-leaf parsley

3 cloves garlic, minced

1½ teaspoons kosher salt

¾ teaspoon freshly ground black pepper

8 ounces low-moisture mozzarella cheese, cut into 12 (¾-inch) cubes

12 small fresh basil leaves, or 6 larger leaves, torn in half, plus ¼ cup loosely packed leaves

1 tablespoon extra-virgin olive oil

1 tablespoon unsalted butter

2 cups Quick-Cook Marinara (about ½ recipe, page 263), cold

Red pepper flakes, for garnish (optional)

DO-AHEAD STRATEGY

The cooked meatballs can be chilled in the bag in an ice water bath (see page 14) for 30 minutes and then refrigerated for up to 1 week. Reheat in a 63°C (145.4°F) water bath for 30 minutes before searing.

CONTINUED >

Preheat your sous vide water bath to 63°C (145.4°F).

In a large bowl, combine the turkey, ricotta, bread crumbs, ½ cup Parmesan cheese, egg, parsley, garlic, salt, and pepper and mix with your hands until the mixture is thoroughly combined.

Divide the turkey mixture into 12 equal portions and shape each portion into a rough disk or patty. Place 1 piece of mozzarella and 1 basil leaf (or ½ leaf) onto the center of each disk, then shape each disk into a smooth sphere a bit smaller than a tennis ball (2½ inches in diameter). Fold the meat around the cheese and basil, pinching the seal shut, and then roll the ball on a clean work surface to shape it evenly. This step is easier if you oil your hands before you shape the balls. Place the balls in a gallon-size freezer-safe ziplock bag in a single layer and then seal using the water displacement method (see page 12). They should fit snugly.

When the water reaches the target temperature, lower the bagged meatballs into the water bath (making sure the bag is fully submerged) and cook for 1 hour.

Remove the bag from the water bath and transfer the meatballs to a plate. Discard the liquid in the bag. Pat the meatballs dry with paper towels.

Heat the oil and butter in a large cast-iron skillet or sauté pan over medium-high heat until the butter has foamed, subsided, and begun to brown. Place the meatballs in the skillet in a single layer (working in batches if necessary) and cook until the undersides are golden brown, 1 to 2 minutes, then flip them with tongs or a spatula and cook until the other sides are browned, about 1 minute more. Transfer the browned meatballs to a warm platter and lower the heat to medium. Immediately add the marinara to the pan—it will sizzle and boil immediately—and cook until it's reduced and thickened slightly, 2 to 3 minutes. Remove the pan from the heat and stir in the remaining ¼ cup basil.

Spoon the sauce over the meatballs, sprinkle with the remaining 2 tablespoons of Parmesan and the red pepper flakes (if using), and serve immediately.

THANKSGIVING TURKEY

From the perspective of a harried Thanksgiving host, cooking a turkey sous vide offers tremendous benefits. It frees up oven space, and the forgiving nature of low and slow cooking offers great flexibility, because even after it's cooked, the turkey can stay in the bath until you're ready to brown and serve, with no sacrifice in quality. More important, cooking turkey gently at a low temperature achieves seriously moist and tender results from a bird that is prone to drying out.

The key to unlocking the juiciest bird is to separate the dark and white meat, which cook at different rates. Often when roasting, by the time the thighs are ready, the breasts will already be woefully overcooked. The sous vide approach lets you stagger their cooking times so both end up perfectly done at the same time. (For this reason, this same method works beautifully for cooking turkey breast on its own.) It's true that you'll have to sacrifice the Norman Rockwell moment of the whole roast bird emerging from the oven, but I say taste trumps romanticism any day—particularly when that day is Thanksgiving. To make this a holiday feast for the ages, serve the turkey along with Sausage Unstuffing (page 270), Easy Herbed Cranberry Sauce (page 269), and Perfect Mashed Potatoes (page 193).

SERVES 8 to 10 as a main course | **SOUS VIDE COOKING TIME:** 10 hours (or up to 19 hours) | **ACTIVE PREP TIME:** 1¼ hours

1 (14- to 16-pound) turkey, preferably fresh, or fully thawed if frozen

1 tablespoon kosher salt

2 teaspoons sugar

Freshly ground black pepper

2 to 3 sage sprigs

½ cup (4 ounces) unsalted butter

GRAVY

6 cups homemade turkey stock using bones, neck, giblets, and wing tips (page 267), or 6 cups store-bought low-sodium turkey broth

2 to 3 shallots, finely minced

1 clove garlic, minced

½ cup all-purpose flour

1 cup dry white wine

½ cup crème fraîche or heavy cream

2 teaspoons chopped fresh sage or thyme, or a mixture

Salt and freshly ground black pepper

DO-AHEAD STRATEGY

The recipe gives ample leeway for fitting into most cooks' plans. If you want to start cooking more than a day in advance, the turkey can be cooked up to 1 week ahead with equally delicious results. Cook the white meat and dark meat according to the recipe and chill them in the bag in an ice water bath (see page 14) for 30 minutes before refrigerating. Reheat in a 60°C (140°F) water bath for 1½ hours.

To butcher your turkey, place it on a clean cutting surface with plenty of space, such as a butcher block or clean countertop. First, remove the packaged gizzards and neck from inside the body cavity and set aside for stock. Using a chef's knife or a boning knife, separate the legs from the body by slicing through the skin where the breast and thigh meet and cutting through the hip joint. Set the legs aside. Next, remove the wings in the same way, slicing through the joint connecting the wing to the back. Remove the wing tips and save for stock, then set the wings aside. Lastly, remove the breasts by sliding the knife along either side of the breastbone, which separates the two sides of the breast, keeping the knife flush with the bone and scraping against it so as not to cut into the meat. Still using the bone as a guide, continue to slice the breasts away from the carcass

CONTINUED >

until you reach the ribs, where the breasts end and you can cut through the skin. At the front end of the bird (by the neck cavity), carve around the wishbone, and you'll have completely separated the breasts from the carcass. Set aside the bones, giblets, neck, and wing tips to use to make stock. (You'll want stock for the gravy and the dressing, see page 270.)

Once the bird is completely sectioned, transfer the breasts, legs, and wings to a large bowl and season with the salt, sugar, and with a few grinds of pepper.

Place the breast halves and 1 sage sprig into a gallon-size freezer-safe ziplock bag and seal using the water displacement method (see page 12). Do the same for the legs and wings (depending on the size of your bird, you may need to put the legs and wings in separate bags; put 1 sage sprig in each bag). At this point, place the turkey pieces in the fridge until you are ready to cook; they will keep well for up to 48 hours. (Not only will this stay in the fridge not hurt, it will actually help season the meat evenly.)

Meanwhile, make your stock for the gravy using the reserved bones, giblets, neck, and wing tips (see page 267). When the stock is done, strain it into a large saucepan and boil it over medium heat until it's reduced by half. If using store-bought turkey broth, you'll want to enrich its flavor by adding the reserved giblets and neck to the broth in a large saucepan and boiling over medium heat until reduced by half. Set aside the reduced stock.

At least 10½ hours before you plan to serve your turkey, preheat your sous vide water bath to 65°C (149°F).

When the water reaches the target temperature, lower the bagged legs and wings into the water bath (making sure the bag is fully submerged) and cook for a minimum of 6 hours or for up to 12 hours (perfect for starting the night before T-day). At this point, keep the breasts in the fridge, as they take considerably less time than the dark meat.

At least 4 hours before you plan to serve the turkey, lower the water bath temperature to 60°C (140°F), letting the dark meat continue to cook in the bath. When the water reaches the new target temperature, add the bagged turkey breasts to the bath. Cook the dark and white meat for an additional 4 hours. At this point, the turkey will be fully cooked and ready to brown. (If you're more than 30 minutes away from serving, the turkey can be kept in the water bath for up to 3 hours longer.)

When you're ready to serve, remove both bags from the water bath, transfer the turkey pieces to a platter or tray, and reserve the cooking juices in the bags for making the gravy.

Using paper towels, pat the turkey pieces thoroughly dry. Melt the butter in a large skillet or sauté pan over medium-high heat until it has foamed, subsided, and begun to brown. Working in batches, add the turkey pieces, skin side down, and sear, using a spoon to baste any skin that doesn't touch the pan with the melted butter, until golden brown and crisp, about 5 minutes per batch. After each batch is browned and crisped, return the pieces, skin side up, to the platter. When all of the pieces have been browned, cover the turkey loosely with aluminum foil to keep warm, or place in a 200°F oven.

Lower the heat under the pan to medium and, using the butter remaining in the pan from browning the turkey, proceed to make the gravy. Add the shallots and garlic, stirring and scraping with a wooden spoon or spatula to dislodge any browned bits stuck to the bottom of the pan, and cook, stirring constantly, until they begin to brown, 2 to 3 minutes. Add the flour, stir with a whisk to work out any lumps, and then cook, stirring constantly, until the flour-and-butter mixture bubbles vigorously, 1 to 2 minutes. It's fine if it browns a bit, but keep it moving so it doesn't burn.

Add the wine to the pan and stir vigorously until the mixture is smooth and bubbling once again, 1 to 2 minutes. Gradually pour in the reduced stock and the reserved turkey cooking juices while whisking constantly to avoid lumps. Once all of the liquid is incorporated, raise the heat to medium-high, bring the mixture to a simmer, and cook, stirring often, for about 5 minutes.

Stir in the crème fraîche and simmer for an additional 5 minutes. The gravy should now be thick enough to coat the back of a spoon. If it isn't, continue simmering until it is. Remove the gravy from the heat, stir in the sage, and season with salt and pepper. Transfer to a gravy boat.

To carve your turkey, transfer the pieces to a large cutting board. Slice the breasts thinly against the grain. For each leg, separate the drumstick from the thigh at the joint. Cut the thigh meat away from the bone and slice it thinly. I don't bother trying to carve meat from the wings or drumsticks; just separate the wings at the joint into sections. Transfer everything to a platter and serve with the gravy on the side.

MEATS

IF EGGS ARE THE GATEWAY TO SOUS VIDE, THEN MEAT IS THE HARD STUFF, offering a dizzying array of possibilities. But don't be intimidated, because there's no steep learning curve to master. Unlike traditional cooking methods—grilling, pan-frying, roasting, you name it—the temperature-controlled heat of sous vide cooks your meat evenly, edge to edge, with no gradient or banding. That means there's no guesswork, no consternated poking or probing, and no worry of overcooking, which is especially reassuring when cooking steaks and roasts. On top of this, the gentler heating causes less damage to the meat proteins (that is, denaturation), so more precious juices stay inside the meat where they belong. This control also opens the door to tenderizing tough cuts while keeping them medium rare. The single most dramatic example of this transformation is Stout-Glazed Short Ribs (page 163), which turns one of the toughest cuts of beef into something sublimely, meltingly tender.

But while sous vide will ensure that your meat turns out deliciously juicy and evenly cooked every time, the temperatures involved are too low to create the flavorful crust formed by direct high heat (see page 9 for an explanation of the Maillard reaction). To have the best of both worlds, you need to give the meat a quick sear to create that coveted golden brown exterior, leaving the inside perfectly cooked. Check out the Perfect Sous Vide Steak (page 145) for one of my favorite searing techniques and a detailed explanation of how to achieve it.

Finally, in addition to guaranteeing consistency and quality, cooking sous vide offers something you might not have thought of: convenience and flexibility. Because meat can be held for hours at the same temperature without any loss of quality, I give a range of cooking times—consider it a kind of buffer zone—for all of the recipes in this section (the same holds true, to a lesser extent, in the "Poultry" chapter). What's more, bagged meat couldn't be easier to chill, store, and reheat (which is why, as much as any of the other reasons, sous vide is so widely used in restaurants). This means you can adapt sous vide to your busy schedule, rather than the other way around.

If you're preparing meat in advance, keep in mind this one caveat, however. If a cut is served medium rare (what I call a "steaklike" cut), you generally want to avoid salting in advance of chilling and reheating. This is because the salt will gradually cure the meat as it sits in the fridge, resulting in a firmer texture akin to deli meat. This isn't inherently bad, of course. For example, it won't be noticeable in the pulled pork on page 133, and it's exactly what you want in the case of the pastrami on page 165. But it will be at odds with the juicy, yielding texture people look for in steaks and roasts. You can easily avoid this by simply salting the meat before searing, when it comes out of the bag.

That's enough sermonizing for now. Let's get to the meat of things.

MOROCCAN LAMB MEATBALLS

Spiced with a fragrant blend of cumin, coriander, thyme, and mint typical of North Africa, these succulent morsels of ground lamb aren't your everyday meatballs. Cooked with the gentle, even heat of sous vide, they need just a quick sear to produce a nice crust. I present them here as an appetizer for a larger group, but they can be served as a main course over rice or couscous, with a side of cucumber salad and maybe a dab of fiery harissa. Whether you call them *kofta*, as they are known in North Africa, or meatballs, I'm confident you'll call them delicious after your first juicy, savory bite.

SERVES 6 to 8 as an appetizer, or 4 as a main course | **SOUS VIDE COOKING TIME:** 1 hour (up to 5 hours) |
ACTIVE PREP TIME: 30 minutes

5 tablespoons extra-virgin olive oil

2 cloves garlic, minced

2 shallots, minced

1 teaspoon ground cumin

¾ teaspoon freshly ground black pepper

½ teaspoon ground coriander

½ teaspoon red pepper flakes

¾ cup dried bread crumbs

½ cup yogurt, homemade (page 260), or whole-milk plain Greek yogurt

1 large egg

2 pounds ground lamb or ground beef

2 teaspoons kosher salt

1 teaspoon chopped fresh thyme

2 tablespoons torn fresh mint leaves, for garnish

1 teaspoon grated lemon zest (from about ½ lemon), for garnish

DO-AHEAD STRATEGY

The cooked meatballs can be chilled in the bags in an ice water bath (see page 14) for 20 minutes and then refrigerated for up to 4 days. Reheat in a 60°C (140°F) water bath for 20 minutes before browning.

CONTINUED >

Preheat your sous vide water bath to 60°C (140°F).

Heat 3 tablespoons of the oil in a small sauté pan over medium heat until it shimmers. Add the garlic and shallots and cook, stirring occasionally, until translucent, softened, and beginning to turn golden brown, about 5 minutes. Stir in the cumin, black pepper, coriander, and red pepper flakes and remove from the heat. Transfer the shallot mixture to a large bowl then whisk in the bread crumbs and yogurt, followed by the egg. Add the lamb, salt, and thyme and mix with your hands until thoroughly combined.

Shape the lamb mixture into spheres a bit larger than a golf ball (about 2 inches in diameter), to make 16 balls. (This step is easier if you oil your hands before you shape the balls.) When all of the balls have been shaped, press down on each ball with the palm of your hand to flatten it slightly, making the balls somewhat patty shaped (this will make them easier to fit in the bag and to sear later on). Transfer the balls to a gallon-size freezer-safe ziplock bag in a single layer and seal using the water displacement method (see page 12).

When the water reaches the target temperature, lower the bagged meatballs into the water bath (making sure the bag is fully submerged) and cook for 1 hour.

Remove the bag from the water bath and transfer the meatballs to a platter or tray. Discard the liquid in the bags and pat the meatballs dry with paper towels.

Heat the remaining 2 tablespoons oil in a large cast-iron skillet or nonstick sauté pan over medium heat until it shimmers. Add the meatballs in a single layer (it's okay if the meatballs touch since they're already cooked) and cook until deep golden brown on the underside, 1 to 2 minutes. Using tongs or a spatula, flip the meatballs over and brown on the second side, 1 to 2 minutes more. (Depending on the size of your pan, you may need to sear the meatballs in two batches, adding more oil as needed.)

To serve, transfer the meatballs to a serving bowl or platter, leaving any excess oil behind in the pan. Sprinkle with the mint and lemon zest.

PRO TIP

Here's a fun fact: salt, not egg, is the primary binding agent in meatballs. Without it, the balls would crumble apart. Mixing salt into ground meat makes the proteins soluble, which basically glues the individual meat bits together once the proteins reach a certain temperature and set.

PORK SATAY WITH PEANUT DIPPING SAUCE

Satay has risen from humble beginnings as a Southeast Asian street food and is now ubiquitous in bars and casual restaurants, even those with no particular Asian allegiance. Unfortunately, popularity doesn't ensure quality, and mediocre examples abound. My version makes sure your satay is always juicy and flavorful, so you'll never get stuck with the short end of the stick. Gently cooking the meat in an aromatic marinade means only a brief grilling is necessary to form a delicious sear, and the marinade takes just moments to become a knockout peanut sauce.

SERVES 4 as an appetizer | **SOUS VIDE COOKING TIME:** 1½ hours (or up to 5 hours) | **ACTIVE PREP TIME:** 20 minutes, plus 5 minutes, to rest

MARINADE

½ cup canned coconut milk, shaken in unopened can before measuring

2 tablespoons light brown sugar

1 to 2 tablespoons store-bought red curry paste (preferably Mae Ploy or Maesri brand, see Resources, page 273)

1 tablespoon fish sauce

1 tablespoon soy sauce

Juice of ½ lime (about 1 tablespoon fresh lime juice)

1½ teaspoons ground turmeric

½ teaspoon ground cumin

½ teaspoon ground coriander

2 (1-inch-thick) boneless pork loin chops, cut lengthwise on the diagonal into ½-inch-thick strips (about 1 pound)

2 tablespoons crunchy peanut butter, or 3 tablespoons coarsely chopped unsalted roasted peanuts

Canola or other mild vegetable oil, for greasing the grill pan or grill rack

2 tablespoons coarsely chopped fresh cilantro, for garnish

4 lime wedges, for serving

DO-AHEAD STRATEGY

The cooked pork can be chilled in the bag in an ice water bath (see page 14) for 20 minutes and then refrigerated for up to 1 week. Adding a couple of extra minutes in the grilling step will be enough to reheat the pork fully.

CONTINUED >

Preheat your sous vide water bath to 57°C (134.6°F).

To make the marinade, in a large liquid measuring cup, whisk together the coconut milk, brown sugar, curry paste to taste, fish sauce, soy sauce, lime juice, turmeric, cumin, and coriander, mixing well.

Place the pork and marinade in a gallon-size freezer-safe ziplock bag and massage the contents until the pork is evenly coated with the marinade. Seal using the water displacement method (see page 12), then press the bag flat so the pork is more or less in a single layer.

When the water reaches the target temperature, lower the bagged pork into the water bath (making sure the bag is fully submerged) and cook for 1½ hours.

Meanwhile, ready the skewers. You will need eight 8-inch skewers, either metal or bamboo. If using bamboo skewers, soak them in water for 30 minutes before loading them to prevent them from burning when over the fire.

When the pork is ready, remove the bag from the water bath and let it rest for 5 minutes. Pour the liquid from the bag into a small saucepan and transfer the pork to a bowl or plate.

Thread the pork pieces onto the skewers (1 or 2 strips per skewer, depending on size).

To prepare the dipping sauce, bring the liquid in the saucepan to a simmer over medium heat, then whisk in the peanut butter and cook, stirring often, until the mixture thickens, about 4 minutes. Remove from the heat, transfer to a small bowl, and set aside.

Preheat a rectangular stove-top grill pan over medium-high heat, or prepare a charcoal or gas grill for direct cooking over medium-high heat. Grease the pan or grill rack with the oil. Place the skewers on the pan or directly over the fire and sear, turning once, until deeply browned (blackened in spots is great) on both sides, about 2 minutes per side.

Transfer the skewers to a platter, sprinkle with the cilantro, and serve with the lime wedges and dipping sauce.

———

PRO TIP

This recipe can be adapted to make chicken satay: substitute skinless, boneless breasts cut against the grain into 1-inch-thick strips and cook in a 60°C (140°F) water bath for 1½ hours.

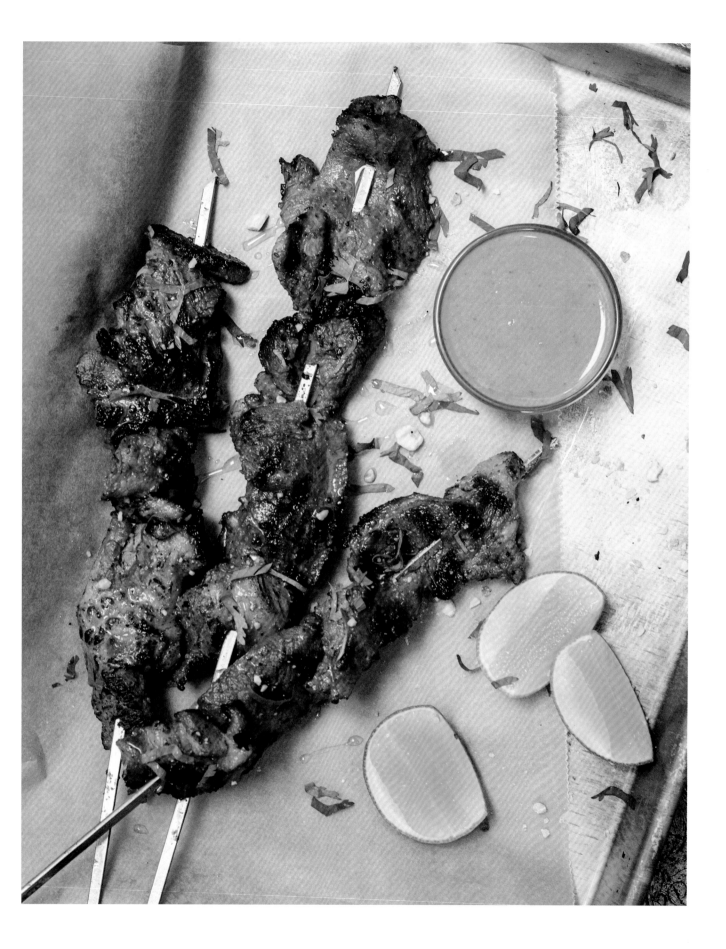

TAIWANESE-STYLE PORK BELLY BUNS

This recipe comes from the crazy-talented Monica Lo, whose beautiful photography graces this book. Her family is from Taiwan, and this is a sous vide version of the pork belly steamed buns or *guo bao* that she grew up with. It's a dish with a long history, and different versions can be found all over China and Southeast Asia. Pickled mustard greens are standard in the Taiwanese version; the option of using sweet yellow pickled daikon radish is particular to her family, rather than traditional.

The star of the dish, of course, is the pork belly. It's cooked at a slightly lower temperature for a longer period of time than the pork belly for my ramen (page 127), making it even softer and more unctuous. The melt-in-your- mouth texture of the meat is in perfect contrast to the pleasant crunchiness of the peanuts and pickles. Aside from the long cooking time and a few ingredients you'll likely have to seek out, these buns are a snap to put together. Frozen steamed buns, pickled daikon, and pickled mustard greens can be found in Chinese grocery stores (see Resources, page 273). The pickles on page 259 would also be delicious in place of the daikon or mustard greens. Five-spice powder contains ground star anise, but the optional whole pod delivers a nice additional pop of flavor.

SERVES 4 as an appetizer | **SOUS VIDE COOKING TIME:** 16 hours (or up to 24 hours) | **ACTIVE PREP TIME:** 15 minutes, plus 10 minutes to rest

1 pound pork belly, in a single piece, skin on or off (according to your preference)

½ teaspoon Chinese five-spice powder

3 tablespoons soy sauce

1-inch piece fresh ginger, thinly sliced (about 2 tablespoons)

1 star anise pod (optional)

¼ cup hoisin sauce

1 tablespoon Sriracha sauce

1 tablespoon coarse sugar (such as turbinado or Demerara), or light brown sugar

1 clove garlic, minced

1 (8-ounce) package steamed buns (*bao*), reheated according to package instructions (8 buns)

½ cup thinly sliced pickled daikon radish or mustard greens

¼ cup roasted unsalted peanuts, coarsely chopped

¼ cup loosely packed fresh cilantro leaves with small stems attached

DO-AHEAD STRATEGY

The cooked pork belly can be chilled in the bag in an ice water bath (see page 14) for 10 minutes and then refrigerated for up to 1 week. Reheat in a 60°C (140°F) water bath for 30 minutes before making the sauce.

CONTINUED >

Preheat your sous vide water bath to 70°C (158°F).

Place the pork belly, five-spice powder, soy sauce, ginger, and star anise (if using) in a gallon-size freezer-safe ziplock bag and seal using the water displacement method (see page 12).

When the water reaches the target temperature, lower the bagged pork belly into the water bath (making sure the bag is fully submerged) and cook for 16 hours. I recommend checking the water bath every few hours to see that the bag is still fully submerged. I also suggest covering the bath with plastic wrap or aluminum foil to minimize evaporation (see page 8 for explanation).

Remove the bag from the water bath and let the pork belly rest for about 10 minutes. Transfer the belly to a cutting board.

To make the sauce, strain the cooking liquid from the bag through a fine-mesh sieve into a medium saucepan and discard the star anise pod and ginger. Using a ladle or large spoon, skim the fat from the surface. Add the hoisin sauce, Sriracha sauce, and sugar to the pan and bring the mixture to a simmer over medium heat. Cook, stirring often, until the mixture is bubbling and thickened, 2 to 3 minutes. Remove from the heat.

Cut the pork belly against the grain into ¼-inch-thick slices. Depending on the size of the piece of pork belly, you may need to cut the slices in half lengthwise so that they fit into the buns.

To assemble, split each bun open at the seam and sandwich 1 or 2 pieces of pork belly, depending on size, inside. Top with some pickled daikon, a drizzle of sauce, and a sprinkle of peanuts and cilantro and serve immediately.

PORK BELLY RAMEN

Myriad styles of broth are found in Japanese ramen shops, from the simplest *shio* (salt-based) pork broth to elaborate versions featuring shrimp and lobster. My broth is miso based, the style most commonly made at home in Japan. It's not strictly traditional, but you'll have no reason to argue with the results: perfectly tender, succulent pork belly and a broth packed with flavor. White or red miso both work for this recipe, and you can buy *awase* miso, which is a mixture of the two.

Feel free to top your bowl of ramen with garnishes other than the ones called for here, such as bamboo shoots or fried garlic, but I highly recommend that you crown it a with gooey-yolked sous vide egg of your choice. A soft, custardy egg cooked at 63°C (page 25) or 75°C (page 30) will melt sensuously into the noodles; for a firmer soft-boiled version, use tea eggs cooked at 85°C (page 36), but skip the marinating step and cut the eggs in half. Any one of these eggs will lift this dish into the culinary stratosphere.

SERVES 4 as a main course | **SOUS VIDE COOKING TIME:** 12 hours (or up to 18 hours) | **ACTIVE PREP TIME:** 25 minutes, plus 10 minutes to rest

PORK BELLY

¼ cup mirin (Japanese sweet cooking wine)

2-inch piece fresh ginger, thinly sliced (about ¼ cup)

2 cloves garlic, thinly sliced

2 green onions, white parts only (reserve the green parts for garnish), cut into 1-inch lengths

¼ cup soy sauce

1 pound pork belly, in a single piece, skin removed

BROTH

4 cups homemade pork stock (page 267; ideally made with neck bones) or store-bought low-sodium chicken broth

¼ cup white or red miso, or a mixture, plus more to taste if needed

½ teaspoon freshly ground white pepper

½ teaspoon toasted sesame oil

4 servings ramen noodles (8 ounces dried or 12 ounces fresh)

1 cup bean sprouts

2 sheets toasted nori, each torn into 4 pieces (8 pieces total)

4 large eggs, cooked sous vide according to your preference (see headnote)

2 tablespoons toasted sesame seeds, for garnish

2 green onions, green part only, thinly sliced, for garnish

1 tablespoon Japanese togarashi or other red pepper flakes, for garnish

DO-AHEAD STRATEGY

The cooked pork can be chilled in the bag in an ice water bath (see page 14) for 20 minutes and then refrigerated for up to 1 week. Reheat in a 60°C (140°F) water bath for 30 minutes before proceeding to make the broth and assembling the bowls of ramen.

CONTINUED >

Preheat your sous vide water bath to 77°C (170.6°F).

To prepare the pork belly, combine the mirin, ginger, garlic, and green onions (white parts only) in a small saucepan over medium-high heat and bring to a boil. Remove from the heat, and add the soy sauce. Place the pork belly in a gallon-size freezer-safe ziplock bag, pour in the mirin mixture, and then seal using the water displacement method (see page 12).

When the water reaches the target temperature, lower the bagged pork belly into the water bath (making sure the bag is fully submerged) and cook for 12 hours. I recommend checking the water bath every few hours to see that the bag is still fully submerged. I also suggest covering the bath with plastic wrap or aluminum foil to minimize evaporation (see page 8 for explanation).

Remove the bag from the water and let the pork belly rest for about 10 minutes. Transfer the pork to a cutting board and set aside. Pour the accumulated cooking juices through a fine-mesh sieve into a liquid measuring cup or bowl and discard the ginger, garlic, and green onions. If desired, using a ladle or large spoon, skim the fat from the surface.

To make the broth for the ramen, pour the cooking juices into a large saucepan, add the stock, miso, white pepper,

and sesame oil, and bring to a rolling boil over medium-high heat. Turn down the heat to medium and continue to cook at a lively simmer (you should see bubbles), whisking until the broth is opaque and completely smooth (no lumps of miso) and slightly reduced, 8 to 10 minutes. Taste the broth. It should be very robust and salty; whisk in more miso if you think the broth needs more oomph. Cover the pan and lower the heat to keep the broth warm until you're ready to serve.

Cut the pork belly against the grain into ¼-inch-thick pieces. At this point, the belly is ready to top your bowl of ramen. However, if you want the pork belly to have a slight textural contrast, arrange it in a single layer on a sheet pan and broil until the pieces take on color and the edges are crisp, 1 to 2 minutes.

When you're ready to serve, cook the ramen noodles in boiling water according to the package instructions, drain, and then divide evenly among four warmed deep soup bowls. If the broth has cooled off, bring it to a simmer again and then ladle it into the bowls. Divide the sliced pork belly, bean sprouts, and nori between the bowls. Top each bowl with an egg and then sprinkle with the sesame seeds, reserved green onions, and *togarashi*.

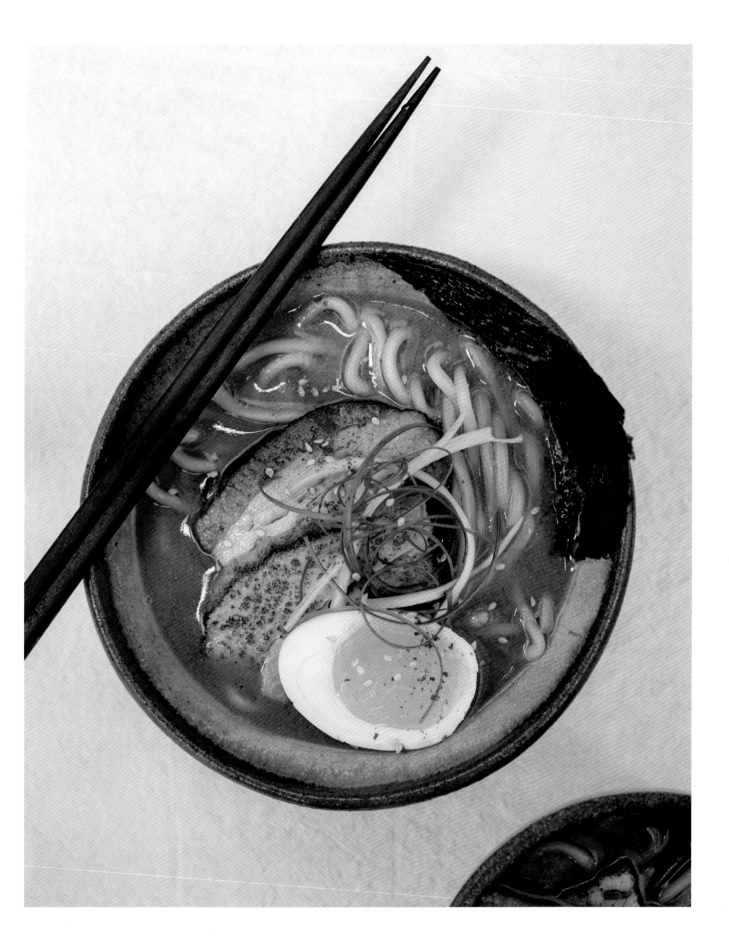

PORK RIB ADOBO

The food of the Philippines is a hybrid born of cross-pollination between foreign Spanish influence and the islands' endemic cuisine. One of its culinary marvels is adobo, a dish whose outward simplicity belies a complex balance of sour, salty, savory, and sweet. This version, which is a distillation of different regional styles, comes from my friend Anthony, sous vide enthusiast and Filipino cook extraordinaire. The best part of this recipe is that while the pork cooks, the juice it releases combines with the marinade to form a marvelously flavorful sauce, no additional steps required. It's almost mandatory to serve this dish with rice; the sauce is crazy good, and you'll want something to soak it up.

SERVES 4 as a main course | **SOUS VIDE COOKING TIME:** 12 hours (or up to 18 hours) | **ACTIVE PREP TIME:** 20 minutes

MARINADE

½ cup coconut, cane, or cider vinegar

¼ cup fish sauce

¼ cup soy sauce

3 cloves garlic, minced

1 tablespoon dark brown sugar

1½ teaspoons freshly ground black pepper

2 bay leaves

1 red Thai or other fresh red chile (such as Fresno or finger), thinly sliced

3 pounds St. Louis–style pork ribs or other meaty rib cut, cut into 3-rib portions if desired

DO-AHEAD STRATEGY

Adobo originated as a form of meat preservation, so it can easily be stored for a later date. The cooked pork ribs can be chilled in the bag in an ice water bath (see page 14) for 20 minutes and then refrigerated for up to 1 week. Reheat in a 60°C (140°F) water bath for 30 minutes.

Preheat your sous vide water bath to 70°C (158°F).

To make the marinade, in a small bowl or liquid measuring cup, combine all of the ingredients and mix well.

Place the pork ribs in a single layer in a gallon-size freezer-safe ziplock bag, pour in the marinade, and seal using the displacement method (see page 12).

When the water reaches the target temperature, lower the bagged ribs into the water bath (making sure the bag is fully submerged) and cook for 12 hours. I recommend checking the water bath every few hours to see that the bag is still fully submerged. I also suggest covering the bath with plastic wrap or aluminum foil to minimize evaporation (see page 8 for explanation).

Remove the bag from the bath and transfer the pork, along with its precious liquid, to a serving platter. Serve with rice on the side and encourage your guests to spoon the glorious adobo sauce on top of their portion.

CAROLINA PULLED-PORK SANDWICHES

Pulled pork is a southern classic that demands vigilance from a pit master, but with sous vide you can take it easy. Cooked in the bag at a low, even temperature, your pork will be moist and tender even if you don't have access to the highest-quality heritage pork used by acclaimed BBQ spots. Not to mention, it would be impossible to barbecue such a small piece of pork shoulder without ending up with pork jerky. Sous vide makes pulled pork practical to prepare in small quantities. Call it the democratization of pulled pork!

This recipe calls for a vinegar-and-chile-based North Carolina–style sauce, with just a small amount of ketchup, which is zingier than the thicker, sweeter barbecue sauce found elsewhere. A garnish of celery leaves, my own quirky addition, adds a nice herbaceous note.

SERVES 4 as a main course | **SOUS VIDE COOKING TIME:** 12 hours (or up to 18 hours) | **ACTIVE PREP TIME:** 25 minutes, plus 5 minutes to rest

SPICE RUB

1 teaspoon kosher salt

1 teaspoon freshly ground black pepper

1 teaspoon smoked paprika

½ teaspoon cayenne pepper

½ teaspoon ground celery seed

1 tablespoon light brown sugar

2 cloves garlic, crushed to a paste with the edge of a knife, or ¼ teaspoon granulated garlic

2 pounds skinless, boneless pork shoulder, in a single piece

1 tablespoon canola or other mild vegetable oil

VINEGAR SAUCE

½ cup cider vinegar

¼ cup ketchup

2 tablespoons apple cider or juice or water

2 tablespoons vinegar-based hot sauce

2 tablespoons light brown sugar

1 teaspoon red pepper flakes

½ teaspoon kosher salt

½ teaspoon freshly ground black pepper

2 cups shredded red or green cabbage, or a mixture

2 tablespoons mayonnaise, homemade (page 262) or store-bought (optional)

4 Kaiser or other soft rolls, split in half

¼ cup loosely packed celery leaves (optional)

DO-AHEAD STRATEGY

The cooked pork can be chilled in the bag in an ice water bath (see page 14) for 30 minutes and then refrigerated for up to 1 week. It can also be prepared though the shredding and seasoning steps and then resealed in a bag. Either way, reheat in a 60°C (140°F) water bath for 30 minutes. The vinegar sauce can be prepared up to 2 weeks in advance and refrigerated, and the slaw can be made up to 1 day ahead and refrigerated.

CONTINUED >

Preheat your sous vide water bath to 77°C (170°F).

While the water is heating, make the spice rub. In a small bowl, mix together the salt, black pepper, paprika, cayenne pepper, celery seed, brown sugar, and garlic. Rub the mixture onto the pork, covering it evenly, then coat the pork evenly with the oil.

Preheat a large cast-iron or nonstick skillet over medium-high heat. Add the pork and sear, turning as needed, until browned on all sides, about 1 minute per side for a total of 4 to 5 minutes.

Transfer the pork to a gallon-size freezer-safe ziplock bag and seal using the water displacement method (see page 12).

When the water reaches the target temperature, lower the bagged pork into the water bath (making sure the bag is fully submerged) and cook for 12 hours. I recommend checking the water bath every few hours to see that the bag is still fully submerged. I also suggest covering the bath with plastic wrap or aluminum foil to minimize evaporation (see page 8 for explanation).

While the pork is cooking, make the vinegar sauce. In a small bowl or a liquid measuring cup, combine all of the ingredients and whisk to dissolve the sugar and salt. Taste and adjust the seasoning with salt if needed.

Up to 2 hours before the pork is ready, make a quick slaw for garnishing the sandwiches. Place the cabbage in a bowl, drizzle with 2 to 3 tablespoons of the vinegar sauce, add the mayonnaise (if using), and toss to coat evenly. Set aside.

When the pork is ready, remove the bag from the water bath and let it rest for 5 minutes. Transfer the pork to a large bowl and pour the cooking liquid into a large liquid measuring cup. If desired, using a ladle or large spoon, skim off the fat from the surface.

Cut the pork against the grain into 2-inch-thick slices, then shred by pulling the slices apart with two forks. Add ¼ cup of the vinegar sauce and ½ cup of the reserved cooking liquid to the shredded meat to moisten it, then taste and adjust with more vinegar sauce if needed.

To assemble the sandwiches, place the bottom halves of the rolls, cut side up, on a work surface and divide the pulled pork evenly among them. Top with the cabbage slaw and a sprinkle of celery leaves, if using. Close with the top halves of the rolls and serve immediately.

PRO TIP

For this recipe, the meat is seared to build flavor before its sous vide bath rather than after, so when it comes out of the bath, it's ready to pull and go, a great technique for other long-cooked meats that end up fall-apart tender.

PUERTO RICAN PERNIL

Pernil, or slow-roasted pork shoulder, is the quintessential dish for midday holiday gatherings in Puerto Rico—think of it as your next-level Christmas ham. For a full Puerto Rican feast, serve it with rice, beans, and fried plantains. Although it's traditionally cooked for many hours over embers in a covered pit, my version allows those of us who don't have a roasting pit to create results that are hard to argue with—extremely tender, juicy meat on the verge of falling apart.

The only thing missing here is the *cuerito* (aka chicharrón), since cooking the shoulder sous vide won't allow you to get the crisp skin that slow roasting will. I doubt you'll hear many complaints, however, as the dish still has a mind-alteringly delicious layer of crispy fat on top. To achieve that ideal crust, the shoulder must have a substantial fat cap. The tangy sofrito seasoning is the big flavor punch here, but you're free to substitute ½ cup of a store-bought version, which is often available at Latin American stores (or see Resources, page 273).

SERVES 8 to 12 as a main course | **SOUS VIDE COOKING TIME:** 36 hours (or up to 48 hours) | **ACTIVE PREP TIME:** 55 minutes, plus 20 minutes to rest

5 to 6 pounds skinless, boneless pork shoulder, in a single piece, ideally with ½- to 1-inch-thick fat cap

1 tablespoon kosher salt

1 tablespoon brown sugar

SOFRITO

2 tablespoons extra-virgin olive oil

6 cloves garlic, minced

2 shallots, minced

Pinch of kosher salt

3 tablespoons chopped fresh cilantro

1 tablespoon chopped fresh oregano, or 1 teaspoon dried oregano

1 teaspoon ground cumin

1 teaspoon freshly ground black pepper

1 tablespoon red wine vinegar

½ cup water

2 tablespoons chopped fresh cilantro, for garnish

8 to 12 lime wedges, for serving

DO-AHEAD STRATEGY

The cooked pork can be chilled in the bag in an ice water bath (see page 14) for 40 minutes and then refrigerated for up to 1 week. To finish, reheat the shoulder in a 60°C (140°F) water bath for 1 hour and then proceed to roast in the oven. Alternatively, roast the pork straight out of the refrigerator starting at 400°F (lower the temperature to 375°F if the roast begins to brown too rapidly) for 1½ to 2 hours. The sofrito can be made in advance and refrigerated for up to 1 week.

CONTINUED >

This dish requires 36 hours to cook, so you will need to plan ahead. Two days prior to serving, put the bagged pork shoulder in the water bath before bed and then take it out of the water bath the morning of the event to finish.

Preheat your sous vide water bath to 60°C (140°F).

Season the pork with the salt and brown sugar, rubbing it into the meat and coating the meat evenly. Place the shoulder in a gallon-size freezer-safe ziplock bag and seal using the water displacement method (see page 12).

When the water reaches the target temperature, lower the bagged pork into the water bath (making sure the bag is fully submerged) and cook for 36 hours. I recommend checking the water bath every few hours to see that the bag is still fully submerged. I also suggest covering the bath with plastic wrap or aluminum foil to minimize evaporation (see page 8 for explanation).

When the pork is ready, remove the bag from the water and let it rest for 10 minutes.

While the pork is resting, make the sofrito. Heat the oil in a small saucepan over medium heat. Add the garlic, shallots, and salt and cook, stirring constantly, until they have softened and turned translucent but have not browned, 3 to 5 minutes. Remove from the heat and stir in the cilantro, oregano, cumin, pepper, and vinegar. Set aside.

Preheat the oven to 425°F.

Transfer the shoulder, fat side up, to a roasting pan. Pour the cooking liquid into a liquid measuring cup or a bowl

and set aside to use in a later step (if desired, using a ladle or large spoon, skim the fat from the surface). Using a sharp knife, score the fat in a crosshatch pattern: make parallel incisions ½ inch apart in one direction, then rotate the pork 90 degrees and repeat the parallel incisions. Be careful not to cut all of the way through the fat into the meat.

Pour or spoon the sofrito mixture on top of the meat, then, using your hands, rub it all over the surface and into the crevices, especially into the scored fat cap. Pour the water and the reserved cooking liquid into the bottom of the roasting pan.

Roast the pork until it turns an even golden brown and the fat on top has crisped (add more water to the pan if needed to prevent scorching), 30 to 40 minutes. Check after the first 10 minutes; if the garlic in the sofrito is browning too rapidly, lower the heat to 400°F.

Remove the pan from the oven, transfer the pork to a cutting board, and let the pork rest for at least 10 minutes before slicing. Using a wooden spoon or spatula, scrape up any browned bits stuck to the roasting pan (adding a little more water if needed to loosen) and then pour the accumulated roasting juices into a liquid measuring cup. Using a ladle or large spoon, skim off the fat from the surface and then strain the juices through a fine-mesh sieve, if desired.

Cut the pork against the grain into slices ¼ to ½ inch thick. Arrange the slices on a serving platter and spoon the roasting juices over the top. Sprinkle with the cilantro and serve with the lime wedges.

PORK CHOPS WITH SUMMER SUCCOTASH

For anyone who has eaten only dry pork chops, sous vide pork chops will be a revelation: they're juicy, tender, and packed with flavor. I prefer the taste and marbling of pork from heritage breeds (like Berkshire) over the typical mass-produced pork, which has been bred to be as lean as possible, but sous vide will produce succulent results in either case. The fat cap is an important element of this recipe, since it renders and is used to cook the vegetables, so be sure to look for a chop with a good amount of fat left on.

This recipe is a good example of how cooking sous vide can be time efficient: the vegetables can be cut while the pork is cooking, so the dish comes together quickly. It's also a great way to showcase summer produce, but pork chops are delicious year-round, so in winter or fall, swap out the corn, beans, and peppers for in-season vegetables such as brussels sprouts and sweet potatoes. Just follow the same procedure for charring them one by one with the rendered pork fat.

SERVES 4 to 6 as a main course | **SOUS VIDE COOKING TIME:** 1 hour (or up to 5 hours) | **ACTIVE PREP TIME:** 40 minutes

4 (1-inch-thick) bone-in loin pork chops (about 3 pounds), with ½-inch-thick fat cap

1 teaspoon ground cumin

¾ teaspoon smoked paprika or regular paprika

1 teaspoon kosher salt

½ teaspoon freshly ground black pepper

1 tablespoon plus 1 teaspoon canola or other mild vegetable oil

SUMMER SUCCOTASH

Kernels from 1 large ear of corn (about 1 cup)

Kosher salt

1 cup cut-up summer beans (such as Romano or wax), in ½-inch pieces

1 cup whole Padrón or shishito peppers, or 1 cup seeded and diced poblano or cubanelle chiles, in ½-inch pieces

1 red bell pepper, seeded and cut into ¼-inch dice

1 small red onion, cut into ¼-inch dice

2 cloves garlic, minced

Juice of ½ lime, (about 1 tablespoon)

2 tablespoons fresh basil, cilantro, or flat-leaf parsley, or a mixture, cut into fine chiffonade

Freshly ground black pepper

DO-AHEAD STRATEGY

The cooked chops can be chilled in the bag in an ice water bath (see page 14) for 15 minutes and then refrigerated for up to 4 days. Reheat in a 58°C (136.4°F) water bath for 30 minutes and then proceed to brown the chops and make the succotash.

CONTINUED >

Preheat your sous vide water bath to 58°C (136.4°F).

Place the pork chops in a gallon-size freezer-safe ziplock bag in a single layer with no overlap (you may need two bags, depending on the size of the chops), then seal using the water displacement method (see page 12).

When the water reaches the target temperature, lower the bagged pork chops into your sous vide bath (making sure the bag is fully submerged) and cook for 1 hour.

When the chops are ready, remove the bag from the water. Line a platter or tray with paper towels and transfer the chops to the platter, discarding the liquid in the bag. Pat the chops thoroughly dry with more paper towels and then season them on both sides with the cumin, paprika, salt, and black pepper. Rub the chops on both sides with 1 teaspoon of the oil, which will help the meat brown evenly in the pan.

Preheat the oven to 175°F. Heat the remaining 1 tablespoon oil in a large cast-iron skillet over medium-high heat until it shimmers. Grab the pork chops with tongs and place them, fat side down, in the pan, holding them together on their side with the tongs to allow the fat cap to render and crisp, 2 to 3 minutes. Once the fat has finished rendering, lay the chops down in the pan and brown (the spices on the meat will cause it to brown quickly), turning once, about 1 minute per side. (Depending on the size of your pan, you may need to cook the chops in two batches.)

Transfer the chops to a heatproof plate or sheet pan and keep warm in the oven until you're ready to serve. The skillet will be coated with rendered pork fat. Pour all but

1 teaspoon of the fat into a small heatproof bowl and set aside to use for cooking the rest of the vegetables. If the chops don't render enough fat to yield 1 teaspoon to cook each vegetable (at least 2 tablespoons total), add olive oil to make up the difference.

Add the corn and a pinch of kosher salt to the skillet and cook over medium-high heat, stirring occasionally, until the kernels blister and char, about 2 minutes. Transfer the corn to a bowl. Repeat this process to cook the remaining succotash vegetables (beans, Padrón peppers, bell pepper, and onion) one at a time, adding 1 teaspoon of the reserved rendered fat (or olive oil) and a pinch of salt to the pan before each addition, and transferring each cooked vegetable to the bowl holding the corn.

When all of the vegetables have been cooked, add 1 teaspoon of the rendered fat to the pan, add the garlic, and sauté over medium-high heat just until aromatic, about 30 seconds. Stir in the reserved cooked succotash vegetables and heat just until warmed through, about 1 minute. Remove the pan from the heat and return the vegetables to the bowl. Stir in the lime juice and basil and season with salt and pepper.

To serve, divide the succotash among individual plates and top with a pork chop. If you are serving more than four people, transfer the pork chops to a cutting board, cut the meat off the bone, slice the meat on a slight diagonal against the grain, and divide the slices among the plates, arranging them on the succotash.

COFFEE-SPICED PORK TENDERLOIN WITH WILD RICE AND RED CABBAGE SLAW

Pork tenderloin is both the leanest and the most delicate cut of meat found on our noble friend the swine. Although this makes it easily overcooked using conventional means, it's ideal for sous vide, where gentle heat gives us juicy results without fail. Here, I heighten the tenderloin's mild flavor with a coffee-based spice blend and pair it with a sweet and savory wild rice and red cabbage slaw, for a satisfying, flavorful meal. I won't hold the fact that it's protein rich and low in fat against it.

The tenderloin in this dish is cooked medium rare, that is, with a pink interior, which I think is the best way eat this cut of pork. It's perfectly safe to eat this way, but if the pink color is a no-go for you, just raise the water bath temperature to 60°C (140°F) and you'll still end up with very moist results.

SERVES 4 as a main course | **SOUS VIDE COOKING TIME:** 1 hour (or up to 5 hours) | **ACTIVE PREP TIME:** 25 minutes, plus 5 minutes to rest

PORK

1 teaspoon kosher salt

½ teaspoon freshly ground black pepper

1 teaspoon light brown sugar

1 teaspoon ground coffee, preferably freshly ground

½ teaspoon ground cumin

½ teaspoon ground cinnamon

½ teaspoon paprika

¼ teaspoon cayenne pepper

1 (1-pound) pork tenderloin, no more than 2 inches in diameter

1 tablespoon canola or other mild vegetable oil

SLAW

½ cup uncooked wild rice

2 tablespoons fresh lemon juice

½ teaspoon coarsely ground caraway or dill seed (optional)

1 shallot, thinly sliced

¼ cup chopped dried cherries or cranberries

2 cups shredded red cabbage (on a box grater or with a sharp knife; about ½ small head)

¼ cup coarsely chopped fresh flat-leaf parsley or dill, or a mixture

3 tablespoons extra-virgin olive oil

Salt and freshly ground black pepper

Flaky sea salt (such as Maldon or fleur de sel) and freshly ground black pepper

DO-AHEAD STRATEGY

If you intend to chill and reheat the tenderloin, I recommend salting the meat after it comes out of the bag (see page 117 for an explanation). The cooked tenderloin can be chilled in the bag in an ice water bath (see page 14) for 10 minutes and then refrigerated for up to 1 week. Reheat in a 55°C (131°F) water bath for about 20 minutes before proceeding with the recipe. The slaw can be made in advance and refrigerated for up to 2 days.

CONTINUED >

Preheat your sous vide water bath to 57°C (134.6°F).

To prepare the pork, in a small bowl, stir together the kosher salt, black pepper, brown sugar, coffee, cumin, cinnamon, paprika, and cayenne, mixing well. Rub the mixture onto the pork, covering it evenly, and then coat the pork evenly with the canola oil.

Place the pork in a gallon-size freezer-safe ziplock bag and seal using the water displacement method (see page 12).

When the water reaches the target temperature, lower the bagged pork into the water bath (making sure the bag is fully submerged) and cook for 1 hour.

While the pork is cooking, cook the wild rice according to the package instructions and set aside to cool until you're ready to make the slaw.

When the pork is ready, remove the bag from the water bath and transfer it to a platter or tray, discarding any residual cooking liquid. Pat the tenderloin dry with paper towels and set aside.

To make the slaw, in a large bowl, combine the lemon juice, caraway, shallot, cherries, and cabbage, stir and toss to mix well, and let sit for 5 minutes. Stir in the cooked wild rice,

parsley, and olive oil and season with salt and black pepper. Set aside.

Heat a cast-iron skillet over medium-high heat. Add the pork loin and sear on the underside until deeply browned, about 1 minute. Roll the loin to the next side and sear for another minute. Continue to sear and roll the loin until the whole surface is browned, 4 to 5 minutes total.

Transfer the pork loin to a cutting board and let rest for 2 to 3 minutes before carving. Cut against the grain into ¼-inch-thick slices.

To serve, spoon the slaw onto a platter and top with pork slices. Sprinkle with the sea salt and black pepper.

PRO TIP

This recipe calls for pork tenderloin, a small muscle that runs alongside the much larger loin muscle. Some grocery stores will inaccurately label boneless pork loin as tenderloin, but the two are a long way apart. Even the largest tenderloins will weigh under 1½ pounds and have a diameter of no more than 2 inches, so don't be fooled by any wily grocery store shenanigans.

THE PERFECT SOUS VIDE STEAK

I consider steak the gold standard of sous vide cooking because it ensures reliable, exact cooking for a cut of meat where doneness counts for everything. This amount of control not only means that I can make *my* perfect steak every time, but that you can customize *your* perfect steak every time, too. I consider 55°C (131°F) the ideal temperature for medium rare when cooking rib eye and other tender steak cuts (for example, strip, top sirloin, tenderloin, and porterhouse). That said, experiment with temperature and let your own taste be your guide. You'll find that even a few degrees up or down can make a dramatic difference. If you or your guests prefer your meat more done, try cooking it at 60°F (140°F) for medium and 65°C (149°F) for medium well. The results will still be far juicier than conventionally cooked steaks.

SERVES 4 as a main course | **SOUS VIDE COOKING TIME:** 1 hour (or up to 5 hours) | **ACTIVE PREP TIME:** 10 minutes, plus 12 minutes to rest

2 (1-inch-thick) boneless rib-eye steaks (about 1 pound each), preferably with fat cap intact

Salt and freshly ground black pepper

1 tablespoon canola or other mild vegetable oil

2 tablespoons unsalted butter

4 to 6 thyme sprigs

1 clove garlic, lightly crushed

DO-AHEAD STRATEGY

If you intend to chill and reheat the steak, I recommend salting the meat after it comes out of the bag (see page 117 for an explanation). The cooked steak can be chilled in the bag in an ice water bath (see page 14) for 20 minutes and then refrigerated for up to 1 week. Reheat in a 55°C (131°F) water bath for 20 minutes and then proceed to the searing step. You can also reheat the fridge-temperature steak directly in the sauté pan or skillet by adding an additional 5 minutes while basting and turning the meat.

CONTINUED >

Preheat your sous vide water bath to 55°C (131°F).

Season the steaks with salt and pepper and then place in a gallon-size freezer-safe ziplock bag and seal using the water displacement method (see page 12).

When the water reaches the target temperature, lower the bagged steaks into the water bath (making sure the bag is fully submerged) and cook for 1 hour.

When the steaks are ready, remove the bag from the water bath and let them rest for 10 minutes. Transfer the steaks from the bag to a platter or tray and pat the meat thoroughly dry with paper towels.

Heat a large, heavy sauté pan or cast-iron skillet over medium-high heat. Once the pan is hot, add the oil and swirl to coat the bottom. Let the oil heat until it shimmers and sends off wisps of smoke, 30 to 60 seconds. Place the meat in the pan and sear until the underside is browned, 30 to 60 seconds. Using tongs, flip the steaks over and brown the second side, 30 to 60 seconds longer. If the steaks have their fat caps, use tongs to hold both steaks upright on their sides, fat pressed against the pan, and render until the fat is crisp and browned, 1 to 2 minutes.

When the steaks are browned on both sides, or after the fat caps are crisped, add the butter, thyme, and garlic (in that order) off to the side of the pan. The butter will sizzle and brown immediately and the thyme will crackle and pop. Once the butter has turned completely brown and has stopped sizzling (meaning all of the water has cooked out), baste the meat: tilt the pan to accumulate the fat on one side, then, using a metal spoon, scoop up the brown butter and distribute it evenly over the meat. As you baste, be sure to flip the meat to brown both sides again as above until the entire surface is a deep, almost mahogany brown, about 30 seconds per side. Depending on the strength of the burner, you may need to flip the meat more than once; just make sure it doesn't rest on any one side longer than 1 minute or it will begin to overcook.

Transfer the meat to a platter or tray and wait for at least 2 minutes before slicing to allow the juices to redistribute after the high-heat searing. Enjoy your steak perfection.

PRO TIP

The technique of basting the steak with butter while in the pan is an excellent method any time you want to achieve a beautifully uniform sear on the stove top. I use it again in Beef Tenderloin with Red Wine Sauce (page 155).

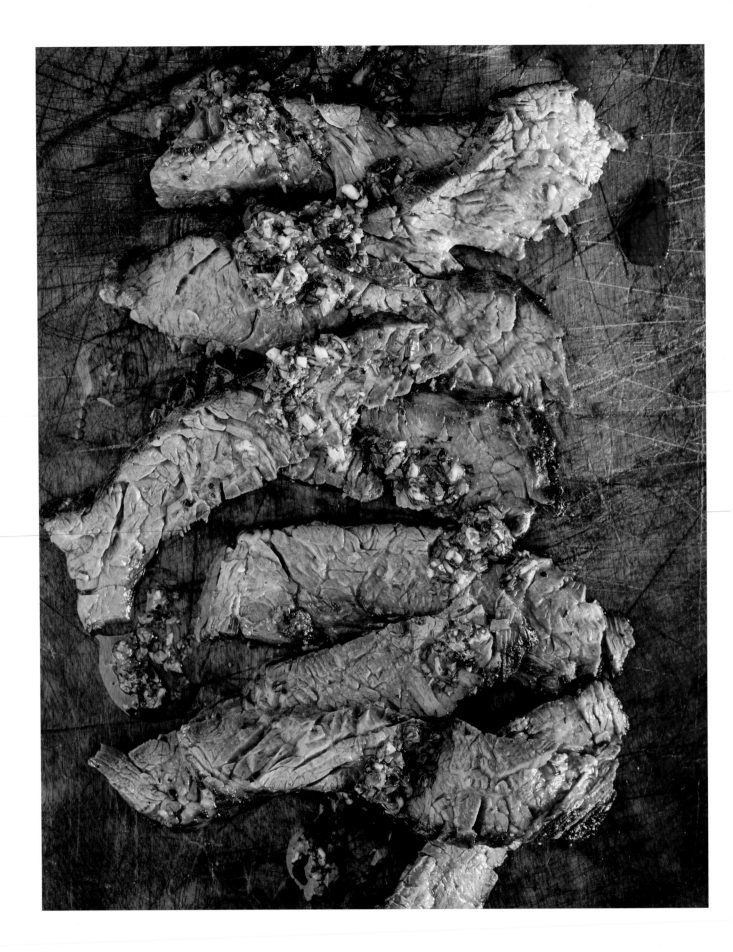

CARNE ASADA WITH CHIMICHURRI SAUCE

Chimichurri, a vibrant, tangy, spicy green sauce made with fresh herbs, garlic, and chile, is the classic condiment for Argentinian mixed grill. Here it is paired with steak, but after you've tasted it, you may find yourself drizzling it on top of just about anything you grill, including poultry, fish, or vegetables.

Skirt steak is an affordable cut that's full of flavor, but it can easily get tough and dry if overcooked. Its thin, uneven shape makes achieving the desired doneness a tricky goal when cooking it over high heat. Cooking it sous vide for an hour at a precise low temperature will ensure rose-colored, medium rare flesh from edge to edge, even for thinner pieces. Finishing your steak with a quick sear on a grill pan is all that's needed to achieve a flavorful char.

SERVES 4 as a main course | **SOUS VIDE COOKING TIME:** 1 hour (or up to 5 hours) | **ACTIVE PREP TIME:** 25 minutes, plus 5 minutes to rest

2 pounds skirt steak, trimmed of excess fat and sinew and cut crosswise into 6-inch-wide pieces

½ teaspoon ground cumin

Salt and freshly ground black pepper

CHIMICHURRI SAUCE

3 cloves garlic, minced

1 shallot, minced

1 medium-hot fresh red chile (such as Fresno or finger) seeded and minced

¾ teaspoon kosher salt

¼ cup red wine vinegar

½ cup extra-virgin olive oil

1½ teaspoons chopped fresh oregano or marjoram, or ½ teaspoon dried oregano

¼ cup chopped fresh cilantro

¼ cup chopped fresh flat-leaf parsley

½ teaspoon ground cumin

½ teaspoon freshly ground black pepper

Pinch of cayenne pepper (optional)

DO-AHEAD STRATEGY

If you intend to cook and chill the steak for storage, I recommend salting the meat after it comes out of the bag (see page 117 for an explanation). The cooked steak can be chilled in the bag in an ice water bath (see page 14) for 15 minutes and then refrigerated for up to 1 week. Bring the steak to room temperature for 30 minutes before the final sear. The *chimichurri* sauce can be made up to 3 days in advance and refrigerated, though the color will dull over time.

CONTINUED >

Preheat your sous vide water bath to 55°C (131°F).

Season the steak pieces evenly with the cumin and then with the salt and pepper. Place the steak in a gallon-size freezer-safe ziplock bag, arranging the pieces in a single layer, and seal the bag using the water displacement method (see page 12).

When the water reaches the target temperature, lower the bagged steak into the water bath (making sure the bag is fully submerged) and cook for 1 hour.

While the steak is cooking, make the *chimichurri* sauce. In a bowl, combine the garlic, shallot, chile, salt, and vinegar and mix well, then let stand for 10 minutes. Stir in the oil, oregano, cilantro, parsley, cumin, black pepper, and cayenne pepper, if using. Taste and adjust the seasoning with salt if needed.

When the steak is ready, remove the bag from the water bath and transfer the steak to a plate. Discard any accumulated cooking liquid in the bag. Pat the steak thoroughly dry with paper towels. Drizzle with 2 tablespoons of the *chimichurri* sauce and, using your hands, rub the sauce into the meat, coating it evenly.

Preheat a stove-top grill pan over medium-high heat. Working in batches, add the steak pieces to the pan and sear, turning once, until nicely browned on both sides, about 1 minute per side. Transfer the finished pieces to a cutting board, tent loosely with aluminum foil, and let rest for 5 minutes.

Cut the steak pieces as thinly as possible on the diagonal against the grain. Arrange the slices on a platter and spoon ¼ cup of the *chimichurri* sauce on top. Pass the remaining sauce at the table.

PRO TIP

The flavor and texture of the chimichurri sauce is best if all of the ingredients are chopped by hand, but in a pinch, they can be thrown together in a food processor or blender and pulsed until coarsely chopped. If using this approach, first roughly chop the garlic, shallot, and chile in the blender, then add the vinegar and the olive oil along with the remaining herbs (double the volume of loosely packed whole leaves) and spices, giving the mixture a few quick pulses to finish blending.

EIGHT-HOUR SKIRT STEAK WITH BALSAMIC MUSHROOMS

Like the carne asada on page 149, this recipe calls for skirt steak cooked at 55°C. The difference lies in the cooking time. Whereas at one hour, the steak is medium rare but with a fairly conventional texture, here you take advantage of the alchemy that transpires during extended sous vide cooking. The skirt steak remains medium rare, but the collagen will have transformed into gelatin, tenderizing the meat. That makes this approach a great option for transforming other flavorful, tougher steak cuts, such as flank, hanger, *bavette*, or tri-tip. To make this recipe in one fell swoop, you'll need to cook the mushrooms at 80°C before lowering the water bath temperature to 55°C for the steak. (Be sure to refrigerate the mushrooms while the steak is cooking.) The fastest way to cool down the water bath is to add ice cubes or cold tap water.

SERVES 4 as a main course | **SOUS VIDE COOKING TIME:** 8 hours (or up to 12 hours) | **ACTIVE PREP TIME:** 15 minutes, plus 5 minutes to rest

2 pounds skirt steak, trimmed of excess fat and sinew and cut lengthwise into 6-inch-wide pieces

1 teaspoon kosher salt

½ teaspoon freshly ground black pepper

1 tablespoon soy sauce

3 tablespoons unsalted butter

2 cloves garlic, minced

1 shallot, minced

Versatile Mushrooms (page 196), drained and liquid reserved separately

2 tablespoons balsamic vinegar

1 teaspoon finely chopped fresh rosemary, for garnish

DO-AHEAD STRATEGY

If you intend to cook and chill the steak for storage, I recommend salting the meat after it comes out of the bag (see page 117 for an explanation). The cooked steak can be chilled in the bag in an ice water bath (see page 14) for 15 minutes and then refrigerated for up to 1 week. Bring the steak to room temperature for 30 minutes before the final sear, adding 2 to 3 minutes to the cooking time to reheat fully. There's no need to reheat the mushrooms. Simply drain them before searing.

CONTINUED >

Preheat your sous vide water bath to 55°C (131°F).

Season the steak pieces evenly with the salt and pepper. Place the steak and soy sauce in a gallon-size freezer-safe ziplock bag, arrange the pieces in a single layer (a little a bit of overlap is fine), and seal using the water displacement method (see page 12).

When the water reaches the target temperature, lower the bagged steak into the water bath (making sure the bag is fully submerged) and cook for 8 hours. I recommend checking the water bath every few hours to see that the bag is still fully submerged. I also suggest covering the bath with plastic wrap or aluminum foil to minimize evaporation (see page 8 for explanation).

Remove the bag from the water bath and let the steak rest for 5 minutes. Transfer the steak pieces to a plate and pat thoroughly dry with paper towels. Reserve the cooking liquid to use later.

Heat the butter in a large sauté pan or skillet over medium-high heat, swirling it as it melts, until it has foamed and the foam has subsided, and then continue cooking until it turns light brown and smells nutty, about 2 minutes. Place the steaks in the brown butter and sear, turning once, until golden brown on both sides, about 1 minute per side. (Depending on the size of your pan, you may need to cook the steak pieces in two batches.) Transfer to a platter or tray, leaving the butter behind in the pan. Keep the steak warm by tenting it with aluminum foil or by placing it into a preheated 200°F oven.

Lower the heat to medium and add the garlic and shallot to the brown butter. Cook, stirring constantly, until they begin to brown, 1 to 2 minutes. Stir in the drained mushrooms and cook for 1 minute more. Add the reserved mushroom liquid and steak cooking juices along with the vinegar to the pan. Bring the mixture to a simmer, and cook until reduced by half, 3 to 5 minutes. Remove from the heat.

To serve, cut the steak on the diagonal against the grain into slices ¼ to ½ inch thick and arrange the slices on a serving platter. Spoon the mushroom mixture on top and sprinkle with the rosemary.

BEEF TENDERLOIN WITH RED WINE SAUCE

This dish hits the sweet spot between easy to prepare and impressive, making it a natural choice for entertaining. When it comes to beef, tenderloin is generally considered the most high-end cut of all. That's especially true in French haute cuisine, where tenderloin's superlatively lean, fine-textured flesh and delicate flavor make it the ideal canvas for any number of luxurious sauces. My take on a classic red wine sauce keeps things simple without stinting on flavor. All you'll need to do to truly make this an entrée par excellence is serve the beef over Perfect Mashed Potatoes (page 193), to soak up every last drop of sauce. I recommend making the potatoes in advance and keeping them warm (or reheating them) in the water bath while the tenderloin is cooking.

SERVES 4 as a main course | **SOUS VIDE COOKING TIME:** 2 hours (or up to 5 hours) | **ACTIVE PREP TIME:** 30 minutes, plus 12 minutes to rest

1 (2-pound) piece beef tenderloin, ideally cut from the center of the fillet

SAUCE

2 tablespoons unsalted butter

1 shallot, minced

1 clove garlic, minced

Pinch of kosher salt

1 cup red wine

¼ cup port

2 cups homemade beef stock (page 267) or store-bought low-sodium beef broth

¼ cup heavy cream

1 to 2 teaspoons coarsely ground black pepper

1 teaspoon chopped fresh thyme

Salt

1 tablespoon canola or other mild vegetable oil

1 tablespoon unsalted butter

4 to 6 thyme sprigs

1 clove garlic, smashed

DO-AHEAD STRATEGY

The cooked tenderloin can be chilled in the bag in an ice water bath (see page 14) for 30 minutes and then refrigerated for up to 1 week. Reheat in a 54°C (129.2°F) water bath for 30 minutes and then season and proceed to the final sear. The red wine sauce can be made up to 1 week in advance and refrigerated.

CONTINUED >

Preheat your sous vide water bath to 54°C (129.2°F).

Place the tenderloin in a gallon-size freezer-safe ziplock bag and seal using the water displacement method (see page 12).

When the water reaches the target temperature, lower the bagged tenderloin into the water bath (making sure the bag is fully submerged) and cook for 2 hours.

About 10 minutes before the beef is ready, begin to make the sauce, which can be finished while the meat is resting. Melt 1 tablespoon of the butter in a saucepan over medium heat. Stir in the shallot, garlic, and salt and sauté, stirring constantly, until translucent and slightly softened, 2 to 3 minutes. Raise the heat to high and add the red wine, port, and stock. Bring to a simmer and cook until the liquid is reduced by about two-thirds, about 15 minutes. Lower the heat to medium, add the cream, and cook, stirring often, until the mixture is thick enough to coat the back of a spoon, 3 to 5 minutes. Turn the heat to its lowest setting and stir in the pepper to taste, thyme, and the remaining 1 tablespoon butter. Taste and adjust the seasoning with salt if needed (if you have used store-bought broth, chances are good that you won't need any). Keep the sauce warm, covered, over the lowest heat possible until the tenderloin is ready to serve.

When the tenderloin is ready, remove the bag from the water bath and let it rest for 10 minutes. Transfer the tenderloin to a platter or tray, pat the meat thoroughly dry with paper towels, and then season with salt. Add the liquid in the bag to the wine sauce.

Heat a large, heavy sauté pan or cast-iron skillet over medium-high heat. Once the pan is hot, add the oil and swirl to coat the bottom. Let the oil heat until it shimmers and sends off wisps of smoke, 30 to 60 seconds. Place the meat in the pan and sear until the first side is browned, 30 to 60 seconds. Turn the piece 90 degrees and brown, about 30 to 60 seconds more. Repeat this two more times until the meat is browned on all sides. (The idea here is to treat the meat as though it is a square that you are turning to brown on all four sides.)

When the meat is browned on the final side, add the butter, thyme sprigs, and garlic (in that order) off to the side of the pan. The butter will sizzle and brown immediately and the thyme will crackle and pop. Once the butter has turned completely brown and stopped sizzling (meaning all of the water has cooked out), baste the meat: tilt the pan to accumulate the fat on one side, then, using a metal spoon, scoop up the fat and distribute it evenly over the meat. As you baste, be sure to flip the tenderloin to brown all of the sides again as above until the entire surface is a deep, almost mahogany brown, about 30 seconds per side. Depending on the strength of the burner, you may need to flip the meat more than once; just make sure it doesn't rest on any one side too long or it will begin to overcook.

Transfer the meat to a platter or tray and wait for at least 2 minutes before slicing to allow the juices to redistribute after the high-heat searing. Slice the meat to the desired thickness (if you cut it about 1 inch thick, everyone can have two 4-ounce portions). Serve over mashed potatoes with the red wine sauce passed at the table.

TRI-TIP STEAK CHILI

Whether you live for football season or just love a good chili, this set-and-forget recipe will let you out of the kitchen and back into the living room to join the party. Cooking chili sous vide will take longer than it would on a burner, but you don't have to watch or stir it, and the results are superior.

Adding the spice blend in stages is a technique I stole from prizewinning cook-off chili recipes. It adds a roundness and depth of flavor that's missing if it's added all at once. If you don't want to make your own spice blend, store-bought chili powder mix is fine. Some commercial mixes contain salt, so check the label and season your chili accordingly. For committed carnivores, this is a dish that can definitely be eaten unadorned, but it's also nice over rice or cheesy grits.

SERVES 4 as a main course | **SOUS VIDE COOKING TIME:** 8 hours (or up to 12 hours) | **ACTIVE PREP TIME:** 30 minutes

SPICE BLEND

1 tablespoon ground cumin

1 tablespoon smoked paprika

1½ teaspoons freshly ground black pepper

½ teaspoon cayenne pepper

½ teaspoon dried oregano

½ teaspoon dry mustard

2 pounds tri-tip or boneless sirloin steak, cut into 1-inch cubes

2 teaspoons kosher salt, plus more as needed

2 tablespoons canola or other mild vegetable oil

1 tablespoon unsalted butter

1 red onion, cut into ¼-inch dice

2 jalapeño chiles, chopped and seeded if desired

3 cloves garlic, minced

1 cup pilsner or other pale lager

1½ cups canned crushed tomatoes (about one 14-ounce can)

2 tablespoons Worcestershire sauce

1 tablespoon molasses

GARNISHES

½ cup shredded Monterey Jack or Cheddar cheese (optional)

2 tablespoons coarsely chopped fresh cilantro (optional)

2 green onions, white and green parts, thinly sliced (optional)

¼ cup sour cream (optional)

DO-AHEAD STRATEGY

The cooked chili can be chilled in the bag in an ice water bath (see page 14) for 30 minutes and then refrigerated for up to 1 week. Reheat in a 55°C (131°F) water bath for 30 minutes before serving with the garnishes.

CONTINUED >

Preheat your sous vide water bath to 57°C (134.5°F).

To make the spice blend, in a small bowl, combine all of the ingredients and mix well. In a large bowl, season the steak with the 2 teaspoons salt and 1 tablespoon of the spice blend, stirring and tossing to coat the pieces evenly.

Heat the oil in a large cast-iron skillet or sauté pan over medium-high heat until it shimmers. Add the steak pieces in a single layer, spacing them at least ½ inch apart so they will brown properly. (Depending on the size of your pan, you may need to brown the steak pieces in two or three batches.) Sear until the first side is deep golden brown, 1 to 2 minutes. Using tongs, flip the pieces and brown on the second side, 1 to 2 minutes more (the spices will help the meat brown quickly). Transfer the seared pieces to a platter or tray, leaving the oil behind in the pan.

Reduce the heat to medium. Add the butter, onion, chiles, and garlic to the pan. Season with a bit more salt to help the mixture soften and cook, stirring frequently, until completely soft and golden brown, about 10 minutes. Stir in 1 more tablespoon of the spice blend and cook, stirring, until fragrant, about 30 seconds. Pour in the beer and scrape the bottom of the pan with a wooden spoon or spatula to dislodge any browned bits. Let the beer boil until reduced by half, 2 to 3 minutes. Stir in the tomatoes, Worcestershire sauce, molasses, and the remaining spice blend and remove from the heat. Taste and adjust the seasoning with salt if needed.

Using a slotted spoon, transfer the seared steak to a gallon-size freezer-safe ziplock bag and then ladle or pour in the sauce mixture. Seal using the water displacement method (see page 12).

When the water reaches the target temperature, lower the bagged steak into the water bath (making sure the bag is fully submerged) and cook for 8 hours. I recommend checking the water bath every few hours to see that the bag is still fully submerged. I also suggest covering the bath with plastic wrap or aluminum foil to minimize evaporation (see page 8 for explanation).

Remove the bag from the water bath and transfer the contents to a warmed serving bowl. Serve with the garnishes, if using, on the side. Game on!

HERB-CRUSTED RACK OF LAMB

Roasted rack of lamb makes an impressive centerpiece. Handsome, yes, but it can also be awfully high maintenance: the attached bones mean that heat penetrates the meat unevenly, and its small size makes it quick to overcook. That's a high-stakes gamble for such a pricey cut. Not one to be fleeced, I turn to a no-fail sous vide approach. With its crunchy herb crust, this little lamb recipe is not only dressed to impress at your next dinner party, it's also a snap to pull off. The meat will stay juicy and evenly pink throughout, even left unwatched for hours (in common with the other recipes in this chapter), making it an ideal no-fuss choice for entertaining. Serve it with a side of Zingy Crushed Potatoes (page 190) or a mix of roasted vegetables, and you'll have a meal to remember.

SERVES 6 to 8 as a main course | **SOUS VIDE COOKING TIME:** 2 hours (or up to 5 hours) | **ACTIVE PREP TIME:** 20 minutes, plus 10 minutes to rest

2 racks of lamb (each with 6 to 8 bones; 2½ to 3 pounds total), trimmed of sinew and excess fat and bones frenched (they're typically sold this way)

3 tablespoons extra-virgin olive oil

1 to 2 cloves garlic, minced

1 cup panko (Japanese-style bread crumbs)

1 tablespoon chopped fresh rosemary or thyme

¼ cup chopped fresh flat-leaf parsley, plus 1 tablespoon, for garnish

Salt and freshly ground black pepper

2 tablespoons Dijon mustard

Flaky sea salt (such as Maldon or fleur de sel)

DO-AHEAD STRATEGY

The cooked lamb can be chilled in the bags in an ice water bath (see page 14) for 30 minutes and then refrigerated for up to 1 week. Reheat in a 55°C (131°F) water bath for 30 minutes before proceeding. The bread-crumb mixture can be made up to 2 days in advance and refrigerated in an airtight container.

Preheat your sous vide water bath to 55°C (131°F).

Place each lamb rack in a gallon-size freezer-safe ziplock bag and seal using the water displacement method (see page 12).

When the water reaches the target temperature, lower the bagged lamb into the water bath (making sure the bag is fully submerged) and cook for 2 hours.

While the lamb is cooking, prepare the crust. Heat the oil and garlic together in a sauté pan over medium-low heat until the garlic sizzles but does not color, about 1 minute.

Add the bread crumbs and stir and toss them to coat them with the oil. Cook, stirring constantly, until the bread crumbs are just beginning to color, 2 to 3 minutes. Remove the pan from the heat and stir in the rosemary, the ¼ cup parsley, and a pinch of salt. Transfer to a platter or tray, spread in an even layer, and let cool to room temperature.

Preheat the oven to 450°F, or preheat the broiler.

Remove the bags from the water bath and let the lamb rest for 5 minutes. Transfer the lamb to a platter or tray and pat thoroughly dry with paper towels, then season with salt and pepper. Discard the liquid in the bags.

Using a brush or your fingers, spread the mustard over the meaty "top" side of the racks. Press the lamb racks, mustard side down, into the plate of bread crumbs, using enough pressure to ensure the crumbs adhere. Some crumbs will be left behind on the plate. Transfer the lamb racks, crumb side up, to a roasting pan or sheet pan. Sprinkle the crumbs left on the plate on top of the racks, then press firmly to form a thick, even crust (some crumbs will fall off, which is fine).

Transfer the lamb to the oven or under the broiler and cook until the crumbs are golden brown, 5 to 10 minutes (depending on your broiler's model, the time may vary even more widely). Keep an eye on the racks, as the crumbs will brown quickly.

Transfer the lamb racks to a cutting board or serving platter and let them rest for 5 minutes. Sprinkle the remaining 1 tablespoon parsley and the sea salt on top of the crust on each rack.

To serve, carve between the bones of each rack to separate the chops, then allot 2-3 ribs per person.

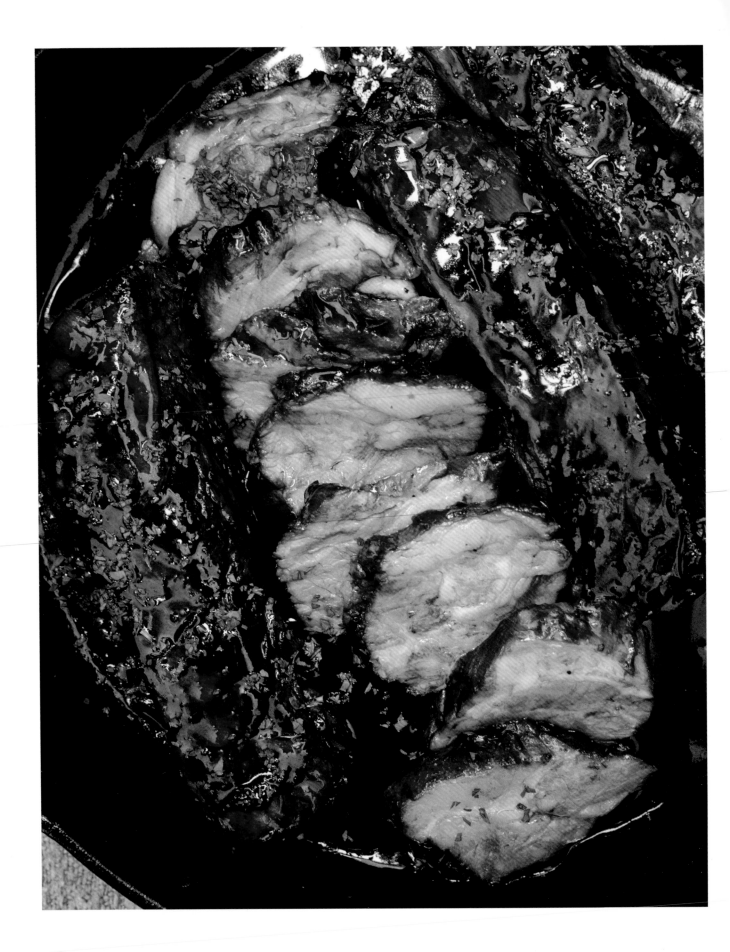

STOUT-GLAZED SHORT RIBS

Short ribs can justifiably be seen as the poster child for sous vide cooking. Cooking the meat slow at such a low temperature for such a long period of time slowly melts the collagen into gelatin, all the while maintaining a perfectly rosy medium rare. It's a shining example of what modern gastronomy can do: achieve something that's only remotely possible using current technology and transform a tough but flavorful cut into the most decadent, unctuous, succulent piece of meat imaginable.

These remarkable ribs call for an equally great sauce, so I turn to my Irish friends to seal the deal with a stout-based glaze. My beer of choice for this dish is a dry Irish stout like Guinness because it has a rich, dark, roasted malt flavor but is low in hops, alcohol, and sugar. As for the rest of the ingredients, I've taken a few cross-cultural liberties. Although the hoisin sauce might seem unnecessarily exotic (and the steak sauce outright blasphemy), it adds a nice depth of flavor and it helps the glaze achieve the desired consistency. The recipe will work without it, but it definitely adds something special. To stick with the Irish theme, I suggest serving the ribs with Perfect Mashed Potatoes (page 193).

SERVES 4 as a main course | **SOUS VIDE COOKING TIME:** 48 hours (or up to 72 hours) | **ACTIVE PREP TIME:** 20 minutes, plus 10 minutes to rest

2 pounds boneless beef short ribs, cut into 4 equal pieces and trimmed of sinew and excess fat

Salt and freshly ground black pepper

2 tablespoons unsalted butter

3 cloves garlic, lightly crushed

1 cup Guinness or other dry stout

1 bay leaf

1½ cups homemade beef stock (page 267) or store-bought low-sodium beef broth

2 tablespoons hoisin sauce or store-bought barbecue or steak sauce (optional)

1 tablespoon dark brown sugar

1 tablespoon chopped fresh flat-leaf parsley

DO-AHEAD STRATEGY

The cooked ribs can be chilled in the bag in an ice water bath (see page 14) for 30 minutes and then refrigerated for up to 1 week. Reheat in a 57°C (134.6°F) water bath for 30 minutes before searing and making the glaze.

CONTINUED >

Preheat your sous vide water bath to 57°C (134.6°F).

Place the short ribs in a gallon-size freezer-safe ziplock bag in a single layer and seal using the water displacement method (see page 12).

When the water reaches the target temperature, lower the bagged short ribs into the water bath (making sure the bag is fully submerged) and cook for 48 hours. I recommend checking the water bath every few hours to see that the bag is still fully submerged. I also suggest covering the bath with plastic wrap or aluminum foil to minimize evaporation (see page 8 for explanation).

When the ribs are ready, remove the bag from the water bath and let the ribs rest for 10 minutes. Transfer the meat to a platter or tray, reserving any cooking liquid in the bag for the glaze. Pat the meat thoroughly dry with paper towels and season with salt and pepper.

Heat a large sauté pan or cast-iron skillet over medium-high heat. When the pan is hot, add 1 tablespoon of the butter, which will sizzle and brown immediately. Carefully place the short ribs, fat side down, in the pan and sear until the underside is golden brown, about 1 minute. Using tongs, flip the pieces and brown for about 1 minute more, then transfer them to a platter or tray.

Drain off and discard all but 1 tablespoon of the fat from the pan and return the pan to medium heat. Add the garlic and cook, stirring occasionally, until lightly browned on both sides, about 2 minutes. Pour in the stout (which will immediately foam and bubble vigorously), add the bay leaf, and scrape the bottom of the pan with a wooden spoon or spatula to dislodge any browned bits. Stir in the reserved cooking liquid, stock, hoisin sauce (if using), and brown

sugar and then let the mixture come to a lively boil (if this takes more than a minute or two, you can raise the heat to medium-high). Reduce the liquid until it has a thick, syrupy consistency and is about one-fourth its original volume, about 15 minutes. (The viscosity you want is somewhere between maple syrup and molasses, that is, pourable but quite sticky.)

Turn down the heat to low and stir in the remaining 1 tablespoon butter until it is completely incorporated. The sauce should be glossy and have a richly sweet, salty taste. Add more salt if needed, or add water or stock to thin it if it's too salty. Remove and discard the bay leaf and garlic cloves. Return the short ribs to the pan and glaze them by spooning the sauce over them until they are completely coated, about 1 minute. The sauce should thicken the tiniest bit more and cling to the meat, forming a glossy surface.

To serve, transfer the ribs to a serving platter and sprinkle with the parsley. Serve with more Guinness and feel the luck o' the Irish.

PRO TIP

This recipe calls for cooking the short ribs for 48 hours because I like the sliceable, steaklike texture that results, but if they're cooked all the way to 72 hours, you'll end up with fall-apart tender meat because the connective tissue will have surrendered completely. If you prefer the longer time, be sure to handle the ribs delicately when you're removing them from the bag so they don't break apart.

KVELL-WORTHY PASTRAMI

Including its 10-day stint in a brine, this pastrami is by far the most time-consuming recipe in this book, but I say good meat comes to those who wait. Furthermore, almost all of the time required is inactive. If you don't want to think that far into the future, however, here is a shortcut: once the brine is in the bag with the beef, you can skip the 10-day curing process and begin the cooking process right away. The meat won't be evenly cured to the middle (if you're using the curing salt, a medium-well brown center will be surrounded by a band of pink), but it will still be delicious, though more akin to a braised brisket than a true pastrami. (Along these same lines, you can leave out the curing salt and the liquid smoke, but you will have strayed even further.) Either way, be sure to enjoy the fruits of your labor piled mile high on deli-style rye bread.

Although it's not widely known outside deli cognoscenti, brisket is not the traditional meat for pastrami. In fact, the neighboring plate or navel cut, preferred for its superior flavor and marbling, holds that distinction. That said, if you can't find navel, there's no reason to fret; brisket will certainly yield excellent results.

SERVES 6 to 8 as a main course | **SOUS VIDE COOKING TIME:** 36 hours (or up to 48 hours) | **ACTIVE PREP TIME:** 15 minutes, plus 10 days to cure (optional)

SPICE MIXTURE

⅓ cup black peppercorns

¼ cup coriander seeds

3 tablespoons yellow mustard seeds

1 tablespoon light brown sugar

BRINE

⅓ cup kosher salt

2½ tablespoons granulated sugar

½ teaspoon pink curing salt (optional, see page 73 for explanation)

1 tablespoon spice mixture

1 bay leaf

1 cup boiling water

1 heaping cup ice cubes

1 teaspoon liquid smoke

1 (4-pound) beef navel or brisket, no more than 3 inches thick

DO-AHEAD STRATEGY

Once the spice mixture has been applied to the cooked pastrami, the meat can be returned to its bag, sealed again using the water displacement method (see page 12), chilled in an ice water bath (see page 14) for 30 minutes, and then refrigerated for up to 2 weeks. Eat it cold or reheat it in a 60°C (140°F) water bath for 30 minutes.

CONTINUED >

To make the spice mixture, combine the peppercorns, coriander seeds, and mustard seeds in a small, dry sauté pan over medium heat and toast, stirring or tossing occasionally, until they are fragrant and begin to pop and smoke, about 5 minutes.

Pour the toasted spices onto a plate and let cool. Working in batches as needed, transfer the spices to a mortar (a blender, spice grinder, or coffee grinder will also work) and grind coarsely, being carefully not to reduce them to a fine powder. Stir or pulse in the brown sugar. The spice mixture will keep in a tightly capped container in a cool place for up to 1 month.

To make the brine, combine the kosher salt, granulated sugar, curing salt, 1 tablespoon spice mixture, bay leaf, and boiling water in a heatproof bowl or large liquid measuring cup and stir to dissolve the salt and sugar. Add the ice and stir until the ice melts and the mixture is cool, and then add the liquid smoke.

Place the beef in a gallon-size freezer-safe ziplock bag, pour in the brine, and seal using the water displacement method (see page 12). Refrigerate the bagged meat in the brine for 10 days. If you decide to skip this brining step, as described in the headnote, you can proceed right to the cooking.

Preheat your sous vide water bath to 65°C (147°F).

When the water reaches the target temperature, lower the bagged brined meat into the water bath (making sure the bag is fully submerged) and cook for 36 hours. I recommend checking the water bath every few hours to see that the bag is still fully submerged. I also suggest covering the bath with plastic wrap or aluminum foil to minimize evaporation (see page 8 for explanation).

When the meat is ready, remove the bag from the water bath and let the meat rest for 10 minutes. Spread the remaining spice mixture onto a platter or tray. Remove the cooked meat from the bag, discarding any liquid (don't pat the meat dry because the moisture will help the spices adhere), and then place the meat on top of the spices. Press and rub the spices into the meat to form an even coating over the entire surface.

At this point, if you're serving the pastrami hot, it's ready to eat. Thinly slice it against the grain, then pile it high on rye bread or daintily shovel it into your mouth. Either way, it's like buttah.

VEGETABLES

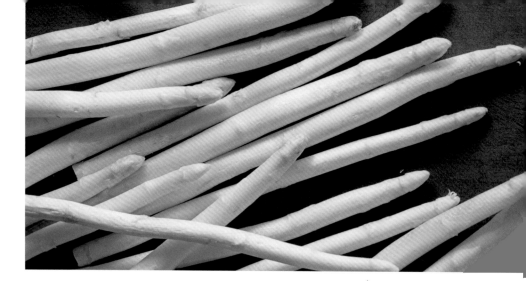

WHEN IT COMES TO SOUS VIDE, VEGETABLES ARE OFTEN RELEGATED TO AFTERTHOUGHT status, but I think they've been sold short. Just try the vibrant-tasting (and vibrant-looking) carrots on page 177 to see how sous vide cooking brings their natural flavor into focus. Or experience the crisp-tender green beans on page 185 to see how blanching green vegetables is easier than ever. You'll be blown away by the ease of making soup, too, like the simple yet luxurious Creamy Winter Squash Soup (page 173), which needs neither watching nor stirring, plus there's no pot to wash. For the coup de grace, try Perfect Mashed Potatoes (page 193), which combine great ease, mouthwatering flavor, and the ideal texture. As a bonus round, get into my newest sous vide crush: mushrooms that are fantastically easy, versatile, and delicious (page 196).

You'll notice that 85°C is a common temperature throughout this chapter, and that's no coincidence: it's the temperature at which cellulose—the complex carbohydrate responsible for a vegetable's rigid structure—breaks down. This process is what causes raw vegetables to transform from firm and crunchy to soft and yielding. Because sous vide allows you to cook at this precise temperature, the chance for error is drastically decreased, making it much easier to avoid overcooked, mushy results.

But temperature control is not the only benefit. Sous vide cooking also helps maintain the nutrients in vegetables. Now, before you think I've lost my way and wandered into the dreaded territory of "health food," let me point out that, when it comes to

vegetables, nutrients are integral to both taste and color. With the vegetables sealed in the bag during cooking, there's nowhere for the good stuff to go, so it stays put in the vegetables themselves.

You'll find three potato recipes here, and with good reason. Even though potatoes are a humble staple, they can be difficult to master. When boiled in water and not closely watched, they can turn into a waterlogged, mealy mess. Cooking potatoes sous vide well below boiling temperature creates just the right texture and undiluted flavor.

Now for some practical advice. Without a vacuum sealer, it can be tricky getting bagged vegetables to sink into the water bath. Fortunately, the solution to this problem is simple: add weight to the bag. Anything from pie weights to clean, smooth stones will work (see page 11). Another unique aspect of cooking vegetables sous vide is that unlike with most other foods, it's possible to use touch to gauge doneness. This is because, as noted above, the breakdown of structural cellulose is the key factor distinguishing raw vegetables from cooked. In other words, once they're soft, they're cooked. In recipes where it's relevant, such as Cauliflower with Garam Masala (page 195) or Zingy Crushed Potatoes (page 190), I encourage you to pinch or poke the vegetable to test for doneness. Consider this a bonus: not only does it put you in greater control of how firm or tender your results are, it also gives you carte blanche to play with your food.

CREAMY WINTER SQUASH SOUP

What I love most about using sous vide to make soup is that you can leave it "unsoupervized," with no risk of it drying out, scorching, or sticking. That means that this flavor-packed soup is extremely low fuss, even more so because there's no dirty pot to clean. Instead of going the usual baking spices route (that is, the clichéd "pumpkin spice"), I've chosen to accentuate the naturally sweet and nutty flavor of the squash with the rich tanginess of crème fraîche, allowing the squash to be the centerpiece of the soup rather than playing second fiddle. Finished with a hit of brightness from fresh herbs and crunchy pumpkin seeds, it's a knockout dish. This recipe will yield delicious results using nearly any winter squash such as kabocha, butternut, red kuri, or delicata.

SERVES 4 as an appetizer | **SOUS VIDE COOKING TIME:** 45 minutes (or up to 1½ hours) | **ACTIVE PREP TIME:** 15 minutes

---

1 medium-small winter squash (about 1½ pounds)

3 cloves Garlic Confit (page 265), or 1 clove garlic, thinly sliced

1 shallot, thinly sliced

2 cups homemade chicken or vegetable stock (page 267) or store-bought low-sodium broth, or water

1 bay leaf

½ cup crème fraîche, plus more for garnish

Salt and freshly ground black pepper

1 tablespoon chopped chives or fresh tarragon leaves, for garnish

¼ cup salted roasted pumpkin seeds, for garnish

DO-AHEAD STRATEGY

The cooked squash mixture (not yet pureed) can be chilled in the bag in an ice water bath (see page 14) for 20 minutes and then refrigerated for up to 1 week (set the bag on a tray or in a bowl in case of leakage) or frozen for up to 2 months. Hold off on adding the crème fraîche until after reheating the squash mixture. When you're ready to serve the soup, reheat the squash in a 70°C (158°F) water bath for 30 minutes and then puree it before adding the crème fraîche.

Preheat your sous vide water bath to 85°C (185°F).

Peel the squash, then halve lengthwise and scrape out the seeds. Cut the halves lengthwise in half again. Turn the squash cut side down and cut crosswise into ½-inch-thick slices. Place the squash pieces, garlic, shallot, stock, and bay leaf in a gallon-size freezer-safe ziplock bag and seal using the water displacement or table-edge method (see page 12). I recommend the latter method for recipes with a relatively large amount of liquid.

When the water reaches the target temperature, lower the bag into the water bath (making sure the bag is fully submerged) and cook for 45 minutes.

Remove the bag from the water bath, discard the bay leaf, and pour the contents of the bag into a blender. Blend on high speed until the mixture is completely smooth. Add the ½ cup crème fraîche and pulse briefly to incorporate, then season with salt and pepper.

To serve, divide the soup evenly among four warmed individual bowls. Garnish each serving with a dollop of crème fraîche, and a scattering of chives and pumpkin seeds.

BEET SALAD WITH GOAT GOUDA AND PISTACHIOS

Although food faddists may have long since declared the duo of beets and goat cheese passé, reports of its demise have been greatly exaggerated. While I happen to think the combo is a classic for good reason, I've mixed things up a little in this recipe. For starters, I've upped the umami ante by switching out the standard fresh goat cheese (chèvre) for sweet, nutty goat Gouda, which you can find in most cheese shops or upscale markets. I've also brightened the beets with ginger and orange zest, and added savory roasted pistachios, which tie everything together and bring a welcome crunch.

Peeling raw beets is markedly less messy than peeling them after roasting or boiling, and because they are sealed in a bag, you don't have to worry about bleeding a lot of flavor (and nutrients) into the water. In addition, cooking the beets with the vinegar and aromatics directly in the bag allows them to absorb the complex flavors more fully than if you simply dress the beets with a vinaigrette before serving. This is a terrific warm salad, but it's also lovely served cold, so feel free to serve the beets at fridge temperature if you've made them ahead of time.

SERVES 4 as an appetizer | **SOUS VIDE COOKING TIME:** 1½ hours (or up to 3 hours) | **ACTIVE PREP TIME:** 20 minutes, plus 10 minutes to rest

1 pound red or golden beets, or a mixture, each about 2 inches in diameter (green tops removed), peeled, and halved lengthwise

2 tablespoons extra-virgin olive oil

2 tablespoons rice vinegar

1 teaspoon honey

Finely grated zest of ½ orange

½ teaspoon peeled, finely grated fresh ginger

1 teaspoon kosher salt

Flaky sea salt (such as Maldon, or fleur de sel) and freshly cracked black pepper

½ cup salted roasted pistachios

4 ounces goat Gouda or other firm aged goat cheese, shaved with a cheese plane or vegetable peeler

2 teaspoons small fennel fronds, for garnish (optional)

DO-AHEAD STRATEGY

The cooked beets can be cooled completely in the unopened bag at room temperature and then refrigerated for up to 2 weeks. Reheat in a 65°C (149°F) water bath for 15 minutes, or serve them straight out of the fridge for a delicious cold salad.

Preheat your sous vide water bath to 85°C (185°F).

Place the beets in a gallon-size freezer-safe ziplock bag and add 1 tablespoon of the oil, the vinegar, honey, orange zest, ginger, and kosher salt. Try to keep the beet halves in a single layer, which is easiest to do if all of the cut sides are face down. Seal using the water displacement method (see page 12).

When the water reaches the target temperature, lower the bagged beets into the water bath (making sure the bag is fully submerged) and cook for 1½ hours. To test if the beets are fully cooked, carefully open the bag (use tongs, as it will be pretty hot) and pierce a beet with the tip of a paring knife. If the knife slides in with only a small amount of resistance, the beets are ready. If it doesn't slide easily, reseal the bag and continue to cook for 30 minutes.

Remove the bag from the water bath and let the beets rest for 10 minutes, then transfer them to a cutting board. Reserve 2 tablespoons of the cooking liquid and discard the rest.

Cut each beet half into 6 to 8 wedges each, about ½ inch thick at its widest point. Toss the wedges into a serving bowl, drizzle with the remaining 1 tablespoon oil and the reserved cooking liquid, and toss to coat evenly. Season with the sea salt and black pepper and then sprinkle with the pistachios, cheese, and fennel fronds, if using.

CARROTS WITH YOGURT–DILL DRESSING AND SUNFLOWER SEEDS

With nothing more than a pinch of salt and few sprigs of dill, these sous vide carrots emerge from their bath in Technicolor, bursting with a sweet carrot flavor and offering a pleasant bite. I like to use a colorful mix of heirloom varieties, but the familiar orange roots won't short you on flavor. Keeping this salad simple allows the undiluted flavor of the carrots to shine through. The yogurt dressing adds a tangy, herbaceous counterpoint to the sweetness of the carrots and nuttiness of the sunflower seeds. If you want to rep your veggie cred to the max, a sprinkle of fennel pollen will add an exotic licorice note, making the dish even brighter. These carrots are terrific whether you serve them warm or at room temperature.

SERVES 4 as a side dish | **SOUS VIDE COOKING TIME:** 1 hour (or up to 2 hours) | **ACTIVE PREP TIME:** 10 minutes, plus 10 minutes to rest

1 bunch slender carrots (about 1 pound), about ¾ inch thick at their widest point, green tops removed and peeled

½ teaspoon kosher salt

2 dill sprigs

1 tablespoon extra-virgin olive oil

DRESSING

¼ cup homemade yogurt (page 260) or store-bought whole-milk plain Greek yogurt

3 tablespoons extra-virgin olive oil

1 tablespoon fresh lemon juice

1 teaspoon honey

2 tablespoons chopped fresh dill

Salt and freshly ground black pepper

¼ cup salted, roasted, and shelled sunflower seeds

2 tablespoons small fresh dill leaves

½ teaspoon fennel pollen (optional)

Flaky sea salt (such as Maldon or fleur de sel)

DO-AHEAD STRATEGY

The cooked and chilled carrots can be refrigerated for up to 1 week. Reheat in a 65°C (149°F) water bath for 15 minutes if serving the carrots warm, or bring to room temperature if serving cold.

Preheat your sous vide water bath to 85°C (185°F).

Place the carrots, kosher salt, dill sprigs, and oil in a gallon-size freezer-safe ziplock bag and roll the carrots around in the bag to coat them evenly. Seal using the water displacement method (see page 12).

When the water reaches the target temperature, lower the bagged carrots into the water bath (making sure the bag is fully submerged) and cook for 1 hour. The carrots should be flexible but not mushy. If they are still rigid, cook them for another 15 minutes.

Remove the bag from the water bath and let the carrots rest in the bag until they are cool enough to handle comfortably, about 10 minutes. If you prefer to serve the carrots cold, place the bagged carrots in an ice water bath (see page 14) for 10 minutes.

While the carrots are cooling, make the dressing. In a small bowl, whisk together the yogurt, oil, lemon juice, honey, and chopped dill, mixing well. Season with the salt and pepper.

Transfer the carrots to a cutting board and cut them in half lengthwise. Discard the dill sprigs and any liquid that has accumulated in the bag.

To serve, spread the dressing in a nice thick layer on the bottom of a platter and arrange the carrots on top. Sprinkle with the sunflower seeds, dill leaves, fennel pollen (if using), and sea salt.

GRILLED ASPARAGUS WITH ROMESCO

If your childhood experience of asparagus involved plates of stringy, mushy horror, this dish will be a revelation. Briefly cooking asparagus sous vide, rather than boiling, results in al dente spears whose bright, grassy flavor and beneficial nutrients are left perfectly intact, not dumped down the drain. The last step of grilling the asparagus gives it a nice char for a final boost of flavor.

Here, I pair the spears with *romesco*, a rustic, boldly flavored Spanish sauce (a distant relative of aïoli) that's traditionally served with grilled vegetables and nicely showcases my Garlic Confit. The recipe makes about double the amount of sauce you'll need, but I guarantee it won't go to waste. It's an incredibly delicious and versatile condiment that stores well to boot. You can put a dollop atop Zingy Crushed Potatoes (page 190) or a rib-eye steak (page 145) or wherever you would normally use salsa. It's that good. Look for the Marcona almonds and piquillo peppers at Spanish markets or online (see Resources, page 273).

SERVES 4 as a side dish | **SOUS VIDE COOKING TIME:** 4 to 12 minutes | **ACTIVE PREP TIME:** 15 minutes

ROMESCO

5 cloves Garlic Confit (page 265), or 2 cloves garlic, thinly sliced

¾ cup roasted salted Marcona almonds, coarsely chopped

1 cup drained roasted jarred piquillo peppers, coarsely chopped (about one 8-ounce jar)

½ cup canned tomato puree

2 tablespoons sherry vinegar

1 tablespoon smoked paprika

½ teaspoon cayenne pepper

⅓ cup extra-virgin olive oil

½ teaspoon freshly ground black pepper

Pinch of kosher salt

1 bunch medium-thick white or green asparagus (about 1 pound; spears about ½ inch thick), tough stems trimmed

1 tablespoon extra-virgin olive oil

Salt and freshly ground black pepper

¼ cup roasted salted Marcona almonds, coarsely chopped, for garnish

2 tablespoon chopped fresh flat-leaf parsley, for garnish

DO-AHEAD STRATEGY

The cooked asparagus can be chilled in the bag in an ice water bath (see page 14) for 10 minutes and then refrigerated for up to 3 days. The asparagus is great served cold, brought to room temp, or reheated on the grill, adding an extra minute or two to warm through completely. The sauce can be made in advance and refrigerated for up to 1 week or frozen for up to 1 month.

CONTINUED >

Preheat your sous vide water bath to 85°C (185°F).

While the water is heating, make the *romesco*. In a blender or food processor, combine all of the ingredients and pulse until a coarse puree forms. Season with additional salt to taste and set aside.

To ensure that your bag sinks, place 1 to 2 pounds of weight into a gallon-size freezer-safe ziplock bag. Add the asparagus and the oil, and seal using the water displacement method (see page 12).

When the water reaches the target temperature, lower the bagged asparagus into the water bath and cook until the spears are just barely firm, about 5 minutes. To test if they are done, squeeze the thick bottom ends; they should feel firm but yield slightly when gently pinched. If they do not yield, cook for an additional 2 minutes. Particularly thick asparagus can take up to 12 minutes, and pencil-thin asparagus can take as little as 4 minutes.

Remove the bag from the water bath and transfer the asparagus spears to a platter or tray. Season with salt and pepper.

Preheat a stove-top grill pan over high heat, or prepare a charcoal or gas grill for direct cooking over high heat. Working in batches if necessary to avoid overlapping, arrange the asparagus spears in a single layer on the grill pan or grill rack and grill, turning as needed, just long enough to char the surface, about 1 minute per side. (The oil that went into the bag with the asparagus is enough for the grilling.)

Transfer the grilled asparagus to a serving platter and spoon a little of the sauce on top. Sprinkle with the almonds and parsley and serve. Pass additional sauce at the table.

SWEET POTATO TACOS

Who says taco time needs to be a meat fiesta? In this recipe, toothsome chunks of sweet potatoes infused with chipotle and cumin take the starring role. The key is cooking the sweet potatoes sous vide, which allows you to achieve a texture that is soft enough not to be crunchy but firm, with just a little bite. Folded up into blistered tortillas with just a sprinkle of Cotija cheese and cilantro on top, these vegetarian tacos are going to make you wish that every day was Taco Tuesday.

SERVES 4 to 6 as a main course | **SOUS VIDE COOKING TIME:** 1 hour (or up to 2 hours) | **ACTIVE PREP TIME:** 25 minutes

2 sweet potatoes (about 1½ pounds), peeled and cut into ½-inch dice (about 4 cups)

3 to 4 chipotle chiles in adobo, seeded (if desired) and chopped

1½ teaspoons ground cumin

1 teaspoon kosher salt

2 tablespoons canola or other mild vegetable oil

12 (6-inch) corn tortillas

Salt and freshly ground black pepper

Juice of ½ lime (about 1 tablespoon)

3 tablespoons minced red onion

½ cup sour cream

½ cup crumbled or grated Cotija cheese or queso fresco

¼ cup coarsely chopped fresh cilantro, for garnish

4 to 6 lime wedges, for serving

DO-AHEAD STRATEGY

The cooked sweet potatoes can be chilled in the bag in an ice water bath (see page 14) for 10 minutes and then refrigerated for up to 1 week. To reheat, remove the sweet potatoes from the bag, discarding the liquid, and continue to the charring step, adding a few additional minutes to ensure the pieces warm through.

CONTINUED >

Preheat your sous vide water bath to 85°C (185°F).

In a large bowl, toss together the sweet potatoes, chiles, cumin, salt, and 1 tablespoon of the oil until the sweet potato pieces are evenly coated with all of the ingredients.

To ensure that your bag sinks, place 1 to 2 pounds of weight into a gallon-size freezer-safe ziplock bag. Add the sweet potato mixture to the bag and seal using the water displacement method (see page 12).

When the water has reached the target temperature, lower the bagged sweet potatoes into the water bath and cook for 1 hour. The sweet potatoes are ready if you can crush the pieces through the bag with a firm pinch.

Remove the bag from the water bath and transfer the sweet potatoes to a plate, discarding the liquid. Set aside.

Heat a large cast-iron skillet over medium-high heat. When the pan is hot, working in batches, heat the tortillas by placing them directly into the skillet and then waiting until they begin to steam and blister, about 20 seconds. Flip them with tongs or a spatula and cook the other side until they again begin to steam and blister, about 30 seconds. Depending on the size of your skillet, you can heat 3 or 4 tortillas at a time. After each batch is heated, transfer the tortillas to a plate and cover them with a kitchen towel or aluminum foil to keep warm.

When all of the tortillas have been heated, and with the pan still over medium-high heat, add the remaining 1 tablespoon oil to the skillet and then add the sweet potato mixture. The pieces do not need to fit in a single layer. Sauté over medium-high heat, stirring occasionally with a wooden spoon, until charred and blackened on the edges, 3 to 5 minutes. Remove from the heat, season with salt and pepper, and then add the lime juice.

To assemble the tacos, spread a small dollop of the sour cream onto the middle of each tortilla. Divide the sweet potato mixture evenly among the tortillas. Top each taco with a sprinkle of the cheese, cilantro, and red onion. Arrange the tacos on individual plates and serve with the lime wedges.

GREEN BEANS AMANDINE

My take on this classic side dish uses sous vide to keep the green beans' pleasantly snappy texture and nutrients intact. As an added bonus, since they aren't cooked directly in water, you won't need to dry them off before sautéing. Dressed with the traditional combo of lemony butter and crunchy almonds, these are green beans you'll be proud to serve, whether as a side dish at a simple meal or as part of an elaborate holiday spread.

Green beans vary widely in size, from slivers no thicker than yarn to behemoths the size of a Sharpie. For this dish, I think that slim, tender haricots verts work best. In a pinch, any kind of string bean will do, though thicker beans can take up to 15 minutes to cook, which will cause them to lose some color.

SERVES 4 as a side dish | **SOUS VIDE COOKING TIME:** 10 minutes (or up to 15 minutes) | **ACTIVE PREP TIME:** 15 minutes, plus 10 minutes to chill

1 pound haricots verts, stem ends snapped

½ teaspoon kosher salt

3 tablespoons unsalted butter

1 tablespoon minced shallot

¼ cup chopped or slivered almonds

1 tablespoon fresh lemon juice

Salt and freshly ground black pepper

Flaky sea salt (such as Maldon or fleur de sel)

DO-AHEAD STRATEGY

After chilling in the ice water bath, the beans can be refrigerated up to 3 days. The final step of sautéing them in the sauce is enough to reheat them.

Preheat your sous vide water bath to 90°C (194°F).

To ensure that your bag sinks, place 1 to 2 pounds of weight into a gallon-size freezer-safe ziplock bag. Add the green beans, sprinkle in the salt, and toss or shake the bag to distribute the salt evenly among the beans. Arrange the beans so they are flat and in a single layer and then seal the bag using the water displacement method (see page 12).

When the water reaches the target temperature, lower the bagged beans into the water bath and cook for 10 minutes. They should yield slightly to firm pressure but still have crunch.

When the beans are ready, immediately transfer the bag to an ice water bath (see page 14) and chill for 10 minutes. Working quickly is important to stop the cooking and preserve the color of the beans. Once the beans are cold, transfer them to a bag, leaving behind any liquid and set aside.

Melt the butter in a large sauté pan over medium heat. Once the butter begins to sizzle and foam, steadily swirl the pan until the butter turns light brown and smells nutty, 1 to 2 minutes. As soon as the butter has browned, immediately stir in the shallot and sauté until translucent, about 1 minute. Add the almonds and cook until they begin to brown, 1 to 2 minutes more. When the almond pieces begin to brown, dump the green beans into the pan all at once and toss and stir with a wooden spoon until they are hot and steaming, 1 to 2 minutes. Remove from the heat, stir in the lemon juice, and season with salt and pepper.

Transfer the beans to a serving platter, spooning any sauce left in the pan on top, sprinkle with sea salt, and eat immediately.

THAI GREEN CURRY
WITH WINTER SQUASH

Good Thai curry is all about creating an intricate balance among contrasting flavors: spicy and sweet, sour and salty. Although the flavor should be complex, making curry at home needn't be. The key to preparing this curry in a hurry is to start with a high-quality store-bought curry paste. You may have been told that it's imperative to make your own, but key aromatics in authentic Thai curry, such as fresh galangal and kaffir lime, can be difficult to find. Since there are no acceptable substitutes for these ingredients, imported pastes have the edge over from-scratch versions made without them. Cooks in Thailand commonly use premade pastes, so even a curry connoisseur will give this recipe a stamp of approval.

Cooking the squash with the curry paste and coconut milk in the bag accomplishes two goals: it creates a tantalizingly fragrant sauce, and the squash turns out perfectly tender but still firm. I like using red kuri squash (a variety from Japan) for this curry, because it most closely resembles the type commonly used in Thailand in terms of taste and texture. It also has the tremendous benefit of not requiring peeling. You'll want to serve this killer curry with plenty of steamed jasmine rice so none of the delicious sauce goes to waste.

SERVES 4 as a main course | **SOUS VIDE COOKING TIME:** 1 hour (or up to 2 hours) | **ACTIVE PREP TIME:** 10 minutes

1 small red kuri or other winter squash (about 1 pound)

1 cup canned coconut milk, shaken in unopened can before measuring

2 tablespoons Thai green curry paste (preferably Mae Ploy or Maesri brand; see Resources, page 273)

2 teaspoons light brown sugar

2 teaspoons fish sauce

1 shallot, thinly sliced

Juice of 1 lime (about 2 tablespoons)

¼ cup loosely packed Thai basil or regular basil leaves

¼ cup salted roasted cashews

DO-AHEAD STRATEGY

The cooked curry can be chilled in the bag in an ice water bath (see page 14) for 20 minutes and then refrigerated for up to 1 week. Reheat in a 70°C (158°F) water bath for 30 minutes.

Preheat your sous vide water bath to 85°C (185°F).

Peel the squash (you can skip peeling if using a red kuri) and cut in half lengthwise. Scrape out the seeds and pulp with a spoon and then cut each half into ½-inch-thick wedges.

In a bowl, whisk together the coconut milk, curry paste, brown sugar, and fish sauce until smooth.

When the water reaches the target temperature, place the squash in a gallon-size freezer-safe ziplock bag and pour the coconut mixture on top. Seal using the water displacement method (see page 12).

Lower the bagged squash into the water bath (making sure the bag is fully submerged) and cook for 1 hour. The squash should be tender enough to pinch apart with gentle pressure. If not, cook for an additional 15 minutes.

Remove the bag from the water bath and transfer the squash and cooking liquid to a serving bowl. Gently stir in the lime juice and the basil leaves and and sprinkle the cashews on top. Serve immediately with rice on the side.

PRO TIP

To make this recipe both vegetarian and vegan, substitute salt to taste for the fish sauce and double-check the label on the curry paste to make sure it doesn't contain shrimp paste, which is a common ingredient.

GLAZED PARSNIPS WITH ROASTED HAZELNUTS

Sous vide offers a dynamite technique for making glazed vegetables. With no need for careful timing, these parsnips are ready to go straight out of the bag, or mashed and blended into the surprisingly delicious Parsnip Cake (page 211). However, if you want to go the distance and achieve a super shiny lacquer, you'll need to transfer them to a sauté pan and reduce the cooking liquid to a thick glaze. I think the final results are worth the effort of washing one dirty pan. Either way, you'll want to seal the deal with a sprinkling of roasted hazelnuts, flaky salt, and fresh chervil.

SERVES 4 as a side dish | **SOUS VIDE COOKING TIME:** 1 hour (or up to 2 hours) | **ACTIVE PREP TIME:** 10 minutes

1 pound parsnips (about 5 medium), peeled, halved lengthwise, then cut into ½-inch pieces on the diagonal

3 tablespoons unsalted butter

2 tablespoons honey

2 tablespoons fresh orange juice or apple juice

1 tablespoon fresh lemon juice

½ teaspoon kosher salt

¼ cup roasted blanched hazelnuts, coarsely chopped or crushed

2 tablespoons fresh chervil, flat-leaf parsley, or tarragon leaves

Flaky sea salt (such as Maldon or fleur de sel)

DO-AHEAD STRATEGY

The cooked parsnips can be chilled in the bag in an ice water bath (see page 14) for 10 minutes and then refrigerated for up to 1 week. The final glazing step will be enough to reheat the parsnips; simply add an additional splash of water to the pan. If you choose to skip the glazing step, simply reheat in a 70°C (158°F) water bath for 20 minutes.

Preheat your sous vide water bath to 85°C (185°F).

To ensure that your bag sinks, place 1 to 2 pounds of weight into a gallon-size freezer-safe ziplock bag. Add the parsnips, butter, honey, orange juice, lemon juice, and salt to the bag and seal using the water displacement method (see page 12).

When the water reaches target temperature, lower the bagged parsnips into the water bath and cook for 1 hour.

Remove the bag from the water bath and transfer the parsnips and their cooking liquid to a large sauté pan or wide stockpot. Cook over medium-high heat, stirring occasionally, until the cooking liquid has reduced to a thick, shiny glaze, 3 to 5 minutes. Remove from the heat.

To serve, transfer the glazed parsnips to a serving bowl or plate and sprinkle with the hazelnuts, chervil, and sea salt.

PRO TIP

Use this recipe as a blueprint for cooking any starchy root vegetable. It will work beautifully with carrots, turnips, rutabagas, or sweet potatoes. Just be sure you cut them into uniform ½-inch pieces.

ZINGY CRUSHED POTATOES

These are my antidote to all of the snooze-worthy potatoes I've encountered in my life. I cook them sous vide until just tender, then smash and panfry them before finishing them with red pepper flakes, green onions, and lime zest, and the results are utterly craveable. With their exotic flavor and comforting creamy, crispy texture, they're like home fries that have studied abroad. As for matching lime and potato, it might seem a little unusual, but as it turns out, the tangy citrus flavor is a wonderful complement to the tuber's subtle earthy sweetness. Try this combo yourself and put boring potatoes in your rearview mirror.

SERVES 4 as a side dish | **SOUS VIDE COOKING TIME:** 1 hour (or up to 2 hours) | **ACTIVE PREP TIME:** 20 minutes, plus 10 minutes to rest

1 pound small, round waxy potatoes (such as German butterball or baby red bliss), scrubbed clean

1 tablespoon unsalted butter

1½ teaspoons kosher salt

4 thyme sprigs

¼ cup olive oil

2 green onions, white and green parts, thinly sliced

½ teaspoon red pepper flakes

Grated zest of 1 lime, for garnish

Flaky sea salt (such as Maldon or fleur de sel) and freshly ground black pepper

DO-AHEAD STRATEGY

The cooked potatoes can be chilled in the bag in an ice water bath (see page 14) for 10 minutes and then refrigerated for up to 1 week. When you're ready to serve them, simply smash the potatoes straight out of the fridge and panfry them. They'll spend long enough in the pan to heat through.

Preheat your sous vide water bath to 85°C (185°F).

Place the potatoes, butter, kosher salt, and thyme sprigs in a gallon-size freezer-safe ziplock bag and seal using the water displacement method (see page 12).

When the water reaches the target temperature, lower the bagged potatoes into the water bath (making sure the bag is fully submerged) and cook for 1 hour. To test for doneness, squeeze a potato through the bag; it should yield to firm pressure. If it doesn't, cook the potatoes for an additional 15 minutes.

Remove the bag from the water bath and let the potatoes rest in the bag until they are cool enough to handle, 5 to 10 minutes. Using a slotted spoon, transfer the potatoes to a platter or tray. Discard any residual cooking liquid and the thyme sprigs. Using the bottom of a mug or tumbler, smash each potato flat to a thickness of about ½ inch to increase the surface area—more to crisp up!

Heat the oil in a large skillet over medium-high heat until it shimmers. Add the potatoes in a single layer and cook until crispy and golden brown on the underside, 5 to 6 minutes. Using a spatula, flip the potatoes over and continue to panfry until the second side is crispy and golden brown, 5 to 6 minutes longer. Add the green onions and red pepper flakes and cook for 1 minute more.

To serve, transfer the crushed potatoes to a platter and sprinkle with the lime zest and with the sea salt and pepper.

BRITISH-STYLE CHIPS

The key to great fried potatoes is the crisp. National allegiances aside, the best technique comes from Belgium, where they are double fried: once to cook them through and once to form a crust. By using sous vide to precook the potatoes, this recipe avoids the need for multiple go-rounds in the deep fryer but still gives you the ideal combination of soft interior and crispy exterior. This owes to the fact that cooked potatoes give off less steam than raw potatoes, and less steam equals a crispier crust. As an additional bonus, you can cook them days ahead of time and store them in the bag until you're ready to fry. Be sure to use a starchy potato like a russet, as waxy potatoes will get too dark before they become crisp. Of course, these chips are a natural to serve with my beer-battered fish on page 59.

SERVES 4 as a side dish | **SOUS VIDE COOKING TIME:** 1 hour (or up to 1½ hours) | **ACTIVE PREP TIME:** 15 minutes

1½ pounds russet potatoes, peeled, halved lengthwise, and cut into wedges ½ inch thick at their widest point (each potato will yield about 12 wedges)

1 tablespoon extra-virgin olive oil

1 teaspoon chopped fresh thyme

1 teaspoon kosher salt, plus more for serving

Canola or other mild vegetable oil, for deep-frying

DO-AHEAD STRATEGY

If you're making the potatoes more than 2 hours in advance of frying, chill them in an ice water bath (see page 14) for 15 minutes and then refrigerate for to 1 week before frying. They can be fried straight out of the fridge, adding just a minute or two to the frying time if needed to brown completely. As with regular fries, these chips won't stay crisp forever after frying. If you want to keep them warm for a short amount of time, they can sit for up to 30 minutes in the 250°F oven, which is a good trick to know when serving them as a side.

Preheat your sous vide water bath to 87°C (188.6°F).

Place the potatoes, olive oil, thyme, and salt in a gallon-size freezer-safe ziplock bag and shake the bag to coat the potatoes evenly with the other ingredients. Seal using the water displacement method (see page 12) and then press down on the bag to distribute the wedges in a single layer (or as close to a single layer as possible).

When the water reaches the target temperature, lower the bagged potatoes into the water bath (making sure the bag is fully submerged) and cook for 1 hour.

Remove the bag from the water bath and set aside the potatoes (still in the bag) at room temperature until you're ready to fry.

When you are ready to fry the potatoes, transfer them from the bag to a platter or tray, discarding any liquid, and thoroughly pat dry with paper towels. Line a second platter or tray with paper towels and place near the stove. Preheat the oven to 250°F.

Pour the canola oil to a depth of about 1½ inches into a deep cast-iron skillet. The oil should come no more than one-third of the way up the side of the pan to ensure that it will not boil over the rim once the potatoes are added. Heat the oil over medium heat until a wooden skewer or bamboo chopstick inserted into the center of the oil bubbles immediately, or the oil registers 350°F on a high-heat thermometer.

Working in batches to avoid crowding, carefully add the potatoes to the hot oil and fry, turning occasionally to prevent sticking, until golden brown and crisp, 4 to 5 minutes. Using a slotted spatula, transfer the chips to the towel-lined platter to blot away any excess oil. Sprinkle with salt to taste, and place in the oven to keep warm. Repeat with the remaining potatoes. Serve hot.

PERFECT MASHED POTATOES

Mashed potatoes are all about creaminess, and to achieve the most luxurious texture, you need to cook the spuds until just tender—and, okay, the butter helps, too. When it comes to the butter, this recipe isn't for the faint of heart. I give a range of buttery goodness below. The lower end of the spectrum will give you firmer American-style mashers (ideal for gravy), and the upper end is a more indulgent French-style pomme de terre puree, for those who laugh in the face of cholesterol. But give me credit, I used restraint. World-renowned French chef Joël Robuchon uses equal parts butter and potato in his version!

SERVES 4 as a side dish | **SOUS VIDE COOKING TIME:** 1 hour (or up to 2 hours) | **ACTIVE PREP TIME:** 15 minutes

1 pound russet or Yukon Gold potatoes, peeled, halved lengthwise, and cut crosswise into ½-inch-thick half-moons

1 teaspoon kosher salt

½ cup heavy cream, whole milk, or crème fraîche, or a mixture

½ to 1 cup (4 to 8 ounces) unsalted butter, at room temperature, cut into ½-inch cubes

DO-AHEAD STRATEGY

The finished mashed potatoes can be prepared, returned to the bag, sealed, cooled in an ice water bath (see page 14) for 20 minutes, and then refrigerated for up to 1 week. Reheat in a water bath anywhere from 54°C (129.2°F) to 70°C (158°F) for 30 minutes. Since you're likely to be serving these potatoes as an accompaniment to one of the main courses in this book, I give you this range so that you can reheat them at the same temperature called for in those recipes.

Preheat your sous vide water bath to 90°C (194°F).

Place the potatoes, salt, and cream in a gallon-size freezer-safe ziplock bag and seal using the water displacement method (see page 12). Press down on the bag so the potatoes sit as flat as possible.

When the water reaches the target temperature, lower the bagged potatoes into the water bath (making sure the bag is fully submerged) and cook for 1 hour.

Remove the bag from the water bath. Set a potato ricer or a food mill fitted with the finest die over a large bowl. Using a ladle, transfer the potato and cream mixture to the ricer or mill and pass it through. (Alternatively, though not ideally, you can use a potato masher.)

Using a wooden spoon or spatula, stir in the butter a few pieces at a time, letting each addition melt and incorporate into the potatoes before adding the next, until all of the butter has been added. Taste and adjust the seasoning with salt if needed and serve immediately.

PRO TIP

To make these potatoes a part of your Thanksgiving feast (or any time you want to make a larger amount of mashed potatoes), you can double (or triple) this recipe; just be sure to divide the uncooked potato mixture between two (or three) bags to ensure that it cooks evenly. Once finished, the mashed potatoes can also be returned to their cooking bags and kept hot for up to 2 hours at 60°C (140°F)—conveniently, the same temperature you'll need to finish cooking your Thanksgiving Turkey (page 111).

CAULIFLOWER WITH GARAM MASALA

This recipe is inspired by *aloo gobi*, a classic Indian cauliflower and potato dish, but to simplify things I leave out the potato. Typically, cooking cauliflower in a pan can be difficult; in order to cook it evenly al dente you need to blanch it first or add water to the pan while sautéing, which inhibits browning and often results in cauliflower that is raw in some places and falling apart in others. Sous vide gives you evenly cooked cauliflower without the need for constant stirring or adding water. Cooking the toasty spices of the garam masala in the bag imparts loads of flavor to the cauliflower and combines with the ghee to form a rich, buttery sauce that delivers an aroma bonanza when the bag is opened. The finished dish is a terrific accompaniment to a meat curry (such as my Chicken Tikka Masala, page 87) dish but it can also easily stand on its own as a main course served with rice and naan.

SERVES 4 as a side dish | **SOUS VIDE COOKING TIME:** 30 minutes (or up to 45 minutes) | **ACTIVE PREP TIME:** 20 minutes

SPICE PASTE

4 tablespoons ghee or canola or other mild vegetable oil

2 teaspoons garam masala

1 teaspoon ground turmeric

1 teaspoon ground cumin

½ teaspoon ground coriander

½ teaspoon Kashmiri red chile powder or red pepper flakes

1 shallot, grated or finely chopped

1-inch piece fresh ginger, peeled and grated or finely chopped (about 1 tablespoon)

2 cloves garlic, finely chopped

1½ teaspoons kosher salt

1 small head cauliflower (about 1½ pounds), broken into bite-size florets (about 4 cups)

Juice from ½ lime (about 1 tablespoon)

Flaky salt (such as Maldon or fleur de sel, optional)

¼ cup loosely packed fresh cilantro leaves, for garnish

DO-AHEAD STRATEGY

I don't recommend cooking the cauliflower in advance (the chilling and reheating would make it too mushy), but the spice paste can be made in advance and refrigerated for up to 1 week or frozen for up to 1 month.

Preheat your sous vide water bath to 83°C (181.4°F).

In a small saucepan, combine all of the spice paste ingredients and heat over medium heat until bubbling. Turn the heat down to low and continue to cook, stirring constantly, until it has taken on a darker shade and the bubbling has subsided, about 5 minutes. At this point, the spice paste should be richly aromatic.

Transfer the spice paste to a large bowl, add the cauliflower, and toss until all of the florets are evenly coated.

To ensure that your bag sinks, place 1 to 2 pounds of weight into a gallon-size freezer-safe ziplock bag. Add the cauliflower and all of the spice paste to the bag and seal using the water displacement method (see page 12). Lower the bagged cauliflower into the water bath and cook for 30 minutes. To check that the cauliflower is done, squeeze one of the florets through the bag; if it yields to firm pressure it's ready. If it doesn't, continue to cook for an additional 10 minutes.

Remove the bag from the water bath and transfer the cauliflower and the cooking liquid to a serving bowl. Add the lime juice, toss the cauliflower once more, and then sprinkle with sea salt, is using, and garnish with cilantro leaves. Serve immediately.

VERSATILE MUSHROOMS

If pressed to pick my favorite sous vide discovery, I'd have to go with mushrooms. Using gentle heat gives mushrooms a fantastic texture that is moist and tender but still toothsome. What's more, the spongelike structure of mushrooms means they readily absorb flavors, so they get imbued with whatever aromatics you put in the bag. Quick, effortless, and packed with flavor, these mushrooms are a sous vide triple threat.

I attached the word *versatile* to these mushrooms for good reason: when finished with balsamic, they're terrific for adding oomph to the Eight-Hour Skirt Steak on page 151, but they're also delicious in scrambled eggs, on a burger, or as a base for a creamy pasta sauce. Simply drain the liquid (save it for adding to sauces, braises, or soups—it's loaded with umami) and then sauté the mushrooms in butter or olive oil, adding whatever herbs or spices you like. Get creative! For this recipe, I chose maitake for its meaty flavor, and oyster and cremini for a variety of textures, but anything from shiitakes to plain ol' button mushrooms will work great.

MAKES 1 to 2 cups cooked mushrooms in liquid | **SOUS VIDE COOKING TIME:** 10 minutes | **ACTIVE PREP TIME:** 5 minutes

8 ounces assorted mushrooms (such as maitake, cremini, and oyster), cut into bite-size pieces

1 tablespoon soy sauce

1 tablespoon extra-virgin olive oil

1 teaspoon fresh thyme leaves

Salt and freshly ground black pepper

Preheat your sous vide water bath to 80°C (176°F).

To ensure that your bag sinks, place 1 to 2 pounds of weight into a gallon-size freezer-safe ziplock bag. In a bowl, combine the mushrooms, soy sauce, oil, and thyme, season with salt and pepper, and toss to coat the mushrooms evenly with the other ingredients. Place the mushroom mixture in the bag and seal using the water-displacement method (see page 12).

When the water reaches the target temperature, lower the bagged mushrooms into the water bath and cook for 10 minutes.

Remove the bag from the water bath and serve the mushrooms immediately.

DO-AHEAD STRATEGY

The mushrooms can be cooled in the bag and refrigerated for up to 1 week. For the skirt steak or for any other dish in which the mushrooms are going to become incorporated into a warm sauce, there's no need to reheat them in the bag.

PRO TIP

Soy sauce might seem out of place here, but it has a great affinity for mushrooms: in small quantities, as in this recipe, it amplifies their earthy, umami flavor while staying out of the spotlight. Soy sauce is the wind beneath maitake's wings.

DESSERTS

I'M NO SLOUCH WHEN IT COMES TO MAKING (OR EATING) SWEETS, so you'd best believe I haven't forgotten about the possibilities of temperature-controlled cooking when making desserts. Although it's true you won't be able to bake a batch of crispy cookies or a fluffy cake using a water bath, for the applications where you can use it, sous vide is unbeatable.

So what desserts will work? As you will see, most of the recipes in this chapter are egg based, and that's no coincidence. The reason for this is that there's nothing better than sous vide for precisely cooking eggs (a point I drive home in the "Eggs" chapter, page 19), and this is no less true when using them as a thickener or binding agent, as in the case of custard. The key to making flawless custard, whether it be a bright, zesty Meyer Lemon Curd (page 207) or rich, intense Chocolate Pots de Crème (page 204), is, of course, to thicken it without curdling. Traditional approaches attempt to accomplish this by heating the egg mixture very gradually. Some recipes call for tempering the eggs or using a double boiler, but even with precautions, a vigilant eye and constant attention are always required to determine the exact moment when the custard is *just* thick enough but not curdled. The precise, gentle heat of sous vide cooking is tailor-made for this purpose: it allows you to cook custards just below the

point at which yolks curdle (85°C). You'll hit the mark every time, and manage this feat with no need to babysit a pot, so banish your fear of curdling and hover no more.

Ice cream gets plenty of attention in this chapter because its versatility offers nearly endless possibilities. On top of being the best tool for making the custard base for ice cream, sous vide is also fantastic for infusing flavors, so it's a great opportunity to customize and embrace your inner Ben or Jerry. I begin the ice cream section with plain ol' vanilla (page 213) and then give you templates for making just about any variation you can dream up, incorporating everything from pistachios in the Nut Butter Ice Cream (page 219) and fruits like apricot in the Catchall Fruit Ice Cream (page 220) to re-creating modern classics like Salted Caramel Ice Cream (page 217).

There's no doubt that eggy desserts take the star billing where sous vide is concerned, but don't miss out on the other, outside-the-box applications you'll find in this chapter. Use sous vide to make the dulce de leche of your dreams (page 225) and poach luscious, fragrant pears (page 208) or incorporate unconventional vegetables like parsnips into your baked goods (page 211). However you use it, I have no doubt you'll be sweet on using sous vide to elevate your dessert repertoire.

VANILLA CRÈME BRÛLÉE

You're going to need a blowtorch to pull off this crème brûlée. Let's be real; recipes that pretend you can do this under a broiler are pure nonsense. A thin, brittle shell of burnt sugar over cool, creamy custard is the sine qua non of crème brûlée, and there's no point in making it any other way. The best a home broiler can turn out is a lackluster crust atop warmed-over custard. No thanks! So if you don't want to deny your crème brûlée dreams, pick up a blowtorch. The good news is that small models designed for the home kitchen (available at most specialty kitchen stores and hardware stores) start at around twenty-five dollars and do a great job of creating the crackly crust. Otherwise, there are plenty of delicious dessert recipes in this book to make instead.

SERVES 4 | **SOUS VIDE COOKING TIME:** 1 hour (or up to 1½ hours) | **ACTIVE PREP TIME:** 10 minutes, plus 3 hours to cool

6 large egg yolks

½ cup granulated sugar

1 vanilla pod, split lengthwise and seeds scraped

Pinch of kosher salt

1½ cups heavy cream

2 tablespoons coarse sugar (such as turbinado or Demerara)

DO-AHEAD STRATEGY

The custards (without the crust) can be made in advance, covered with plastic wrap, and refrigerated for up to 5 days. When you're ready to serve, torch them according to the directions.

Preheat your sous vide water bath to 83°C (181.4°F).

In a bowl, whisk together the egg yolks, granulated sugar, vanilla seeds, and salt until smooth (you will still see specks of vanilla) and then whisk in the cream and add the vanilla pod.

Pour the mixture into a quart-size freezer-safe ziplock bag and seal using the water displacement or table-edge method (see page 12). I recommend the latter method for recipes with a relatively large amount of liquid.

When the water reaches the target temperature, lower the bagged custard into the water bath (making sure the bag is fully submerged) and cook for 1 hour.

Remove the bag from the water bath and give it a shake to redistribute the contents. Snip off a corner from the bag and evenly divide the mixture among four 4-ounce ramekins or crème brûlée dishes, leaving behind the vanilla pod. Tap the bottom of each dish against the countertop to smooth out the top and remove any air bubbles, and then transfer the ramekins to the fridge and chill for at least 3 hours. (If refrigerating the custards for longer than 3 hours, wrap them with plastic wrap.)

When you're ready to serve, sprinkle the coarse sugar over the custards (about 1½ teaspoons per custard), gently spreading the sugar with a back of a spoon to create a thin even layer. Depending on the size of the ramekins (and thus the surface area of the custard), you may need slightly more or less sugar—you want just enough to cover the custard.

Point the blowtorch directly at the surface of the sugar (the tip of the flame should almost touch the sugar) and move the flame back and forth until all of the sugar is melted and browned, 30 to 60 seconds. Serve immediately.

CHOCOLATE POTS DE CRÈME

Chocolate *pot de crème* is the little black dress of desserts. Both simple and sophisticated, it can be adorned with a pinch of Mexican cinnamon or ground coffee if you're feeling jazzy, but it's wonderfully decadent just as it is. With just a hint of sweetness, a deep chocolate flavor, and a seductively rich, silky texture, this dessert is sure to impress.

I love giving these chocolaty treats as gifts because they come in their own individual packages, take no extra work to make a double or triple batch, and are guaranteed to turn out perfect every time. Bear in mind, cooking them in glass vessels does require some special attention. If you add the jars to the water bath after it has reached 80°C, the glass runs the risk of cracking due to heat shock. To avoid that, you need to put them in the water bath before it's hot. As a result, I don't give an exact cooking time because it will depend on how long the water takes to heat up. This isn't really a big deal, however, because a little more time in the water bath won't overcook the custard.

SERVES 4 | **SOUS VIDE COOKING TIME:** About 1½ hours (or up to 2 hours) | **ACTIVE PREP TIME:** 5 minutes, plus 3 hours to cool

---

2 cups heavy cream

4 ounces highest-quality bittersweet chocolate, coarsely chopped

3 tablespoons sugar

1 teaspoon vanilla extract

Pinch of kosher salt

4 large egg yolks

Flaky sea salt (such as Maldon or fleur de sel, optional)

DO-AHEAD STRATEGY

The cooked pots de crème can be refrigerated for up to 1 week.

In a saucepan, bring 1½ cups of the cream to a simmer over medium heat. Remove from the heat and whisk in the chocolate, sugar, vanilla, and salt until completely smooth. Whisk in the egg yolks one at a time, mixing well after each addition, and then transfer the mixture to a large liquid measuring cup for easy pouring.

Divide the chocolate mixture evenly among four 4-ounce mason jars (or other sealable heatproof glass containers). Cap each container with a lid. Tighten each lid just enough to form a seal without exerting any pressure, "finger-tight."

Fill your sous vide water bath, then place the sealed jars in the bath, resting them on the bottom. Set the bath to 80°C (176°F).

Once the water has reached the target temperature (20 to 30 minutes), cook the custards for 1 hour.

Using tongs, carefully remove the jars from the water (watch out, as they're hot!). Transfer the jars to the fridge and allow the custards to cool until fully set, at least 3 hours.

To serve, using a bowl and a whisk, whip the remaining ½ cup cream until soft peaks form. Unscrew the tops and sprinkle each custard with a pinch of the sea salt and then top with a dollop of the whipped cream.

MEYER LEMON CURD

Despite the name, when it comes to curd, like all custards, you don't actually want it to curdle, and thus sous vide works like a charm. I love Meyer lemons for their complex, herbaceous flavor, but the great thing about this recipe is that any variety of citrus will work: lime, grapefruit, orange—whatever strikes your fancy. Note that different citrus fruits have different acidity and sugar levels, however, so you'll want to adjust the amount of sugar accordingly. Slather this on top of toast, fill a prebaked tart shell, or eat it straight out of the jar.

MAKES about 3 cups | **SOUS VIDE COOKING TIME:** 1 hour (or up to 1½ hours) | **ACTIVE PREP TIME:** 10 minutes, plus 10 minutes to cool and 2 hours to chill

1½ cups sugar

½ teaspoon kosher salt

3 tablespoons finely grated Meyer lemon zest (from about 4 lemons)

1 cup Meyer lemon juice (from about 4 lemons)

4 large eggs

2 large egg yolks

½ cup (4 ounces) unsalted butter, melted and cooled

DO-AHEAD STRATEGY

The cooked curd will keep in an airtight container in the refrigerator for up to 2 weeks.

Preheat your sous vide water bath to 83°C (181.4°F).

In a blender, combine the sugar, salt, and lemon zest and process until the mixture is a fine powder, about 1 minute. Add the lemon juice, eggs, egg yolks, and butter and process on low speed until the mixture is thoroughly blended.

Pour the mixture into a gallon-size freezer-safe ziplock bag and seal using the water displacement or table-edge method (see page 12). I recommend the latter method for recipes with a relatively large amount of liquid.

When the water reaches the target temperature, lower the bag of curd into the water bath (making sure the bag is fully submerged) and cook for 1 hour.

Remove the bag from the water bath and let the curd cool for 10 minutes at room temperature. At this point, the curd can be transferred to a container of your choice. Refrigerate for at least 2 hours to chill before using.

SPICED POACHED PEARS

This is my riff on traditional poached pears. Poaching the pears sous vide traps all of the heady spice aromas together with their liquid, so when you open the bag, you end up with a ready-to-roll luscious sauce to serve over ice cream, and the gentle cooking produces pears that are perfectly succulent, yet never mushy. It's my go-to elegant dessert when I'm cooking for a crowd because it can be easily doubled, cooked in advance, and reheated just before serving.

SERVES 4 | **SOUS VIDE COOKING TIME:** 30 minutes (or up to 1 hour) | **ACTIVE PREP TIME:** 10 minutes

3 tablespoons light brown sugar

2 tablespoons unsalted butter

1 tablespoon fresh lemon juice

1 tablespoon bourbon or dark rum

1 teaspoon peeled, grated fresh ginger, or pinch of ground ginger

Pinch of kosher salt

1 vanilla pod, split lengthwise and seeds scraped

1 star anise pod

2 ripe but firm pears, peeled, halved lengthwise, and cored

1 pint vanilla ice cream, homemade (page 213) or store-bought

1 tablespoon fresh tarragon leaves, for garnish (optional)

Preheat your sous vide water bath to 85°C (185°F).

In a small saucepan, combine the brown sugar, butter, lemon juice, bourbon, ginger, salt, and vanilla seeds (not the pod) and place over medium heat. Stir with a whisk until the butter has melted and the sauce is completely smooth. Add the star anise and vanilla pod and remove from the heat.

Place the pears in a gallon-size freezer-safe ziplock bag, pour in the sauce, and seal using the water displacement method (see page 12).

When the water reaches the target temperature, lower the bagged pears into the water bath (making sure the bag is fully submerged) and cook for 30 minutes.

Remove the bag from the water bath and transfer the pears and the cooking liquid to a bowl. Remove and discard the anise and vanilla pod. To cut the pears into a fan design, place them on a cutting board and then cut parallel slices lengthwise ¼ inch thick through the fat part of each pear half, leaving the stem end intact, then press gently to fan the slices apart.

To serve, scoop the ice cream into bowls, top with a fanned pear half, and drizzle the sauce over the top. Garnish with the tarragon, if using.

DO-AHEAD STRATEGY

The cooked pears can be refrigerated in the bag for up to 1 week (there's no need to cool down in an ice water bath). Reheat in a 60°C (140°F) water bath for 15 minutes before serving.

PRO TIP

If you have only rock-hard pears, don't fret. Just cook them longer, checking every 15 to 30 minutes, until they are tender.

PARSNIP CAKE

If you look closely, you'll recognize the glazed parsnips from the "Vegetables" chapter. Yep, that's right. Turns out that you can make your cake and eat it, too (without guilt!), knowing you're getting an extra serving of vegetables. This is essentially a carrot cake recipe with parsnips swapped in, but because raw parsnips, unlike carrots, would be too tough to put directly into the batter, I turn to sous vide to soften them up first. It's a fantastic approach to use whenever you're baking with other hard vegetables, such as pumpkin or sweet potato.

This cake is also egg free, and if you leave the butter and the honey out of the glazed parsnips recipe and choose to skip the frosting, it will even be vegan! In spite of that, this is not a recipe for a "healthy" parsnip cake: it's incredibly moist delicious, and it leaves absolutely nothing to be desired. My pumpkin spice–scented bitters will add a boost of flavor, but substituting vanilla extract is fine. Don't leave this one just for dessert: spoon the batter into muffin pans for scrumptious breakfast pastries (even sans frosting).

MAKES one 9-inch cake or 18 muffins | **SOUS VIDE COOKING TIME:** 1 hour, plus 15 minutes to cool (for parsnips) | **ACTIVE PREP TIME:** 45 minutes including baking time, plus 30 minutes to cool

Cooking spray, for greasing cake pan

BATTER

¾ cup coconut oil or canola or other mild vegetable oil

Glazed Parsnips (page 189), cooled in the bag

1 cup firmly packed light brown sugar

¼ cup granulated sugar

¼ cup maple syrup

1 teaspoon vanilla extract

1 teaspoon Pumpkin Spice Bitters (page 233) or vanilla extract

2 tablespoon finely grated orange zest (from about 1 large orange)

1¾ cups all-purpose flour

1 teaspoon baking powder

1 teaspoon baking soda

½ teaspoon salt

1 teaspoon ground cinnamon

¼ teaspoon ground ginger, or 1 tablespoon peeled, finely grated fresh ginger

¼ teaspoon freshly grated or ground nutmeg

FROSTING

8 ounces cream cheese, at room temperature

6 tablespoons unsalted butter, at room temperature

Pinch of kosher salt

1 teaspoon fresh lemon juice

1 cup confectioners' sugar

½ cup toasted unsweetened coconut flakes, for garnish (optional)

DO-AHEAD STRATEGY

If you want to make this recipe from start to finish, be sure to factor in at least 1 hour to cook the glazed parsnips in a 85°C (185°F) water bath and another 15 minutes to let them cool down before you add them to the batter (skip the final stove-top glazing step). Otherwise, the cooked parsnips can be refrigerated for up to 1 week. The frosted cake or muffins can be loosely wrapped with aluminum foil or plastic wrap and refrigerated for up to 5 days.

CONTINUED >

Preheat your oven to 350°F. Grease a 9-inch cake pan, or line 18 muffin cups with paper liners.

To make the batter, pour the oil into a food processor, followed by the cooked parsnips and their cooking liquid, brown sugar, granulated sugars, and maple syrup and pulse until the mixture is a coarse puree, with the largest pieces of parsnip no bigger than ¼ inch.

Transfer the mixture to a large bowl and whisk in the vanilla, bitters, orange zest, flour, baking powder, baking soda, salt, cinnamon, ginger, and nutmeg until fully incorporated.

If making a cake, pour the batter into the prepared cake pan, using a rubber spatula to get all of the batter. If making muffins, use a 2-ounce scoop to fill each prepared muffin cup. Place the cake pan or muffin pans on a sheet pan.

Bake until the top has set and browned and a skewer inserted into the center comes out clean, 20 to 25 minutes for the muffins and 35 to 40 minutes for the cake. Transfer to a rack and let cool in the pan until no longer warm to the touch, at least 30 minutes.

While the cake or muffins are cooling, make the frosting. In a bowl, combine the cream cheese, butter, salt, and lemon juice and mix with a wooden spoon or rubber spatula until the mixture is completely smooth. Sift in the confectioners' sugar, and beat vigorously until the mixture is smooth and fluffy, 2 to 3 minutes. At this point, you can place the frosting in a tightly sealed container and refrigerate it for up to 5 days before using.

When the cake has cooled, remove from the pan and place it on a serving plate. Using a butter knife or offset spatula, spread the frosting on the top and sides. Alternatively, remove the muffins from the pans and spread the frosting on top of each. Sprinkle with the toasted coconut, if using.

HASSLE-FREE VANILLA ICE CREAM

Making ice cream using a sous vide machine is a complete game changer. Not only do you get perfectly cooked custard without the risk of curdled yolks, it also takes almost no work to achieve: no tempering, no patient stirring over low, low heat, *nada*. Just drop the bag in the water and wait, and you'll have perfect results.

I can never get enough of homemade ice cream, so I'm including plenty of options in this chapter. Feel free to use this vanilla ice cream recipe as a blank canvas for all your ice cream–making endeavors. Vanilla does a great job of subtly enhancing the flavors of other complementary ingredients, but there are some instances where the flavors might clash. For this reason, I make vanilla an optional ingredient in the other ice cream recipes that follow. Other aromatic ingredients I like to use in lieu of vanilla are citrus zests; coffee beans; spices such as cardamom pods, ginger, cinnamon sticks, and coriander; and herbs such as mint, lemongrass, bay, basil, and thyme. Add these at your discretion when whipping up your own inspired creamy creations, and be sure to strain the custard to remove any coarse bits before pouring it into the ice cream machine.

You can also make any fruit-flavored ice cream by swapping out some of the milk for a juice or puree. Feeling boozy? Up to 2 tablespoons of nearly any alcoholic beverage can be stirred into the base after chilling. Some of my favorites are Cognac, *amaro*, Grand Marnier, amaretto, and crème de cassis. The only ingredient I wouldn't recommend you omit is the honey (or corn syrup), as it greatly improves the texture of ice cream because the glucose helps prevent the formation of larger ice crystals, resulting in a smoother end product.

MAKES about 1 quart | **SOUS VIDE COOKING TIME:** 1 hour (or up to 1½ hours) | **ACTIVE PREP TIME:** 10 minutes, plus at least 45 minutes to chill

6 large egg yolks

¾ cup sugar

1 tablespoon honey or light corn syrup

1 vanilla pod, split lengthwise and seeds scraped, or 1 teaspoon vanilla extract

Pinch of salt

1½ cups whole milk

1½ cups heavy cream

2 tablespoons bourbon

DO-AHEAD STRATEGY

The cooked base can be refrigerated for up to 1 week before freezing.

CONTINUED >

Preheat your sous vide water bath to 85°C (185°F).

In a large bowl, whisk together the egg yolks, sugar, honey, vanilla seeds (or extract), and salt until thoroughly combined. Whisk in the milk and cream, then add the vanilla pod, if using.

Pour this ice cream base into a gallon-size freezer-safe ziplock bag and seal using the water displacement or table-edge method (see page 12). I recommend the latter method for recipes with a relatively large amount of liquid.

When the water reaches the target temperature, lower the bagged ice cream base into the water bath (making sure the bag is fully submerged) and cook for 1 hour.

When the base is ready, transfer the bag to an ice water bath (see page 14) and chill for at least 45 minutes, or refrigerate the bag for at least 6 hours. Either way, the ice cream base must be fully chilled before freezing.

When ready to freeze, pass the ice cream base, which has now thickened to a custard, through a sieve and remove the vanilla pod (if used). Freeze the custard base in an ice cream machine according to the manufacturer's instructions or freeze without an ice cream machine as directed below.

Transfer the ice cream to an airtight freezer-safe container and place in the freezer. Because it lacks the stabilizers used in many commercial varieties, the texture of homemade ice cream is best if stored for no more than 1 week.

HOW TO FREEZE WITHOUT AN ICE CREAM MACHINE

I learned this hack from the formidable food scientist Harold McGee.

In a large container, mix together 1 pound salt and 3 quarts water, stirring until the salt dissolves. Split the brine equally between two new gallon-size ziplock bags. Lay the bags flat in the freezer and freeze overnight.

The next day, lay a kitchen towel on a countertop and sandwich the bag of chilled ice cream custard base between the bags of brine that spent overnight the freezer. (The brine will be below 32°F, but the salt will prevent the water from forming ice crystals.) Cover with additional kitchen towels to insulate. Leave the covered bags on the counter for about 30 minutes, at which point the ice cream base should be frozen. Be sure to save the bags of brine in the freezer for future sous vide ice cream adventures! If desired, transfer the ice cream to an airtight freezer-safe container for easier scooping.

CHOCOLATE ICE CREAM

If you've ever experienced a bad breakup, you already know that chocolate ice cream is essential. This recipe is a variation on my basic vanilla ice cream recipe, but here, along with adding cocoa powder, I've spiked it with a coffee-flavored liqueur, a synergistic combination that brings out the chocolaty notes. You might be surprised to see that I call for cocoa powder. The reason I don't use melted chocolate is that cocoa butter is waxy at freezer temperature, which would ruin the velvety texture of the finished ice cream—and that would break my heart.

MAKES about 1 quart | **SOUS VIDE COOKING TIME:** 1 hour (or up to 1½ hours) | **ACTIVE PREP TIME:** 10 minutes, plus at least 45 minutes to chill

6 large egg yolks

⅓ cup high-quality natural or Dutch-processed cocoa powder

¾ cup sugar

1 tablespoon honey or light corn syrup

1 vanilla pod, split lengthwise and seeds scraped, or 1 teaspoon vanilla extract (optional)

Pinch of salt

1½ cups whole milk

1½ cups heavy cream

1 tablespoon coffee-flavored liqueur (optional)

DO-AHEAD STRATEGY

The cooked base can be refrigerated for up to 1 week before freezing.

Preheat your sous vide water bath to 83°C (181.4°F).

In a large bowl, whisk together the egg yolks, cocoa powder, sugar, honey, vanilla seeds or extract (if using), and salt until thoroughly combined. Whisk in the milk and cream, then add the vanilla pod, if using.

Pour this ice cream base into a gallon-size freezer-safe ziplock bag and seal using the water displacement or table-edge method (see page 12). I recommend the latter method for recipes with a relatively large amount of liquid.

When the water reaches the target temperature, lower the bagged ice cream base into the water bath (making sure the bag is fully submerged) and cook for 1 hour.

When the base is ready, transfer the bag to an ice water bath (see page 14) and chill for at least 45 minutes, or refrigerate the bag for at least 6 hours. Either way, the ice cream base must be fully chilled before freezing.

When ready to freeze, add the liqueur (if using) and the pass the ice cream base, which has now thickened to a custard, through a sieve and remove the vanilla pod (if used). Freeze the custard base in an ice cream machine according to the manufacturer's instructions, or freeze without an ice cream machine as directed on page 214.

Transfer the ice cream to an airtight freezer-safe container and place in the freezer. Because it lacks the stabilizers used in many commercial varieties, the texture of homemade ice cream is best if stored for no more than 1 week.

SALTED CARAMEL ICE CREAM

Some cynics claim that salted caramel has jumped the shark—a victim of its own success. But when properly made, the perfectly balanced combination of sweet and salty is still one of my favorite indulgences. This recipe is a perfect way to show off your homemade *dulce de leche*, but high-quality store-bought caramel or butterscotch sauce will also give you great results. The key to this recipe is to add the salt immediately before the base is frozen so the salt crystals don't dissolve, giving you flecks of salt in the finished ice cream.

MAKES about 1 quart | **SOUS VIDE COOKING TIME:** 1 hour (or up to 1½ hours) | **ACTIVE PREP TIME:** 10 minutes, plus at least 45 minutes to chill

6 large egg yolks

⅔ cup Dulce de Leche (page 225) or store-bought caramel or butterscotch sauce

1 vanilla pod, split lengthwise and seeds scraped, or 1 teaspoon vanilla extract (optional)

1½ cups whole milk

1½ cups heavy cream

1 teaspoon flaky sea salt (such as Maldon or fleur de sel), plus more to taste

DO-AHEAD STRATEGY

The cooked base can be refrigerated for up to 1 week before freezing.

Preheat your sous vide water bath to 83°C (181.4°F).

In a large bowl, whisk together the egg yolks, Dulce de Leche, and vanilla seeds or extract (if using) until thoroughly combined. Whisk in the milk and cream and then add the vanilla pod, if using.

Pour this ice cream base into a gallon-size freezer-safe ziplock bag and seal using the water displacement or table-edge method (see page 12). I recommend the latter method for recipes with a relatively large amount of liquid.

When the water reaches the target temperature, lower the bagged ice cream base into the water bath (making sure the bag is fully submerged) and cook for 1 hour.

When the base is ready, transfer the bag to an ice water bath (see page 14) and chill for at least 45 minutes, or refrigerate for at least 6 hours. Either way, the ice cream base must be fully chilled before freezing.

When ready to freeze, pass the ice cream base, which has now thickened to a custard, through a sieve and remove the vanilla pod (if used). Stir in the sea salt. Freeze the custard base in an ice cream machine according to the manufacturer's instructions, or freeze without an ice cream machine as directed on page 214.

Transfer the ice cream to an airtight freezer-safe container and place in the freezer. Because it lacks the stabilizers used in many commercial varieties, the texture of homemade ice cream is best if stored for no more than 1 week.

NUT BUTTER ICE CREAM

I am nuts for this ice cream, which you can steer in several directions. If you're feeling like a kid, kick it old school and blend in peanut butter. This is an instance in which the smooth texture of processed creamy peanut butter (such as Skippy or Jif), will yield a better texture than natural creamy peanut butter, though the latter will work (as will other nut butters). For something more cosmopolitan, slip in some pistachio paste. Nutella also works great—hey, it's dessert after all.

MAKES about 1 quart | **SOUS VIDE COOKING TIME:** 1 hour (or up to 1½ hours) | **ACTIVE PREP TIME:** 10 minutes, plus at least 45 minutes to chill

6 large egg yolks

¾ cup sugar

1 tablespoon honey or light corn syrup

1 vanilla pod, split lengthwise and seeds scraped, or 1 teaspoon vanilla extract (optional)

Pinch of salt

1½ cups whole milk

1½ cups heavy cream

⅓ cup smooth nut butter, pistachio paste, or Nutella

1 tablespoon amaretto or other nut-flavored liqueur (optional)

DO-AHEAD STRATEGY

The cooked base can be refrigerated for up to 1 week before freezing.

Preheat your sous vide water bath to 83°C (181.4°F).

In a large bowl, whisk together the egg yolks, sugar, honey, and vanilla seeds or extract (if using), and salt until thoroughly combined. Whisk in the milk and cream. Add the nut butter and, using an immersion blender, blend until the mixture is smooth. Add the vanilla pod, if using.

Pour the ice cream base into a gallon-size freezer-safe ziplock bag and seal using the water displacement or table-edge method (see page 12). I recommend the latter method for recipes with a relatively large amount of liquid.

When the water reaches the target temperature, lower the bagged ice cream base into the water bath (making sure the bag is fully submerged) and cook for 1 hour.

When the base is ready, transfer the bag to an ice water bath (see page 14) for at least 45 minutes, or refrigerate at least 6 hours. Either way, the ice cream base must be fully chilled before freezing.

When ready to freeze, add the amaretto (if using) to the ice cream base and then pass the base, which has now thickened to a custard, through a sieve and remove the vanilla pod (if used). Freeze the custard base in an ice cream machine according to the manufacturer's instructions, or freeze without an ice cream machine as directed on page 214.

Transfer the ice cream to an airtight freezer-safe container and place in the freezer. Because it lacks the stabilizers used in many commercial varieties, the texture of homemade ice cream is best if stored for no more than 1 week.

CATCHALL FRUIT ICE CREAM

I love the flaming orange hue of this ice cream when it's made with apricot, but you can use this recipe as a blueprint for any fruit-flavored ice cream, and it even works with certain vegetables. Simply swap in nearly any juice, jam, puree, or even chopped fresh fruit of the season for the apricot jam. Peach jam, apple cider, applesauce, any kind of berry puree (or jam), roasted pear, celery or beet juice (this is actually good), and roasted pumpkin puree are all good choices. Citrus juice is an exception, as adding the full ¾ cup would cause the base to curdle. For citrus and other highly acidic ingredients, such as rhubarb and passion fruit, I recommend adding no more than 1½ tablespoons. The way around this (and an especially delicious solution) is to use up to ¾ cup citrus curd (like my Meyer Lemon Curd, see page 207), which won't break the custard.

MAKES about 1 quart | **SOUS VIDE COOKING TIME:** 1 hour (or up to 1½ hours) | **ACTIVE PREP TIME:** 10 minutes, plus at least 45 minutes to chill

---

6 large egg yolks

¾ cup sugar

1 tablespoon honey or light corn syrup

1 vanilla pod, split lengthwise and seeds scraped, or 1 teaspoon vanilla extract (optional)

Pinch of salt

¾ cup apricot puree, juice, or jam

1 tablespoon fresh lemon juice

¾ cup whole milk

1½ cups heavy cream

DO-AHEAD STRATEGY

The cooked base can be refrigerated for up to 1 week before freezing.

Preheat your sous vide water bath to 85°C (185°F).

In a large bowl, whisk together the egg yolks, sugar, honey, vanilla seeds or extract (if using), and salt until thoroughly combined. Whisk in the apricot puree and lemon juice until thoroughly blended, and then whisk in the milk and cream. Add the vanilla pod, if using.

Pour the ice cream base into a gallon-size freezer-safe ziplock bag and seal using the water displacement or table-edge method (see page 12). I recommend the latter method for recipes with a relatively large amount of liquid.

When the water reaches the target temperature, lower the bagged ice cream base into the water bath (making sure the bag is fully submerged) and cook for 1 hour.

When the base is ready, transfer the bag to an ice water bath (see page 14) and chill for at least 45 minutes, or refrigerate the bag for at least 6 hours. Either way, the ice cream base must be fully chilled before freezing.

When ready to freeze, pass the ice cream base, which has now thickened to a custard, through a sieve and remove the vanilla pod (if used). If you're using a coarse-textured jam and you'd like chunks of fruit in the ice cream, skip the sieving step and simply remove the vanilla pod (if used). Freeze the custard base in an ice cream machine according to the manufacturer's instructions, or freeze without an ice cream machine as directed on page 214.

Transfer the ice cream to an airtight freezer-safe container and place in the freezer. Because it lacks the stabilizers used in many commercial varieties, the texture of homemade ice cream is best if stored for no more than 1 week.

CINNAMON-APPLE ICE CREAM

Living in California, I don't get to enjoy fall's beautiful foliage or brisk weather anymore, but I still enjoy playing along with the seasons. Nothing says autumn like the flavors of cinnamon and apple, so I bring them together in this ice cream. It's delicious on its own or serve with homemade mulled cider and bitters as a sophisticated adult dessert, which I like to call an Appogato (page 222).

MAKES about 1 quart | **SOUS VIDE COOKING TIME:** 1 hour (or up to 1½ hours) | **ACTIVE PREP TIME:** 10 minutes, plus at least 45 minutes to chill

6 large egg yolks

¾ cup sugar

1 tablespoon honey or light corn syrup

1 vanilla pod, split lengthwise and seeds scraped, or 1 teaspoon vanilla extract (optional)

Pinch of salt (optional)

¾ cup apple butter or pureed applesauce

1½ cups heavy cream

¾ cup whole milk

2 (3-inch-long) cinnamon or cassia sticks, or ½ to 1 teaspoon ground cinnamon

DO-AHEAD STRATEGY

The cooked base can be refrigerated for up to 1 week before freezing

Preheat your sous vide water bath to 85°C (185°F).

In a large bowl, whisk together the egg yolks, sugar, honey, vanilla seeds or extract (if using), ground cinnamon, and salt until thoroughly combined. Whisk in the apple butter until well blended, then whisk in the cream and milk. Add the vanilla pod and cinnamon sticks (if using).

Pour this ice cream base into a gallon-size freezer-safe ziplock bag and seal using the water displacement or table-edge method (see page 12). I recommend the latter method for recipes with a relatively large amount of liquid.

When the water reaches the target temperature, lower the bagged ice cream base into the water bath (making sure the bag is fully submerged) and cook for 1 hour.

When the base is ready, transfer the bag to an ice water bath (see page 14) to chill for 45 minutes, or refrigerate the bag for at least 6 hours. Either way, the ice cream base must be fully chilled before freezing.

When ready to freeze, pass the custard through a sieve and remove the vanilla pod (if used) and the cinnamon sticks. Freeze the custard base in an ice cream machine according to the manufacturer's instructions, or freeze without an ice cream machine as directed on page 214.

Transfer the ice cream to an airtight freezer-safe container and place in the freezer. Because it lacks the stabilizers used in many commercial varieties, the texture of homemade ice cream is best if stored for no more than 1 week.

PRO TIP

Most people are surprised to learn that the spice they know as cinnamon is in fact cassia. Although both cinnamon and cassia are the bark of members of the Cinnamomum genus, cinnamon comes from the species C. verum, whereas cassia comes from C. cassia. I prefer true cinnamon (also called Mexican or Ceylon cinnamon) in fruit desserts, particularly those made with apple, because it has a softer, more floral aroma than the hotter, spicier cassia. Either will work here, but if you can find true cinnamon (commonly available at Latin markets, or see Resources, page 273), give it a try.

APPOGATO

This is my take on an *affogato*, a classic Italian dessert in which a shot of hot espresso is poured over vanilla ice cream (the term *affogato* appropriately means "drowned"). The effect is a delightful and ephemeral hot-cold combo. In this version, I double down on the apple, using both my sous vide–infused cider and my sous vide Cinnamon-Apple Ice Cream, and then I boost it with a little extra spice and bitterness (and caffeine!) from sous vide–infused Coffee-Cardamom Bitters. I think the Italians would approve.

SERVES 4 | **ACTIVE PREP TIME:** 20 minutes to reheat the mulled cider

1 pint Cinnamon-Apple Ice Cream (page 221)

Coffee-Cardamom Bitters (page 223)

2 cups Mulled Apple Cider (page 253), with or without brandy

Ground cinnamon, for serving

DO-AHEAD STRATEGY

To pull this dessert off on the fly, the components need to be made ahead of time. The ice cream and the bitters can made up to 1 week in advance. The mulled cider can be made either 45 minutes before you want to serve the dessert (since it's ready to use immediately after straining) or well in advance and reheated 20 minutes before serving.

If the mulled cider is not still hot, reheat the bagged cider in a water bath set to 70°C (158°F) for 20 minutes.

To serve, using an ice cream scoop, divide the ice cream evenly among four coffee cups or parfait glasses. Top each serving of ice cream with a dash or two (or more, if you like bitters!) of the bitters, if using. Pour ½ cup of the hot cider over each cup of ice cream, sprinkle with a little ground cinnamon, and serve immediately.

DULCE DE LECHE

Anyone who has made *dulce de leche* at home will probably leap to ask, "Why should I spend fifteen hours making it sous vide when I can make it in a few hours by sticking a can in a pot of boiling water on the stove or in even less than an hour in a pressure cooker?" The answer is twofold: First and foremost, cans of condensed milk should not be heated at all because they are lined with BPA, a chemical that can leach into the milk and is known to have a variety of harmful effects. Second, there's always a risk that the can will explode due to the heat. On a more delicious note, transferring the condensed milk to a new container allows us to add spices like vanilla or cinnamon while the milk caramelizes. That's reason enough for me!

Homemade *dulce de leche* is delicious straight outta the jar, but it's also incredible as a component of other desserts, such as the filling for Alfajores (page 226) or the flavoring for Salted Caramel Ice Cream (page 217). If you can't wait that long, simply warm it up and pour it over ice cream. Mmmm. Dulce-de-licious.

MAKES about 1½ cups | **SOUS VIDE COOKING TIME:** 15 hours | **ACTIVE PREP TIME:** 5 minutes, plus 20 minutes to cool

1 (14-ounce) can sweetened condensed milk

½ vanilla pod, split lengthwise and seeds scraped

1 (3-inch) cinnamon stick (optional)

Pinch of kosher salt

DO-AHEAD STRATEGY

The cooked sauce can be transferred to a mason jar or other airtight sealable container and refrigerated for up to 2 weeks. If serving warm, reheat the bags or jars in a 60°C (140°F) water bath until pourable, about 15 minutes.

Preheat your sous vide water bath to 85°C (185°F).

Place the condensed milk, vanilla seeds and pod, cinnamon (if using), and salt into a quart-size freezer-safe ziplock bag and seal using the water displacement or table-edge method (see page 12). I recommend the latter method for recipes with a relatively large amount of liquid.

When the water reaches the target temperature, lower the bagged milk into the water bath (making sure the bag is fully submerged) and cook for 15 hours.

When the milk is ready, it will have thickened and caramelized to a deep golden brown. Remove the bag from the water bath and let the contents cool for 20 minutes. Remove the vanilla pod and cinnamon stick (if used) from the bag.

If you do not plan to devour the sauce immediately, reseal it in the bag or transfer it to a mason jar or other airtight container and refrigerate for up to 1 month.

PRO TIP

Although the sauce can be cooked directly in mason jars (and looks awfully cute in them), I've found that it's easiest to cook it in ziplock bags because there's no worry about getting the proper seal or having the glass crack in the water bath.

ALFAJORES

Alfajores are a confection with centuries of history behind them. They first originated in Spain as a type of spiced honey-almond cookie, but have since spawned a panoply of widely divergent variations throughout Latin America. My favorite version of *alfajores* hails from Argentina, and that's the one I give you here. Filled with homemade *dulce de leche* and dusted with confectioners' sugar, these melt-in-your-mouth, citrus-scented cookies are a wonderful treat to have on hand. Of course, I can't promise that they'll last very long. Speaking of time, you'll need to plan ahead, as the *dulce de leche* called for needs to cook for 15 hours.

MAKES about 24 sandwich cookies | **ACTIVE PREP TIME:** 30 minutes to chill, 20 minutes to bake

¾ cup (6 ounces) unsalted butter, at room temperature

¾ cup granulated sugar

1 teaspoon kosher salt

2 large eggs

1 tablespoon fresh orange juice

1 tablespoon fresh lemon or lime juice

2 teaspoons finely grated orange zest

1 teaspoon finely grated lemon or lime zest

1 tablespoon rum (optional)

½ cup cornstarch

2½ cups all-purpose flour

1 teaspoon baking powder

Cooking spray, for greasing sheet pans

1½ cups Dulce de Leche (page 225), made with cinnamon, cold or at room temperature

2 tablespoons confectioners' sugar, for dusting

DO-AHEAD STRATEGY

As noted in the instructions, the unbaked dough can be kept in the fridge for up to 1 week, or portioned and frozen for up to 1 month. The finished *alfajores* can be stored in an airtight container for up to 3 days at room temperature or refrigerated for up to 1 week.

In a large bowl, combine the butter, granulated sugar, and salt and beat with a wooden spoon until smooth. Add the eggs one at a time, beating after each addition until incorporated. Mix in the orange and lemon juices and zests and the rum, if using.

Sift together the cornstarch, flour, and baking powder into a bowl. Add the flour mixture to the butter mixture and mix until well blended. Cover and refrigerate the dough for at least 30 minutes or for up to 1 week before baking.

Position two racks in the center of the oven and preheat the oven to 350°F. Lightly spray two sheet pans with cooking spray.

Using a tablespoon or a ½-ounce ice cream scoop, scoop the dough into small balls and drop onto the prepared sheet pans, spacing them at least 1 inch apart. You should have about 48 balls. Using the palm of your hand, flatten each ball into a ¼-inch-thick disk. At this point, the disks can be frozen on the trays for at least 2 hours and then transferred to an airtight container and kept in the freezer for up to 1 month before baking.

Bake the cookies, rotating the pans back to front after 8 minutes so they bake evenly, until golden brown on the bottom and very lightly browned on top, 15 to 20 minutes. Transfer the cookies to a wire rack and let cool completely, at least 10 minutes.

When you're ready to serve the *alfajores*, turn half of the cookies flat side up. Spoon a 2-teaspoon-size dollop of the *dulce de leche* onto each overturned cookie. Place the remaining cookies, flat side down, on top and press gently until the filling just peeks out at the edges. Transfer the filled cookies to a serving plate and lightly dust the tops with the confectioners' sugar.

COCKTAILS AND INFUSIONS

SOUS VIDE IS A GREAT TOOL FOR STEPPING UP YOUR GAME when it comes to home drinking (I mean that in terms of quality, not quantity). The fundamental reason for this is that ethyl alcohol boils at a much lower temperature than water. This means that when booze is heated, the bulk of the alcohol content will evaporate before the water even comes to a simmer—no good at all. The difficulty is that heat is important if you want to dissolve sugar quickly and infuse flavor. So if, for example, you'd like to make your own liqueur, you would typically have to do so at room temperature, which can take as long as a month. Because sous vide cooking is done in a sealed container, it is easy to reap the benefits of controlled infusion without the risk of cooking off precious alcohol.

After extensive research, I've crafted a pretty kick-ass collection of sous vide infusions (alcoholic and otherwise): next-level syrups, liqueurs, and bitters that will get you well on your way to a well-stocked bar (or help you nail your next Dark and Stormy). When it comes to choosing the right base alcohol to make these infusions, keep it simple. I don't recommend using the cheapest brands, as they can be harsh tasting. Select something midrange; for vodka, I wouldn't spend more than twenty or thirty dollars for a bottle. When it comes to the brown liquors—bourbon, whiskey, rye, and the like—the same rules apply. I advise against using jugs marked only XXX, but your bourbon doesn't have to be distilled by Kentucky virgins and aged for a hundred years. As for tequila, the main thing to look for is bottles that say "made from 100 percent blue agave," as opposed to "made with agave." The latter is typically grain alcohol with flavor added, to which I say no, gracias.

All of the alcohol infusions in this book are made at 60°C, which I think offers the best of both worlds: it's low enough to ensure a gentle infusion (avoiding cooked flavors or overextraction) but still speedy (for most, only an hour is required—lightning fast for

an infusion!), with the added bonus that the combination of temperature and time is sufficient to pasteurize the liquid, which is particularly valuable when infusing perishable ingredients like citrus juice.

Because the infusions are made at under 75°C, they can be safely made in glass bottles or mason jars without risk of the glass cracking. That means you can make them and store them in the same aesthetically pleasing container. You will just need to add 30 minutes to the cooking time to account for the lower conductivity of the glass container over the freezer bags. However, at higher temperatures, such as with the syrups at 85°C, the glass can shatter unless it has been heat treated. For this reason, I recommend that you use freezer bags to infuse your syrups. You can always transfer them to pretty bottles afterward.

You'll also find a collection of "sous-perior" cocktails that employ these boozy building blocks. Because mixologists tend to be a bit persnickety about this sort of thing, I want to be clear that these are my spins on the classics, rather than misfired attempts at faithful versions. Barflies desperately seeking Sazeracs will fall for my Big Easy Does It (page 250), a rye-based elixir spiked with sous vide Fennel Liqueur (page 249) and Pink Peppercorn and Hibiscus Bitters (page 232), while pumpkin spice fans (you know who you are) will light up over my Dark and Stormy (page 240) enlivened with a dash of Pumpkin Spice Bitters (page 233). And although the recipes give instructions for a single perfect cocktail, I'm not suggesting you drink alone. Nearly all of them can be doubled and will still fit into a standard-size cocktail shaker. If you want to make more than double, go ahead and mix multiple batches, just like a pro. The exception to this is the Piña Kayada (page 245), which won't fit into a shaker if doubled. If you want to make a big batch, just follow the blender instructions.

Okay, enough talk. Now let's get shaking.

Bitters are essential to any decent bar and indispensible in many classic cocktails. In fact, an Old-Fashioned (whiskey, sugar, and bitters) is known as such because adding sugar and bitters to a spirit was the original form that cocktails took—the archetype from which all others derive. In this light, the rising popularity of house-made bitters can be seen as an inevitable result of the craft cocktail revolution. More important, the precise temperature of sous vide cooking produces consistently excellent results in exponentially shorter times than the typical room-temperature infusion. This means that it has never been easier to make your own tinctures and concoctions. What follows is just a sample of some of my favorites, which you should look on as a springboard for limitless variation and exploration. So join in on the fun of making your own bespoke beverages and keep the bitterness confined to your glass.

PINK PEPPERCORN AND HIBISCUS BITTERS

Try this rosy-hued, peppery infusion in place of Peychaud's bitters in classic cocktails (as I do with the Big Easy Does It on page 250), or use it to help to regular lemonade slip into something pink.

MAKES ½ cup | **SOUS VIDE COOKING TIME:** 1 hour (or up to 2 hours) | **ACTIVE PREP TIME:** 10 minutes, plus 30 minutes to cool

¼ cup dried hibiscus flowers or hibiscus herbal tea (such as Red Zinger, about 4 bags cut open)

Zest of ½ lemon, removed in strips with a vegetable peeler, including some of the bitter white pith

Zest of ½ orange, removed in strips with a vegetable peeler, including some of the bitter white pith

1 tablespoon pink peppercorns

Pinch of saffron threads (optional)

1 tablespoon sugar

½ cup vodka

Preheat your sous vide water bath to 60°C (140°F).

Place all of the ingredients in a quart-size freezer-safe ziplock bag and seal using the water displacement or table-edge method (see page 12). I recommend the latter method for recipes with a relatively large amount of liquid.

When the water reaches the target temperature, lower the bag into the water bath and cook for 1 hour.

Remove the bag from the water bath and place on the countertop. Let cool to room temperature, about 30 minutes.

Strain the liquid through a fine-mesh sieve into a small bottle or jar to remove the spices (a bitters bottle with an eyedropper is great for this; the bottles can be purchased online). Cap tightly and store at room temperature out of direct sunlight for up to 6 months.

PUMPKIN SPICE BITTERS

Use this seasonally inspired infusion in place of Angostura bitters in classic cocktails (like the Dark and Stormy, page 240) or to boost your baked goods (like the Parsnip Cake, page 211). The chile is a quirky addition, but I think it's a great asset for flavor and color.

MAKES ½ cup | **SOUS VIDE COOKING TIME:** 1 hour (or up to 2 hours) | **ACTIVE PREP TIME:** 10 minutes, plus 30 minutes to cool

3-inch piece fresh ginger, thinly sliced

2 cinnamon sticks

1 guajillo or ancho chile, stemmed, seeded, and cut into ½-inch-wide strips

1 teaspoon whole allspice berries (about 20)

½ teaspoon whole cloves (about 12)

1 whole nutmeg, crushed with the flat of a heavy knife or the bottom of a pot

½ vanilla pod, split lengthwise and seeds scraped (optional)

1 tablespoon honey

½ cup bourbon or other whiskey

Preheat your sous vide water bath to 60°C (140°F).

Place all of the ingredients in a quart-size freezer-safe ziplock bag and seal using the water displacement or table-edge method (see page 12). I recommend the latter method for recipes with a relatively large amount of liquid.

When the water reaches the target temperature, lower the bag into the water bath and cook for 1 hour.

Remove the bag from the water bath and place on the countertop. Let cool to room temperature, about 30 minutes.

Strain the liquid through a fine-mesh sieve into a small bottle or jar to remove the spices (a bitters bottle with an eyedropper is great for this; the bottles can be purchased online). Cap tightly and store at room temperature out of direct sunlight for up to 6 months.

COFFEE–CARDAMOM BITTERS

Like the other two bitters recipes, this one is great as a component in a variety of cocktails. It's also the secret ingredient in my Appogato (page 222), where it adds a bittersweet, spicy depth. For those who are truly unfazed by bitterness, I recommend sipping it on its own as a digestive, like an Italian *amaro*.

MAKES ½ cup | **SOUS VIDE COOKING TIME:** 1 hour (or up to 2 hours) | **ACTIVE PREP TIME:** 10 minutes, plus 30 minutes to cool

¼ cup whole coffee beans (the darker the roast, the more bitter the end result)

1 teaspoon black peppercorns

6 green cardamom pods, lightly cracked

½ cup dark rum

2 tablespoons dark brown sugar

Preheat your sous vide water bath to 60°C (140°F).

Place all of the ingredients in a quart-size freezer-safe ziplock bag and seal using the water displacement or table-edge method (see page 12). I recommend the latter method for recipes with a relatively large amount of liquid.

When the water reaches the target temperature, lower the bag into the water bath and cook for 1 hour.

Remove the bag from the water bath and place on the countertop. Let cool to room temperature, about 30 minutes.

Strain the liquid through a fine-mesh sieve into a small bottle or jar to remove the spices (a bitters bottle with an eyedropper is great for this; the bottles can be purchased online). Cap tightly and store at room temperature out of direct sunlight for up to 6 months.

HOME-INFUSED GIN

Infusing vodka to taste like gin is yet another crafty way to incorporate sous vide into your bartending toolkit. Technically speaking, the result isn't gin because the aromatics are added before distillation when making true gin. That said, the flavor is practically indistinguishable from gin, and the aromatics come through especially bright and clear. What's more, you're able to customize the blend of spices and herbs (from allspice to bay leaf to cinnamon) to create something that reflects your personal preferences. Look on the following recipe as a guide that features some commonly used gin botanicals. Juniper is the only essential, as it's the defining characteristic of gin.

MAKES about 1 quart | **SOUS VIDE COOKING TIME:** 1 hour (or up to 2 hours) | **ACTIVE PREP TIME:** 10 minutes, plus at least 30 minutes to cool

4 cups vodka

¼ cup (1 ounce) juniper berries

1 tablespoon coriander seeds

1 teaspoon white or black peppercorns (black will darken the gin slightly)

1-inch piece fresh ginger, thinly sliced (about 1 tablespoon)

1 lemongrass stalk, dry outer leaves and tip removed, bruised with the back of a knife and cut into 2-inch lengths

5 green cardamom pods, lightly cracked

2 thyme sprigs

Zest of 1 lemon, removed in strips with a vegetable peeler, including as little of the bitter white pith as possible

Preheat your sous vide water bath to 60°C (140°F).

Place all of the ingredients in a gallon-size freezer-safe ziplock bag and seal using the water displacement or table-edge method (see page 12). I recommend the latter method for recipes with a relatively large amount of liquid.

When the water reaches the target temperature, lower the bag into the water bath and cook for 1 hour.

Remove the bag from the water bath and chill in an ice water bath (see page 14) for 30 minutes, in the freezer for 1 hour, or in the refrigerator for 2 hours.

Strain the liquid through a fine-mesh sieve into a bottle or mason jar to remove the spices. Like all of the infused spirits, this gin will keep indefinitely at room temperature. But if you want to be able to make a proper gin and tonic at the drop of a hat, it's best to keep the gin in the refrigerator or freezer.

HOMEMADE TONIC SYRUP

Although the idea of making your own tonic syrup might seem overly ambitious, if you're willing to go all out for the best G&T of your life, this homemade option will blow commercially prepared versions (think Canada Dry and Schweppes) out of the water. The hardest part of this recipe is procuring cinchona bark, which is what makes tonic, tonic. Although it's not a readily available ingredient, it can be found in specialty stores or ordered online (see Resources, page 273).

MAKES 1½ cups | **SOUS VIDE COOKING TIME:** 1 hour (or up to 2 hours) | **ACTIVE PREP TIME:** 10 minutes, plus at least 30 minutes to cool

2 cups sugar

2 cups water

½ cup (2 ounces) cinchona bark

Zest of 1 grapefruit, removed in strips with a vegetable peeler, including some of the bitter white pith

1 tablespoon dried lavender (optional)

1 teaspoon citric acid powder, or ¼ cup fresh lemon juice

Preheat your sous vide water bath to 60°C (140°F).

Place all of the ingredients in a freezer-safe gallon-size ziplock bag and seal using the water displacement or table-edge method (see page 12). I recommend the latter method for recipes with a relatively large amount of liquid.

When the water reaches the target temperature, lower the bag into the water bath and cook for 1 hour.

Remove the bag from the water bath and chill in an ice water bath (see page 14) for 30 minutes, in the freezer for 1 hour, or in the refrigerator for 2 hours.

Strain the liquid through a fine-mesh sieve into a bottle or mason jar to remove the spices. The syrup can be refrigerated for up to 2 weeks or frozen for up to 2 months.

TYPE A G&T

I was introduced to the idea of creating a bespoke sous vide gin and tonic from my friend Eamon Rockey, the cocktail whiz behind Betony, a Michelin-starred restaurant in Manhattan. This version lets you micromanage every aspect of the drink, down to a home-infused gin and from-scratch tonic syrup. For those who don't want to go the extra mile to make their own tonic, store-bought will work just fine; just use 6 ounces to replace the syrup and soda. Be sure to have all of the ingredients at refrigerator temperature to avoid diluting the cocktail once the ice is added.

MAKES 1 cocktail

2 ounces Home-Infused Gin (page 234)

1 ounce Homemade Tonic Syrup (page 235)

5 ounces soda water

1 lime wedge

1 Thai basil leaf, for garnish (optional)

3 to 4 juniper berries, for garnish (optional)

Fill a Tom Collins glass with ice cubes and pour in the gin and the tonic syrup. Top with the soda water, and give the drink a stir with a bar spoon or straw to combine the ingredients. Squeeze the lime wedge into the drink and then drop it into the glass. (I prefer this to the usual custom of resting the wedge on the rim, to be squeezed by the guest. This way there's less mess for the person enjoying the drink.) Garnish with the Thai basil and juniper berries, if using.

HOMEMADE GINGER SYRUP

Ginger syrup has become an essential tool in the mixologist's arsenal, and this recipe can hang with the best of them: biting and spicy and with an intense ginger flavor. Sous vide improves the results by allowing the syrup to cook without evaporation, which lets you maintain the ratio of liquid to sugar (important for making consistent syrups) and prevents the loss of aromatics into the air, producing a more pronounced flavor. If you're a ginger lover like me, substitute this anywhere you might use honey or simple syrup.

MAKES 1½ cups | **SOUS VIDE COOKING TIME:** 30 minutes (or up to 1 hour) | **ACTIVE PREP TIME:** 5 minutes, plus at least 10 minutes to cool

4 ounces fresh ginger (about four 3-inch pieces), sliced ⅛ inch thick (about 1 cup)

1 cup coarse sugar (such as turbinado or Demerara), or ½ cup each granulated sugar and lightly packed light brown sugar

1 cup water

Preheat your sous vide water bath to 85°C (185°F).

Place all of the ingredients in a gallon-size freezer-safe ziplock bag and seal using the water displacement or table-edge method (see page 12). I recommend the latter method for recipes with a relatively large amount of liquid.

When the water reaches the target temperature, lower the bag into the water bath and cook for 30 minutes.

Remove the bag from the water bath and chill in an ice water bath (see page 15) for 10 minutes, in the freezer for 30 minutes, or in the refrigerator for 1 hour.

Pour the liquid and ginger pieces into a blender and process until a smooth puree forms. Strain through a fine-mesh sieve into a bottle or mason jar, pressing against the solids with the back of a spoon or ladle to extract as much liquid from the pulp as possible. The syrup can be stored in the refrigerator for up to 2 weeks or in the freezer for up to 2 months.

DARK AND STORMY

This recipe calls for a dark rum with a molasses-forward taste. Gosling's Black Seal rum is the traditional choice for this classic cocktail, and Myers's dark rum will work, but Cruzan Black Strap rum is my preference. I like to use soda water along with my own ginger syrup in place of the usual ginger beer for a nice boost in both fresh ginger flavor and effervescence, and my Pumpkin Spice Bitters add a splash of color and spicy depth of flavor to finish the drink.

MAKES 1 cocktail

2 ounces dark rum

1 ounce Homemade Ginger Syrup (page 239)

¾ ounce fresh lime juice

2 ounces soda water

2 dashes (about ½ teaspoon) of Pumpkin Spice Bitters (page 233; optional)

1 mint sprig, for garnish (optional)

Combine the rum, ginger syrup, and lime juice in a cocktail shaker, fill with ice, cover, and shake until cold (about 10 seconds of vigorous shaking). Strain into a Tom Collins glass filled with ice, then top with the soda water followed by the bitters, if using. Slap the mint sprig (if using) against the palm of your hand to release the aroma and then slide the stem into the drink, leaving the leaves sticking out.

PENICILLIN

The Penicillin is a relatively recent invention, created by Sam Ross of Milk & Honey, a New York City cocktail bar, but it has since spread to all corners of the bar-osphere and is now rightfully considered a modern classic. Once you taste its surprising combination of smoky, spicy, and bright flavors, you'll see why. It's the perfect excuse for whipping up a batch of ginger syrup. I call for two types of Scotch for this recipe, and it's not because I'm indecisive. Setting aside their technical differences, the main functional distinction between them is taste: the most notable feature of blended Scotches is their smoothness, whereas Islay Scotches are smoky. By combining the two in this drink, you capture the best of both aspects.

MAKES 1 cocktail

2 ounces blended Scotch whisky

¾ ounce Homemade Ginger Syrup (page 239)

¾ ounce fresh lemon juice

½ ounce Islay Scotch whisky

2 pieces candied ginger, threaded onto a cocktail skewer (optional)

Combine the blended Scotch, ginger syrup, and lemon juice in a cocktail shaker, fill with ice, and shake until cold (about 10 seconds of vigorous shaking). Strain into an Old-Fashioned glass filled with ice, gently pour the Islay Scotch on top, place the candied ginger (if using) on the rim, and cure what ails ye. I promise, you'll feel better right quick.

PANDAN-INFUSED CREAM OF COCONUT

Before I dive in, let me clarify some terms to save you from going coconuts. Cream of coconut is essentially a coconut-flavored syrup, not to be confused with coconut cream or coconut water. If you've ever enjoyed a piña colada, chances are it was made with Coco López, the cream of coconut used as the basis for the Puerto Rican original. By making it from scratch with unsweetened coconut milk, not only do you maximize freshness and control the amount of added sugar, but you also get the chance to infuse it with additional flavor in the form of *pandan*, a type of tropical grass. Owing to its appealing sweet smell (akin to that of jasmine or basmati rice), *pandan* is widely used in Southeast Asian cuisines to flavor sweets such as *kaya*, a coconut jam popular in Malaysia and Indonesia, which was my inspiration here.

MAKES 1½ cups | **SOUS VIDE COOKING TIME:** 30 minutes (or up to 1 hour) | **ACTIVE PREP TIME:** 5 minutes, plus at least 10 minutes to cool

10 pandan leaves, cut into 2-inch lengths (about 2 ounces or 1 cup, loosely packed)

1½ cups canned coconut milk, shaken in unopened can before measuring (1 can plus enough water to total 1½ cups)

½ cup sugar

¼ cup honey

2 drops of pandan extract (optional)

Preheat your sous vide water bath to 85°C (185°F).

Combine all of the ingredients in a gallon-size freezer-safe ziplock bag and seal using the water displacement or table-edge method (see page 12). I recommend the latter method for recipes with a relatively large amount of liquid.

When the water reaches the target temperature, lower the bag into the water bath and cook for 30 minutes.

Remove the bag from the water bath and chill in an ice water bath (see page 14) for 10 minutes, in the freezer for 30 minutes, or in the refrigerator for 1 hour. Pass the liquid through a fine-mesh sieve into a bottle or mason jar to remove the *pandan* leaves. The cream of coconut can be stored in the refrigerator for up to 1 week or in the freezer for up to 1 month.

PRO TIP

Pandan *extract and* pandan *leaves are widely available in Southeast Asian grocery stores (the latter is usually sold frozen, which is perfectly acceptable). You can also find both online (see Resources, page 273).*

PIÑA KAYADA

If you like piña coladas, but are leery of getting caught in the rain, whip up a batch of this iconic cocktail (no beach required). I breathe new life into this hit from the '80s by using my *pandan*-infused cream of coconut, a decidedly twenty first-century touch. I also add a splash of lime juice, which makes for a more balanced drink. You can whip this up in a blender to make a big batch, but I've included amounts for a single serving in brackets, which can be made like a shaken cocktail. So put on some salsa music and blend (or shake) to the beat.

MAKES 4 to 6 cocktails

2 cups (4 ounces) pineapple juice, nectar, or puree, homemade (see Pro Tip) or store-bought

¾ cup (1½ ounces) Pandan-Infused Cream of Coconut

¾ cup (1½ ounces) white rum

¼ cup (½ ounce) fresh lime juice

About 3 cups crushed ice, if blending

1 pineapple chunk and knotted pandan leaf per cocktail, each speared on a cocktail skewer (optional)

If you're making a pitcher's worth, combine all of the ingredients, except the pineapple chunk and pandan leaf, in a blender and mix on high speed until the ice is incorporated. Pour into chilled glasses.

If shaking a single-serving cocktail, combine all of the ingredients in a cocktail shaker, fill with ice, and shake until cold (about 10 seconds of vigorous shaking). Strain into a chilled glass (or hollowed-out pineapple) and add the garnish, if using. Imagine an island breeze, and enjoy.

PRO TIP

To make your own pineapple juice, purchase already peeled and cored fresh pineapple (or peel and core your own) and then puree in a blender and strain through a fine-mesh sieve.

GRAPEFRUIT AND EARL GREY TEQUILA

It's common knowledge that citrus is a great match for tequila, but grapefruit, in particular, really shines, bringing out the grassy and floral notes found in good tequila. When I found out that the bergamot used to flavor Earl Grey tea is packed with the same aromatic compounds that give grapefruit its signature taste, I felt like I was really on to something. The resulting elixir is basically a fancified margarita mix (only much, much better), with the triple sec and tequila already added in. If, like me, you love smoky, earthy flavors, use any good-quality mezcal.

MAKES about 1 quart | **SOUS VIDE COOKING TIME:** 1 hour (or up to 2 hours) | **ACTIVE PREP TIME:** 10 minutes, plus at least 30 minutes to cool

1 quart blanco tequila or mezcal

Zest of 1 grapefruit, removed in strips with a vegetable peeler, including as little of the bitter white pith as possible

¾ cup grapefruit juice (from about 1 large grapefruit)

Zest of 1 orange, removed in strips with a vegetable peeler, including as little of the bitter white pith as possible

¼ cup fresh orange juice (from about 1 orange)

⅔ cup light agave syrup, or 1 cup sugar

1 tablespoon loose-leaf Earl Grey tea

Preheat your sous vide water bath to 60°C (140°F).

Place all of the ingredients in a gallon-size freezer-safe ziplock bag and seal using the water displacement or table-edge method (see page 12).

When the water reaches the target temperature, lower the bag into the water bath and cook for 1 hour.

Remove the bag from the water bath and chill in an ice water bath (see page 14) for 30 minutes, in the freezer for 1 hour, or in the refrigerator for 2 hours. Pass the liquid through a fine-mesh sieve into a bottle or mason jar to remove the zest and tea leaves. The liqueur can be stored in the refrigerator for up to 2 weeks or in the freezer indefinitely.

GRAPEFRUIT AND EARL GREY MARGARITA

As already noted, my sweetened and infused tequila works basically like a premade margarita mix: just add a little fresh lime juice and you've got a fiesta. This fortuitously delicious combination of oh-so-proper Earl Grey tea and tequila (a famously, let us say, *unruly* quaff) is something I imagine would have limbered up even the Iron Lady (aka Margaret Thatcher). For that reason, I like to think of this drink as Rowdy Margaret. (Marga…rita. Rowdy…Margaret…get it?)

MAKES 1 cocktail

Kosher salt, for salting the glass rim (optional)

3 ounces Grapefruit and Earl Grey Tequila (opposite)

¾ ounce fresh lime juice

1 strip grapefruit zest, removed using a vegetable peeler

Chill a martini glass or cocktail coupe. To salt the rim of the glass, spread a layer of salt onto a small plate or in a small, shallow bowl. Dampen the rim of the chilled glass with a dab of water or lime juice, then dip the glass into the plate of salt.

Combine the tequila and lime juice in a cocktail shaker. Fill with ice, shake until cold (about 10 seconds of vigorous shaking), and then carefully strain into the salt-rimmed glass. Garnish with the grapefruit zest.

FENNEL LIQUEUR

This is my take on a homemade anisette (popular examples of this type of liqueur include pastis, Pernod, Herbsaint, and Sambuca), and it has a wonderfully fresh, herbaceous, anisey taste that, I acknowledge, is a flavor people tend to either love or hate. I happen to fall on the love end of the spectrum, but either way, you should view this recipe as a template to make an herbal liqueur with herbs of your choosing. Anything from lemon balm to basil will work, but for stronger-flavored, woody herbs like rosemary and lavender, be aware that you'll have to scale back the quantities dramatically (2 to 3 rosemary sprigs would be sufficient for this recipe). The seeds are optional, but they will add a greater depth of flavor.

MAKES about 1 quart | **SOUS VIDE COOKING TIME:** 1 hour (or up to 2 hours) | **ACTIVE PREP TIME:** 10 minutes, plus at least 30 minutes to cool

4 cups vodka

1 cup loosely packed fresh fennel fronds (no thick stalks; from about 1 fennel bulb), fennel flowers, or tarragon leaves, or a mixture

1 cup sugar

2 teaspoons aniseeds, or 1 tablespoon fennel seeds (optional)

Preheat your sous vide water bath to 60°C (140°F).

Place all of the ingredients in a gallon-size freezer-safe ziplock bag and seal using the water displacement or table-edge method (see page 12). I recommend the latter method for recipes with a relatively large amount of liquid.

When the water reaches the target temperature, lower the bag into the water bath and cook for 1 hour.

Remove the bag from the water bath and chill in an ice water bath (see page 14) for 30 minutes, in the freezer for 1 hour, or in the refrigerator for 2 hours. Pass the liquid through a fine-mesh sieve into a bottle or mason jar to remove the herbs and seeds. The liqueur can be stored at room temperature, out of direct sunlight, for up to 2 months or in the freezer indefinitely.

A LI'L LESSON ON LIQUEURS

The liqueur recipes in this chapter are a fusion of the methods I use for making sous vide syrups and infused alcohols, offering a sort of two-for-one: dissolving the sugar and gently infusing flavor. Traditional homemade liqueurs, which are infused at room temperature, can take weeks to make, and during that time musty or vinegary flavors can develop, especially when using fresh herbs or fruit. In contrast, sous vide not only extracts clean, pure flavor, it also pasteurizes and delays spoilage. It's a clear win.

BIG EASY DOES IT

The Sazerac is one of the oldest cocktails around, an enduring classic that originated in New Orleans in the so-called Golden Age of Cocktails (between 1860 and Prohibition) and has since become so iconic that it serves as a symbol for the Big Easy itself.

Admittedly, this is not a traditional Sazerac, and although hard-line aficionados might be scandalized, it's a safe bet that anyone who loves the classic will enjoy this fresh-faced version. It works well with any brown liquor: rye whiskey, Cognac, or bourbon. If you're not using my recipe for fennel-flavored liqueur, it's okay to substitute a store-bought anisette or absinthe. You may need to adjust the quantity, however, as sweetness levels and intensity will vary. Likewise, Peychaud's bitters can be used in lieu of my homemade bitters.

MAKES 1 cocktail

2½ ounces rye whiskey, Cognac, or bourbon

½ ounce Fennel Liqueur (page 249)

3 dashes (about ¾ teaspoon) of Pink Peppercorn and Hibiscus Bitters (page 232)

1 strip lemon zest removed using a vegetable peeler

1 fennel frond (optional)

Pour the rye, liqueur, and bitters into a mixing glass (or the bottom half of a cocktail shaker). Fill the glass with ice cubes and stir with a bar spoon or straw until the mixture is very cold and the edges of the ice cubes have melted, about 30 seconds.

Strain the mixture into a chilled Old-Fashioned glass. With the yellow facing down, squeeze the lemon zest strip a few inches above the drink to release its essential oils, then discard. (This is the traditional way to finish a Sazerac, as you want only the aroma from zest and none of the bitterness.)

Garnish with the fennel frond, if desired, and let the good times roll.

MULLED APPLE CIDER

Because 70°C is a good serving temperature for a hot drink but is below the boiling point of alcohol, it's the perfect temperature at which to infuse and serve boozy wintery drinks like mulled wine and spiced cider. (This same recipe would work with red wine swapped in for the cider.) For that reason, once you've strained out the spices (to prevent overextraction and bitterness), the cider can be returned to the bag (or transferred to sealable heat-safe mason jar or bottle) and kept in the water bath at 70°C practically indefinitely without degrading, which makes it great for holiday gatherings or for a bitterly cold night alone. It's critical that you use whole spices to infuse the cider, as ground ones would create an undesirable gritty mouthfeel.

SERVES 4 | **SOUS VIDE COOKING TIME:** 45 minutes (or up to 1½ hours) | **ACTIVE PREP TIME:** 5 minutes

4 cups apple cider or apple juice

½ cup apple brandy (such as applejack or Calvados), (optional)

2 tablespoons dark brown sugar

1 whole nutmeg, crushed with the flat of a heavy knife or a pot bottom

15 whole cloves (about ½ teaspoon)

3 (3-inch-long) cinnamon sticks

Zest of 1 orange, removed in strips with a vegetable peeler, including as little of the bitter white pith as possible

2 star anise pods

Preheat your sous vide water bath to 70°C (158°F).

Place all of the ingredients in a gallon-size freezer-safe ziplock bag and seal using the water displacement or table-edge method (page 11). I recommend the latter method for recipes with a relatively large amount of liquid.

When the water reaches the target temperature, lower the bagged cider ingredients into the water bath and cook for 45 minutes.

Remove the bag from the water bath. Strain the cider through a fine-mesh sieve into a heatproof pitcher or a large liquid measuring cup to remove the spices.

The hot cider is now ready to drink or to pour over ice cream in the Appogato (page 222). The strained cider can also be cooled and stored in the same bag or a tightly capped mason jar. It will keep in the refrigerator for up to 2 weeks or in the freezer for up to 2 months.

If you've cooled the cider, reheat in a 70°C (158°F) water bath for 20 minutes. If you don't include the brandy, it can be heated on the stove top. I don't recommend stove-top heating for the boozy version, however, because if the cider reaches too high a temperature, the alcohol will burn off, defeating the whole purpose!

PRO TIP

As with all of my beverage infusions, this recipe should be seen as a guide rather than a canonical formula. If you have a blend of spices you like for mulling, go ahead and swap it in.

BASICS, SAUCES, AND CONDIMENTS

I LOVE BEAVERING AWAY IN THE KITCHEN TO PREPARE ELABORATE MEALS, but some days, it's all I can do to get dinner on the table. The do-ahead strategies I've included in every recipe are designed to help in that regard, but sometimes it's nice to just be able to pull out a little something that will transform an everyday meal into a great one. That's why I always have an arsenal of sauces, condiments, and other basics in my fridge that can be called upon at a moment's notice to enliven a simply cooked chicken breast or to slather on top of a burger. There's no shame in using premade versions of these basics for the recipes in this book (and for that reason I call for either homemade or store-bought), but when you have a little extra time in the kitchen, why not try making them yourself? Like many other sous vide dishes, they're easier to pull off than you may think.

The following recipes are what I consider the building blocks of a well-stocked pantry (but for safety's sake, please store them in the fridge!), and are the ones called for over and over again in this collection of recipes. Think of them as the secret sauce for a great meal.

You will likely be surprised to find sous vide instructions for some of these preparations. Stocks, pickles, sauces, and even yogurt are actually easier to make in a water bath than by conventional methods, and the final results are often superior. Once you try cooking my marinara sauce (page 263) or my cranberry sauce (page 269) in a bag, you'll never go back to the splattered stove-top method again.

The precise temperature control of sous vide not only helps produce great-tasting results, it also improves the quality and safety of certain foods, a real boon when preparing make-ahead pantry items. My version of Garlic Confit (page 265), for instance, drastically reduces the risk of botulism, thus extending its shelf life, and my mayonnaise (page 262) deploys pasteurized eggs in lieu of raw ones. In both cases, you end up with delicious condiments that are a big step above store-bought and that can be enjoyed worry free.

My hope is that by sharing these recipes with you, and by pulling back the veil to give you a glimpse into the way *I* incorporate sous vide into my cooking repertoire, you'll be inspired to make it part of *yours.*

QUICK PICKLES

If you're a fan of pickling vegetables, you'll be an instant convert to my faster and less messy technique. Precisely heating the vegetables with the pickling liquid dissolves the salt and sugar and simultaneously gives you total control over the final texture of the pickles. Next, because you use a bag rather than a jar, it's much easier to immerse the vegetables and you use less liquid. Benefits all around! If you really like the twee look of pickles lined up in mason jars, feel free to transfer them after they're done.

The flavor of these pickles is sweet, sour, and salty, somewhere between bread and butter pickles and kosher dill pickles. I like them as an all-purpose sandwich (and snacking) pickle—with my pastrami (page 165), for example—but you should feel to adjust the salt, sugar, and spices to your taste. The procedure will be the same.

MAKES about 1 quart | **SOUS VIDE COOKING TIME:** 5 minutes (or up to 10 minutes) | **ACTIVE PREP TIME:** 10 minutes, plus 30 minutes to cool

1 cup cider, rice, or white wine vinegar

¼ cup sugar

4 teaspoons kosher salt

1 teaspoon black or white peppercorns, or a mixture

½ teaspoon coriander seeds

3 dill sprigs

1 clove garlic, lightly crushed

Pinch of red pepper flakes

1 English or 4 Persian cucumbers, cut on the diagonal into ¼-inch-thick slices (about 4 cups)

DO-AHEAD STRATEGY

Once cooled, the pickles can be refrigerated for up to 3 weeks, either stored in the bag or transferred to mason jars. If you're using jars, make sure the vegetables are covered by the pickling liquid; you may need to top them with a small weight (such as a saucer) to keep them submerged. The pickles will become gradually become more sour over time.

Preheat your sous vide water bath to 80°C (176°F).

In a bowl or a large liquid measuring cup, combine the vinegar, sugar, salt, and peppercorns and stir to mix.

Place the coriander, dill, garlic, red pepper flakes, and cucumber slices in a gallon-size freezer-safe ziplock bag and pour in the pickling liquid. Seal using the water displacement or table-edge method (see page 12). I recommend the latter method for recipes with a relatively large amount of liquid.

When the water reaches the target temperature, lower the bagged cucumbers into the water bath and cook for 5 minutes.

Remove the bag from the water bath and set aside to cool for at least 30 minutes. The pickles are ready to eat as soon as they've cooled.

PRO TIP

You can use this recipe as a blueprint for pickling other types of vegetables, though they may need to be cooked for a longer period of time. For tender vegetables such as radishes and onions, the cooking time will be the same. For sturdier vegetables like beets and carrots, the process will take at least 30 minutes. In any case, make sure you cut your vegetables no thicker than ¼ inch so that they can properly absorb the pickling liquid.

FOOLPROOF HOMEMADE YOGURT

Despite what the hundreds of products lining the supermarket dairy shelves might suggest, making your own yogurt is dead simple. You'll need to start with yogurt with live active cultures, so check the label to be sure. If you made the yogurt yourself, it definitely contains live cultures, and all you need to do is to save at least ¼ cup of it for making your next batch. Typical yogurt recipes call for scalding milk on the stove top to change the structure of its proteins, which is what allows the milk to thicken once it has been cultured. But using the stove requires vigilant pot watching to avoid risking scorched milk or a rubbery skin. Sous vide gets the same results effortlessly.

How long you sous vide the yogurt is a matter of preference. The longer the time period, the thicker and more sour the yogurt will be. The yogurt will be done at the 4-hour mark (it will thicken somewhat as it cools), but for a thicker, tangier yogurt, leave it in the water bath for up to 8 hours. This recipe can also be halved or doubled with no adjustment in time. Once you have a steady supply of fresh yogurt, the possibilities are endless: use it to make the dressing for the carrot salad on page 177, to create kick-ass breakfast parfaits, or to mix up a mango lassi.

MAKES about 1 quart | **SOUS VIDE COOKING TIME:** 5 to 10 hours, depending on your taste preference | **ACTIVE PREP TIME:** 5 minutes, plus 3½ hours to cool

4 cups whole milk

2 tablespoons nonfat milk powder (optional)

¼ cup whole-milk plain yogurt with live active cultures, store-bought or from a previous batch you've made

DO-AHEAD STRATEGY

The yogurt can be stored in the refrigerator for up to 2 weeks.

Preheat your sous vide water bath to 85°C (185°F).

Combine the milk and milk powder, if using, in a gallon-size freezer-safe ziplock bag and seal using the water displacement or table-edge method (see page 12). I recommend the latter method for recipes with a relatively large amount of liquid.

When the water reaches the target temperature, lower the bagged milk into the water bath (making sure the bag is fully submerged) and cook for 1 hour.

Remove the bag from the water bath and set aside until warm but not hot to the touch, about 30 minutes. (If you want to be precise, a thermometer should register 110°F to 120°F, but as long as it's cool enough to touch, it will be fine.) While the milk is cooling, lower the temperature of the water bath to 46°C (114.8°F).

Once the milk has cooled, add the yogurt, mix well to combine thoroughly, and then reseal using the water displacement or table-edge method. (You can mix in the yogurt by either whisking it into the milk in the bag, or by adding it to the bag, resealing the bag, and then massaging the contents to distribute the yogurt evenly.)

Once the water reaches the new target temperature, lower the bag back into the water bath and leave it in the water bath to culture for 4 hours or up to 9 hours, according to your taste preference.

Remove the bag from the water bath and refrigerate for at least 3 hours, until cold, before using. If desired, pour or spoon (depending on thickness) the finished yogurt into mason jars or an airtight container for storage.

RISK-FREE MAYONNAISE

When it comes to flavor, homemade mayonnaise beats the pants off store-bought. But few folks outside of culinary school bother to make it for two main reasons: concerns about eating raw eggs and fear of eternal whisking. Happily, sous vide vanquishes both of those obstacles with ease. This recipe relies on a blender and a pasteurized egg to do the heavy lifting. As is the case in my sous vide–assisted hollandaise (see page 26), the solution lies in using a whole egg. By pasteurizing the egg at 57°C for 2 hours, you end up with an egg that's safe to eat, but can be used just like a raw egg. The addition of the extra liquid and volume provided by the egg white makes emulsifying the mayo in a blender a snap. If you don't have a blender, you can make this by hand by whisking it in a bowl, but it won't end up quite as thick. Slather this mayo on your favorite sandwiches or use it to make the tartar sauce for Beer-Battered Fish and Chips (page 59).

MAKES about 1½ cups | **ACTIVE PREP TIME:** Less than 5 minutes

1 "Raw" Pasteurized Egg (page 22)

2 teaspoons Dijon mustard

1 tablespoon fresh lemon juice or cider vinegar

½ teaspoon salt

1½ cups canola or other mild vegetable oil

Following the directions on page 22, crack the egg into a blender or food processor and add the mustard, lemon juice, and salt. Blend on low speed until completely smooth. With the motor running, slowly pour in the oil, at first only few drops at a time, then in a thin stream as the mixture begins to thicken, until all of the oil is incorporated; at this point, you've got mayo. Transfer to an airtight container and refrigerate.

DO-AHEAD STRATEGY

The finished mayo can be refrigerated for up to 2 weeks.

QUICK-COOK MARINARA SAUCE

Sous vide is a fast, easy way to make a delicious, tangy marinara. This quick-cooking method takes the raw edge off of the garlic while still imparting its aroma, and leaves the bright flavors of barely cooked tomato intact. The added benefit, of course, is no messy pot or stove top spattered with red sauce to clean up afterward. Marinara, unlike long-cooked tomato sauce, or *sugo*, is meant to be light bodied; if you want a thicker sauce, transfer the marinara to a saucepan and cook over medium heat for a few minutes to reduce it slightly. This sauce freezes well, so keep it on hand to use as a tasty sauce for pasta or over my turkey meatballs (page 109).

MAKES 4½ cups | **SOUS VIDE COOKING TIME:** 30 minutes (or up to 1½ hours) | **ACTIVE PREP TIME:** 5 minutes

1 (28-ounce) can whole San Marzano tomatoes

1 teaspoon red pepper flakes

2 cloves garlic, minced

1 teaspoon fresh thyme or oregano leaves

Salt and freshly ground black pepper

DO-AHEAD STRATEGY

The cooked and chilled sauce can be refrigerated for up to 1 week or frozen for up to 2 months. Reheat the refrigerated sauce on the stove top; frozen sauce can be reheated in a 60°C (140°F) water bath for 45 minutes.

Preheat your sous vide water bath to 90°C (194°F).

Place the tomatoes, red pepper flakes, garlic, thyme, and salt and black pepper to taste in a gallon-size freezer-safe ziplock bag and crush the tomatoes slightly to break them up. Seal using the water displacement or table-edge method (see page 12). I recommend the latter method for recipes with a relatively large amount of liquid.

When the water reaches the target temperature, lower the bagged tomatoes into the water bath (making sure the bag is fully submerged) and cook for 30 minutes.

Remove the bag from the water bath. The marinara is now ready to use, but it can also be cooled in an ice water bath (see page 14) for 20 minutes and then refrigerated or frozen.

PRO TIP

Sous vide setups are great for thawing frozen foods, particularly items like soups, stocks, and sauces like this one that are primarily liquid. You can safely thaw any in a water bath (provided that you've stored it in a freezer-safe bag) at any temperature above 55°C (131°F).

GARLIC CONFIT

I like to think of garlic confit as roasted garlic's refined cousin: its subtler flavor makes it a much more versatile supporting character—for instance, adding depth to my *romesco* (see page 179)—but without losing its garlicky indulgence for those who just want to spread whole luscious, sweet cloves onto slices of baguette.

A NOTE ON STORAGE AND SAFETY: If you're not going to eat this garlic confit within a few days, I have a word of caution. Because it's grown in dirt, garlic (any vegetable, really) is exposed to a common soil bacterium called *Clostridium botulinum.* If stored for long enough under airless conditions (like being submerged in oil), this bacteria will produce a toxin that causes the illness botulism. Moreover, it's a tough li'l bugger, capable of surviving boiling and of growing at fridge temp. But before I scare you off altogether, fret not: my version includes a few simple precautions that will ensure that you minimize risk. Namely, removing the garlic cloves from the oil and blotting them dry before sprinkling them with salt, which impedes the growth of harmful botulinum bacteria. This means you can safely double or triple the recipe and always have this flavor-packed trade secret on hand. And you can rest easy to boot, albeit perhaps with a hint of garlic breath.

MAKES about ⅓ cup | **SOUS VIDE COOKING TIME:** 1½ hours (or up to 4 hours) | **ACTIVE PREP TIME:** 5 minutes, plus 10 minutes to chill

1 head garlic (about 12 cloves), separated into cloves, peeled, and root ends and any discoloration trimmed away

¼ cup extra-virgin olive oil

4 thyme sprigs

1 teaspoon kosher salt (for storage)

DO-AHEAD STRATEGY

If you have followed the chilling and storage preparation instructions precisely, the confit will keep in the refrigerator for up to 3 weeks.

Preheat your sous vide water bath to 88°C (190.4°F).

To ensure that your bag sinks, place 1 to 2 pounds of weight into a quart-size freezer-safe ziplock bag. Add the garlic cloves, olive oil, and thyme and seal using the water displacement or table-edge method (page 11). I recommend the latter method for recipes with a relatively large amount of liquid.

When the water reaches the target temperature, lower the bagged garlic into the water bath and cook for 1½ hours.

When the garlic is ready, transfer the bag to an ice water bath (see page 14) and chill for 10 minutes. Using a slotted spoon, transfer the garlic cloves to a plate, leaving the oil behind in the bag and discarding the thyme sprigs. Using paper towels, pat the garlic cloves completely dry, transfer them to an airtight container lined with a fresh paper towel, and then sprinkle with the salt, tossing the cloves gently to coat them evenly. Store in the refrigerator.

The garlic oil can be stored in the freezer (either left in the bag or transferred to an airtight container) for up to 2 months. It thaws quickly at room temperature and will add instant garlicky depth when drizzled over bruschetta, tossed with pasta, or whisked into a vinaigrette. Consider it a delicious bonus by-product!

HOMEMADE STOCK

You might wonder why something as simple as stock requires a sous vide makeover. The reason is simple: freedom. Making homemade stock using sous vide means not having to keep a watchful eye over the pot. I love that you can leave the stock simmering away while you're out of the house and even overnight without fear of it boiling over. What's more, the heat is so precise that even though you don't skim the stock during cooking, the result is clear and bright tasting. Needless to say, this stock is vastly superior to anything from a can or box.

Making stock is an act of resourcefulness, great for utilizing leftover bones and meat scraps (which can be frozen until you've accumulated enough to make a batch). You can make it with veal, pork, poultry, or beef bones, or a mixture of the four, but for the richest stock, I recommend using bones with some meat still attached from cuts with lots of connective tissue. Veal, beef, pork neck and rib bones, and chicken necks, backs, and wings produce the best flavor and body but are by no means a requirement.

MAKES about 6 cups | **SOUS VIDE COOKING TIME:** 6 hours (or up to 24 hours) | **ACTIVE PREP TIME:** 20 minutes

1 tablespoon canola or other mild vegetable oil (if making a brown stock)

2 to 3 pounds assorted meaty bones and/or meat scraps

1 yellow onion, peeled and halved through the stem end

1 carrot, peeled, halved lengthwise, and cut crosswise into 3-inch pieces

1 celery stalk, cut into 3-inch pieces

3 cloves garlic, peeled but left whole

6 cups water

3 flat-leaf parsley stems

3 thyme sprigs

½ teaspoon white or black peppercorns, or a mixture

1 bay leaf

DO-AHEAD STRATEGY

Once strained and cooled, the stock can be refrigerated in the bag for up to 1 week or frozen for up to 2 months. The stock can be thawed in a water bath at 55°C (131°F) or above for 30 minutes or until it returns to its liquid state. A microwave or the stove top will work fine, as well.

CONTINUED >

Preheat your sous vide water bath to 85°C (185°F).

If you're making a brown stock (see Pro Tip below), heat the oil in a large skillet or sauté pan over high heat. Add the bones and cook until browned, 3 to 5 minutes per side, flipping at least once. (Depending on the size of your bones and/or scraps, this could take up to 10 minutes total. Don't worry about browning them evenly, however, as this is only about building flavor.) Transfer the bones and/or scraps to a plate or bowl, leaving the oil behind in the pan.

With the pan still over high heat, add the onion, carrot, and celery and cook, turning as needed, until deeply browned, about 3 minutes per side. Stir in the garlic, cook for 1 minute more, and then remove from the heat.

Pour or spoon off any fat left in the pan (there might not be a lot) and place the pan back on the stove top over high heat. Add 1 cup of the water and scrape the bottom of the pan with a wooden spoon or spatula to loosen any browned bits.

Place the remaining 5 cups water and the parsley, thyme, and peppercorns in a gallon-size freezer-safe ziplock bag. Add the browned bones, vegetables, and any collected juices to the bag and seal using the water displacement or table-edge method (page 11). I recommend the latter method for recipes with a relatively large amount of liquid.

If you're making a white stock, omit the vegetable oil. Place all of the ingredients into the bag without browning and seal using the water displacement or table-edge method.

When the water reaches the target temperature, lower the bagged bones and vegetables into the water bath (making sure the bag is fully submerged) and cook for 6 hours.

Remove the bag from the water bath and strain the liquid through a fine-mesh sieve (or a colander lined with cheesecloth) into a large bowl to remove all of the solids. Discard the solids. If desired, using a ladle or large spoon, skim off any fat that floats to the top. The stock is ready to use at this point. If you plan to store it for any period of time, proceed to the next step.

Return the liquid to a freezer-safe ziplock bag (you can reuse the bag the stock was cooked in; just rinse it out with water) or any other airtight container. Chill the stock in an ice water bath (see page 14) for 30 minutes before storing it in the refrigerator or freezer (any fat in the stock will solidify and can be lifted off).

————

PRO TIP

Browning the bones and vegetables will result in what French cuisine refers to as a "brown stock." This step is optional; it adds depth of flavor and a rich color, but there are times (in the squash soup on page 173, for instance) when a subtler "white stock" flavor is preferable. I give directions for both styles above. You can also follow either method to make a vegetable stock by simply omitting the bones, doubling the quantity of vegetables, and cooking for only 2 hours.

EASY HERBED CRANBERRY SAUCE

Cranberry sauce is the Rodney Dangerfield of a turkey dinner: it gets no respect. But as this recipe demonstrates, it doesn't take a lot of effort to turn what can potentially be a humdrum accompaniment into an attention-grabbing condiment. The addition of anisette or a DIY herbal liqueur might make your teetotaling relatives blush, but I think it adds an interesting licorice-y dimension of flavor (particularly when paired with fresh tarragon). That said, the liqueur and the tarragon could also be left out to produce a more straightforward version that's still quite delicious.

This recipe isn't the easiest cranberry sauce that could grace your Thanksgiving table—for that, simply use a can opener—but my sous vide version does have the great advantages of freeing up precious burner space and eliminating the need to dirty one more pot. It even comes in an already-sealed container to store the sauce if you want to make it ahead.

MAKES about 2 cups | **SOUS VIDE COOKING TIME:** 1½ hours (or up to 3 hours) | **ACTIVE PREP TIME:** 5 minutes, plus 15 minutes to cool

8 ounces fresh or frozen cranberries (about 2 cups), thawed if frozen

¾ cup sugar

½ cup honey

Juice of 1 lime (about 2 tablespoons)

1 tablespoon peeled grated or minced fresh ginger (from about a 1-inch piece)

1 tablespoon Fennel Liqueur (page 249) or anisette

½ teaspoon freshly ground black pepper

Pinch of kosher salt

1½ teaspoons chopped fresh tarragon or thyme, or a mixture (optional)

DO-AHEAD STRATEGY

The cooked and cooled sauce can be refrigerated for up to 2 weeks.

Preheat your sous vide water bath to 85°C (185°F).

If using thawed cranberries, drain off any excess liquid. Place the cranberries, sugar, honey, lime juice, ginger, liqueur, pepper, and salt in a gallon-size freezer-safe ziplock bag and shake the bag so the contents are evenly distributed. Seal using the water displacement method (see page 12).

When the water reaches the target temperature, lower the bagged cranberries into the water bath (making sure the bag is fully submerged) and cook for 45 minutes.

Remove the bag from the water bath and set it on a countertop. Place a kitchen towel over the bag and then smash the cranberries in the bag using your hands. Return the bagged cranberries to the bath and cook for 45 minutes more.

Remove the bag from the water bath and set aside on a countertop for 15 minutes to cool. Transfer the sauce to a serving bowl and stir in the tarragon, if using. Serve at room temperature or cold.

SAUSAGE UNSTUFFING

Sous vide makes stuffing a snap to make ahead and then cook (or reheat) along with your turkey. It even cooks at the same temperature as the turkey breasts. Cooking the stuffing in a bag also keeps everything moist and prevents the vegetables from turning to mush, so you end up with juicy sausage bits, crunchy diced vegetables, and tender pieces of bread when the stuffing hits your holiday table. What's more, this is an incredibly forgiving dish; once the bag is in the water bath, the stuffing can stay unattended for hours with no loss of quality, allowing you to tend to your other dishes—a real boon when you're pulling off an elaborate holiday feast. This technically qualifies as a dressing and not a stuffing because it isn't cooked inside a bird, but I'm sure your guests won't argue with the results (and it is "stuffed" into a ziplock bag).

SERVES 8 to 10 as a side dish | **SOUS VIDE COOKING TIME:** 2 hours (or up to 6 hours) | **ACTIVE PREP TIME:** 50 minutes

10 cups bread pieces, cut in 1-inch cubes or coarsely torn (about 1 large loaf; see Pro Tip, opposite)

1 tablespoon canola or other mild vegetable oil

1 pound mild pork sausage (such as breakfast sausage or sweet Italian), removed from casings

1 turkey liver, chopped (optional)

¾ cup (6 ounces) unsalted butter

1 large yellow onion, cut into ½-inch dice

4 celery stalks, cut into ½-inch dice

1 carrot, peeled and cut into ½-inch dice

3 cloves garlic, minced

1 cup dry white wine

1 cup roasted and peeled chestnuts (store-bought is fine), coarsely chopped (optional)

¼ cup chopped fresh flat-leaf parsley

3 tablespoons chopped fresh sage or thyme, or a mixture

About 6 cups turkey stock, homemade (page 267) or store-bought

Salt and freshly ground black pepper

3 large eggs, lightly beaten

DO-AHEAD STRATEGY

The bread can be toasted up to 2 days before you make the stuffing, cooled, and stored in an airtight container at room temperature. The finished stuffing itself can also be made in advance; once cooked, chill it in an ice water bath (see page 14) for 30 minutes and then refrigerate for up to 1 week. Reheat in the bag in a 60°C (140°F) water bath for 1 hour. For your Thanksgiving game plan, the stuffing can be made the day before the big day, or thrown together while the dark meat is cooking, depending on which is more convenient.

At any point up to 2 days before you plan on making your stuffing (including while your water bath is heating), toast the bread. Preheat the oven to 350°F. Spread the bread in a single layer on two or three large sheet pans and toast until lightly browned and crispy on the outside, 15 to 20 minutes. Let cool to room temperature then transfer to an airtight container until needed.

Preheat your sous vide water bath to 60°C (140°F).

Heat the oil in a large sauté pan over medium-high heat until it shimmers. Crumble the sausage meat into the pan, add the liver (if using), and cook, undisturbed, until the bottom of the meat is golden brown, 3 to 5 minutes. Break up the sausage with a wooden spoon (you want the sausage in small bite-size pieces) and cook, stirring, until the sausage and liver are browned on all sides, 2 to 3 minutes longer. Transfer the sausage and liver to a large bowl, leaving behind any fat in the pan.

Lower the heat to medium, add the butter, and stir until the butter has melted, about 1 minute. Add the onion, celery, carrot, and garlic and sauté, stirring occasionally, until the vegetables have begun to soften and brown but still have some bite, about 5 minutes. Pour in the wine and scrape the bottom of the pan with a wooden spoon or spatula to loosen any browned bits. Bring to a simmer and cook until the wine has reduced by about half, 2 to 3 minutes. Remove from the heat.

Transfer the vegetable mixture to the bowl holding the sausage. Stir in the bread, chestnuts (if using), parsley, and sage. Pour in the stock, 1 cup at a time, stirring gently with a wooden spoon after each addition until the bread is well moistened but not swimming in stock (you don't want any excess stock at the bottom of the bowl). Depending on the type of bread, you may need only 3 to 4 cups stock. Season the mixture to taste with salt and pepper and then stir in the eggs.

Place the stuffing mixture in a gallon-size freezer-safe ziplock bag and seal using the water displacement method (see page 12). At this point, the stuffing can be refrigerated for up to 24 hours or cooked immediately.

When the water reaches the target temperature, lower the bagged stuffing into the water bath (making sure the bag is fully submerged) and cook for 2 hours.

Remove the bag from the water bath, transfer the stuffing to a serving dish, and serve immediately. Alternatively, if you like your stuffing with a crispy crust, transfer the stuffing to a buttered broiler-proof baking, place into a preheated 400°F oven (or under a broiler), and cook until the top is golden brown, 5 to 10 minutes.

PRO TIP

Any kind of good-quality bread will work for this, from a plain white Pullman loaf to a rustic country-style bread. I prefer a blend of brioche and sourdough rye. Please don't use those ghastly store-bought croutons masquerading as "stuffing mix."

MEASUREMENT CONVERSION CHARTS

VOLUME

U.S.	IMPERIAL	METRIC
1 tablespoon	½ fl oz	15 ml
2 tablespoons	1 fl oz	30 ml
¼ cup	2 fl oz	60 ml
⅓ cup	3 fl oz	90 ml
½ cup	4 fl oz	120 ml
⅔ cup	5 fl oz (¼ pint)	150 ml
¾ cup	6 fl oz	180 ml
1 cup	8 fl oz (⅓ pint)	240 ml
1¼ cups	10 fl oz (½ pint)	300 ml
2 cups (1 pint)	16 fl oz (⅔ pint)	480 ml
2½ cups	20 fl oz (1 pint)	600 ml
1 quart	32 fl oz (1⅔ pints)	1 l

TEMPERATURE

FAHRENHEIT	CELSIUS/GAS MARK
250°F	120°C/gas mark ½
275°F	135°C/gas mark 1
300°F	150°C/gas mark 2
325°F	160°C/gas mark 3
350°F	175°C or 180°C/gas mark 4
375°F	190°C/gas mark 5
400°F	200°C/gas mark 6
425°F	220°C/gas mark 7
450°F	230°C/gas mark 8
475°F	245°C/gas mark 9
500°F	260°C

LENGTH

INCH	METRIC
¼ inch	6 mm
½ inch	1.25 cm
¾ inch	2 cm
1 inch	2.5 cm
6 inches (½ foot)	15 cm
12 inches (1 foot)	30 cm

WEIGHT

U.S./IMPERIAL	METRIC
½ oz	15 g
1 oz	30 g
2 oz	60 g
¼ lb	115 g
⅓ lb	150 g
½ lb	225 g
¾ lb	350 g
1 lb	450 g

RESOURCES

Most of the ingredients called for in this book are readily available at your local Mexican bodega, Asian market, Indian spice shop, or the international aisle at a growing number of mainstream grocery stores. But if you can't track them down on foot, don't despair. You can find nearly any specialty ingredient online and have it shipped to your door. Here is a list of some of my favorite online resources for hard-to-find ingredients and specialty foods.

ALL-AROUND

Amazon
www.amazon.com
Caribbean jerk seasoning, cinchona bark, coconut vinegar, *pandan* leaves, premade mole sauces, *toban djan, yuzu* juice, *yuzu kosho*, etc.

Earthy Delights
www.earthy.com
(855) 328-8732
Yuzu juice, *yuzu kosho*, high-quality soy sauces, dried chiles (ancho, pasilla, and *guajillo*), fleur de sel

JAPANESE

Asian Food Grocer
www.asianfoodgrocer.com
(888) 482-2742
High-quality soy sauce, *shichimi togarashi*

MEXICAN

Alegro Foods
www.alegrofoods.com
Dried chiles (ancho, pasilla, and *guajillo*), prepared moles, Mexican (Ceylon) cinnamon

PHILIPPINE

Phil-Am Food
www.philamfood.com
(201) 963-0455
Pandan leaves, coconut vinegar

SPANISH

Despaña Brand Foods
www.despanabrandfoods.com
(888) 779-8617
Serrano ham, *pimenton*, Marcona almonds, *piquillo* peppers

SPECIALTY MEAT PRODUCTS

D'Artagnan
www.dartagnan.com
(800) 327-8246
Moulard duck legs, Pekin and Muscovy duck breasts, rendered duck fat, curing salt, quail

SPICES

Kalustyan's
www.kalustyans.com
(800) 352-3451
Mexican (Ceylon) cinnamon, Madras curry powder, cinchona bark, sumac, za'atar, various whole and ground Indian spices

Penzey's Spices
www.penzeys.com
(800) 741-7787
Dried chiles (ancho, pasilla, and *guajillo*), *pimenton*, Mexican (Ceylon) cinnamon, Madras curry powder, cinchona bark, sumac, za'atar, various whole and ground Indian spices

Walkerswood Caribbean Food
www.walkerswood.com
(876) 926-6449
Caribbean jerk seasoning

THAI

ImportFood.com
www.importfood.com
(888) 618-8424
Mae Ploy and Maesri Thai curry paste

ABOUT THE AUTHORS

AUTHOR BIOGRAPHY

Lisa Q. Fetterman is the founder and CEO of Nomiku, makers of the first home immersion circulator. She has been honored at the White House Maker Faire, and was named on both *Forbes* and *Zagat Survey*'s 30 Under 30 lists for her pioneering work in the food space. Lisa earned a BA in journalism from New York University and honed her culinary sensibilities working at some of the top restaurants in the country, including Babbo and Jean-Georges in New York and Saison in San Francisco.

CO-AUTHOR BIOGRAPHY

Meesha Halm is the author of *The Balsamic Vinegar Cookbook*, *Savoring the Wine Country*, and more than twenty restaurant guides. She has been the local editor for *Zagat Survey* for 16 years, and her writing and food videos can be seen on The Food Network, Bravo, and Tastemade. Prior to her work as a writer, she was a cookbook editor at Collins Publishing.

CO-AUTHOR BIOGRAPHY

Scott Peabody is a professional chef with more than a decade of experience. He attended the Culinary Institute of America in Hyde Park before cutting his teeth in New York City, toiling in the kitchens of renowned chefs Jean-Georges Vongerichten and Thomas Keller, where he was initiated into the mysteries of sous vide cooking. Scott provided the recipes and culinary direction for this book.

PHOTOGRAPHER BIOGRAPHY

Monica Lo is an experienced creative director and food photographer. She holds a degree in communication design at Pratt Institute, trained at The Institute of Culinary Education, and was mentored by Andrew Scrivani of the *New York Times*. Monica provided the photography and art direction for this book.

ACKNOWLEDGMENTS

FROM LISA:

There are so many people to thank for helping make this cookbook happen, I am so fantastically lucky to know some of the most awesome people in the wide world of food. As Julia Child put it, people who love to eat are always the best people. In no particular order, I want to specifically thank

The team at Ten Speed Press, for seeing the huge potential of home sous vide cooking, understanding my vision for this book, and helping it become a reality.

Dominique Crenn and Karen Leibowitz, for writing this book's lovely, thoughtful foreword.

Leslie Jonath, my producer for this book, for her indomitable positivity and enthusiasm. Gold star!

Ethel Brennan, prop stylist extraordinaire, for helping make the photo shoot a towering success.

Andrew Schloss, for his diligent recipe testing.

Joey Wan, for capturing our good sides in the team bio photos.

Mary Mar Keenan of MMclay, for lending her beautiful ceramics to use in photos.

Chubo Knives, for the gift of their gorgeous Japanese steel.

Heritage Foods USA, for providing amazingly delicious turkey and pork shoulder.

Bruce Hill of Chef's Press, for furnishing handsome kitchen weights (for when the bags wouldn't sink).

Renan Ticzon of Lundy Way aprons, for helping the team look sharp (and tidy) while we slaved over our water baths.

The entire amazing Nomiku team: Patrick Wong, Tiffany Chan, Chris Palia, Alex Krolick, Caitlin Enomoto, and Grace Ellen Miller, for being the best.

My husband and co-founder, Abe Fetterman, for being my right hand.

Last but certainly not least, I owe my deepest thanks to the best team of collaborators I could have asked for: my co-author Meesha Halm, for taking the sous vide plunge with me and keeping this project on track; Scott Peabody, my second co-author and this book's chef-in-residence, for developing (and cooking) all these fantastic recipes and making them soigné; Monica Lo, photographer and art director, for making this book such a thing of beauty.

FROM MEESHA:

My eternal gratitude to my devoted husband Jon Fox and our children Olive and Jude, for their love and support, and for gamely riding along (albeit with some skepticism) on this sous vide odyssey through all the recipe mishaps and late night writing sessions (or as they called it, "sous hell").

FROM SCOTT:

My heartfelt thanks to everyone who gave me advice and endured my griping when finishing this cookbook seemed like a positively Herculean task (you know who you are), but especially to Jose Rodriguez, my lovely photo shoot assistant, pernil advisor, fellow sybarite, and partner in crime.

INDEX

Copyright © 2016 by Lisa Q. Fetterman
Photographs copyright © 2016 by Monica Lo

Published in the United States by Ten Speed Press, an imprint of the Crown Publishing
Group, a division of Penguin Random House LLC, New York.
www.crownpublishing.com
www.tenspeed.com

Ten Speed Press and the Ten Speed Press colophon are registered trademarks
of Penguin Random House LLC.

Library of Congress Cataloging-in-Publication Data
Names: Fetterman, Lisa Q., author. | Halm, Meesha, author. | Peabody, Scott, author.
Title: Sous vide at home the modern technique for perfectly cooked meals / by Lisa Q.
    Fetterman with Meesha Halm and Scott Peabody ; photography by Monica Lo.
Description: First edition. | Berkeley, CA : Ten Speed Press, [2016] | Includes bibliographical
    references and index.
Identifiers: LCCN 2016007211 (print) | LCCN 2016016632 (ebook)
Subjects: LCSH: Sous-vide cooking. | LCGFT: Cookbooks.
Classification: LCC TX690.7 .F48 2016 (print) | LCC TX690.7 (ebook) | DDC 641.5/87—dc23
LC record available at https://lccn.loc.gov/2016007211

Hardcover ISBN: 978-0-399-57806-9
eBook ISBN: 978-0-399-57807-6

Printed in China

Design by Hope Meng

10 9 8 7 6 5 4 3 2 1

First Edition